J. Moffett

STRAIGHT LEFT
An Autobiography

PADDY DEVLIN

THE
BLACKSTAFF
PRESS

BELFAST

• A BLACKSTAFF PAPERBACK ORIGINAL •

Blackstaff Paperback Originals present new writing, previously
unpublished in Britain and Ireland, at an affordable price.

First published in 1993 by
The Blackstaff Press Limited
3 Galway Park, Dundonald, Belfast BT16 0AN, Northern Ireland

This book has received support from the
Cultural Traditions Programme of the
Community Relations Council, which aims to encourage
acceptance and understanding of cultural diversity.

© Text, Paddy Devlin, 1993
© Foreword, Chris Ryder, 1993
All rights reserved

Typeset by Paragon Typesetters, Queensferry, Clwyd

Printed in Ireland by ColourBooks Limited

A catalogue record for this book
is available from the British Library

ISBN 0-85640-514-0

CONTENTS

*To my long-suffering family —
my wife Theresa,
my daughters Anne, Moya and Patricia,
and my sons Joe and Peter —
who unfairly have had to carry
the burden of my sins
as well as their own*

FOREWORD

Few British or Irish politicians involved in the affairs of Northern Ireland over the last twenty-five years have avoided clashing with the burly figure of Paddy Devlin. One Home Secretary was assaulted with a rolled-up copy of the *Daily Express* and several secretaries of state and their junior ministers have been threatened with punches, told to 'get stuffed' or worse. Political opponents and colleagues alike have suffered torrential tongue-lashings when their views did not coincide with the passion of his own.

A senior civil servant, now retired, who witnessed many of these exchanges describes Devlin as the coarsest man who has ever faced the British government. Uncensored expletives usually punctuated his conversations with the density of dried fruit in a barnbrack. But rather surprisingly the same official believes that Devlin was effective and genuine. 'He gained a lot of respect the longer we knew him and worked with him.'

The many people who really know, cherish and respect Paddy Devlin have long recognised that behind his blusterous façade and hair-trigger temper, there beats a big and warm heart, which is the powerhouse of a singularly compassionate and visionary man. In his heyday no problem was too trivial for him to resolve; no deadlock too solid for him to tackle with his unique pragmatism and common sense; and no person too humble to receive his selfless, undivided attention.

His driving anti-sectarianism and lack of bigotry gave him the singular distinction of being a politician who could go unmolested into the hardest heartlands of both unionism and nationalism and be greeted on first name terms.

His life, which he recounts here for the first time, is a remarkable self-mapped achievement. Only one other figure from a nationalist background, his longtime political ally Gerry Fitt, has beaten a similar path from modest origins in Belfast's disadvantaged slums to ministerial office and the corridors of power at Stormont.

But Paddy Devlin's journey is all the more remarkable for the way in which his personal and political philosophy evolved. Starting as a youthful activist with the outlawed Irish Republican Army, he carved out an individual political culture which brought him, through the trade union movement, into socialism and the belief that only social and economic equality would smother the tribal divisions in Northern Ireland and unite the workers against the bosses, creating conventional right–left politics.

It has been a personal misfortune for Paddy Devlin, and a ruinous loss for Northern Ireland, that he belonged to a gifted but blighted political generation who were prevented by bigotry and backwardness from achieving their full potential and making a lasting contribution to solving the myriad social, political, security and economic problems that have scarred Northern Ireland for far too long.

Gerry Fitt, Austin Currie, Ivan Cooper and Paddy O'Hanlon, like Paddy Devlin, were all talented politicians who transformed the civil rights campaign into the political force they named the Social Democratic and Labour Party. In their radical and most successful days, in the early 1970s, they brought a new tolerance, breadth of vision and dynamism to the frozen political wasteland at Stormont. (Their successors have, unfortunately, lost the focus of this vision.)

Together with forward-looking unionists, most notably Brian Faulkner, they created the power-sharing Executive in 1974, the most promising political framework for stability since Ireland had been partitioned in the early 1920s. Their joint courage and vision were, however, maimed within months by a British general election and a loyalist general strike, a devastating uppercut which still handicaps the hunt for reconciliation and consensus.

As a result, Paddy Devlin, like his contemporaries, was forced into the political wilderness by the reassertion of the divisive nationalist and unionist standpoints. Consequently he has been able to leave only a fingerprint on Irish history, rather than the deep footprint of which he was capable. His life, values and experience, outlined here, do however provide thought and inspiration for a future generation. If they succeed where he failed, I know he will be happy.

CHRIS RYDER
HILLSBOROUGH
JULY 1993

1

BIRTH, BOXING
AND BUTCHERY

The great Ulster poet John Hewitt has described Belfast as 'that river-straddling, hill-rimmed town'. While his imagery is geographically accurate, it portrays far too tranquil a picture of the volatile, turbulent city where I was born and have spent virtually all my life. I much prefer the words of Louis MacNeice, who says that Belfast is 'devout and profane and hard'.

It is actually a place of extremes. Over the years I have seen extraordinary acts of selflessness and generosity and witnessed the most incredible hatred and intolerance. Poverty and unemployment have demoralised and crippled whole families while, often only a few streets away, conspicuous and selfish extravagance is the norm.

Belfast has long been a religiously divided city. Its rigid sectarian barriers, mental as well as physical, have blighted the lives and hopes of successive generations. It is an ineradicable stain on its history that the community has tolerated the tribal killers on both sides. We cannot even agree on a common version of our history. Our fatal divisions are dated back to the Easter Rising in 1916, the United Irishmen in the 1790s or the outcome of the Battle of the Boyne in 1690. The merits of these views, and many others, have been more than adequately probed by academics, historians and other pundits, so without attributing any historical significance to the timing, I will start my story at what I think is the most appropriate point: the beginning of my own lifetime.

In 1922, after the most recent two decades of Troubles, twenty-six Irish counties secured their independence from Britain, and a Free State, with its own parliament and government, was established in Dublin. The nationalist minority in the six northern counties of the island, who were outnumbered some two to one by the unionist majority, were abandoned to their uncertain fate under a regional unionist-controlled parliament in Belfast. The unionists had belligerently opposed Home Rule for Ireland because that would, they said, be tantamount to 'Rome Rule' – imposing on them an unacceptable Catholic way of life and values.

When I was born at the family home in 46 Lady Street on the Falls Road on 8 March 1925, the new Northern Ireland was still coming to terms with partition. It was hoped this was the final solution to reconcile the conflicting objectives of unionists and nationalists in Ireland.

We were not a Belfast family. The Devlins originally hailed from Tyrone and then moved to Randalstown, Co. Antrim, near the shores of Lough Neagh. My paternal grandfather, Patrick Devlin, was a railway worker, an engine driver according to some of my elderly relatives, although he is simply described as a mechanic in contemporary records. The family apparently settled in Belfast when he moved to the goods yard at Grosvenor Road, at the rear of the Great Northern Railway terminus at Great Victoria Street, Belfast. Around 1880, they took up residence a short distance away, at 59 Baker Street, later living at several other addresses in the area called the Pound Loney, at the bottom of the Falls Road.

Patrick Devlin married Mary Donnelly, a weaver, at St Joseph's Church in Belfast on 4 February 1885. Over the next ten years, before he died on 12 October 1895, aged only forty-two, they had five children: John, born on Christmas Day in the wedding year; Margaret, 1888; Mary Ann, 1890; Thomas, 1891;

2

and Mary, 1894. The second youngest, Thomas, was my father.

Thomas married Anna Lillis, born December 1902 and some twelve years his junior, at St Peter's Pro-Cathedral in Belfast on 20 April 1924. She was the daughter of Patrick Lillis, a labourer, and Rose Burns, a spinner. As far as I can trace back, the Lillis strand of the family appears to have its origins in the Cookstown area of Co. Tyrone until they moved to Belfast in the late 1800s. The first positive trace I can find of them in the records shows them living at 7 Quadrant Street in 1902. Several women members of the family had worked in the linen mills for years and endured the hardships that that entailed.

My newly married parents moved into 46 Lady Street, a house occupied by two of my aunts, where I was born, the eldest of seven children. Two years after my birth came Mary, followed in due course by Rose, Anna, Tommy, Margaret and Bobby. Margaret later followed Tommy out to Australia. She has since died but he still lives there.

My earliest memories are therefore of Lady Street, which ran parallel to Albert Street, off the Pound Loney. It was a cobble-stoned, terraced street of small houses, each with a kitchen and livingroom downstairs and two small bedrooms upstairs. Water came from a single cold tap in a stone sink behind the door; there was a pit in the back yard for refuse and an outside lavatory. Every Saturday night we were taken into the small room off the kitchen one at a time to have a bath with water that had been boiled on the stove during the day.

Our daily lives were governed by the bells of St Peter's, which as the crow flies was only a couple of hundred yards away from the house. The chimes every fifteen minutes were a constant reminder of our routine, dictating where we should be or what we should be doing. Attendance at one church ceremony or another was virtually an everyday commitment, with regular mass, confession and communion every week, and a midweek confraternity meeting. For a time, under pressure from my aunts who wanted me to emulate the boy next door, I reluctantly trained to be an altar boy but I dropped out before being finally accepted. Another unwelcome involvement came when the family pushed me into playing the cymbals with the West Belfast Accordion Band for a few months. My Uncle Jimmy played the big drum with the band and I was dragged along until they could get someone else and I was able to escape.

With memories of the regular sectarian pogroms and incursions by unionist mobs that littered Belfast's history still kept alive by the reminiscences of the older members of the community, you were always ready to spring to the defence of the church and the area. We heard stories of the conduct of the Orangemen towards the church and the priests and of an attack on the bishop's house at Bankmore Street which filled me with dread throughout my childhood days. Each summer the stories from the old people seemed to be proved right when the Orange bands and their thunderous Lambeg drums were heard coming from the direction of the nearby Grosvenor Road. I can well remember experiencing such a sense of terror in my body that I ran to hide under the bed.

The stories told to boys like myself concerned local heroes who had fought to protect the chapel and Catholic people. I never found out if the tales were entirely true but they certainly influenced our thinking. I remember, even in the late twenties, my mother going out each night to put on the window shutters. I well understood that they were designed to stop the Orange mobs and the feared, all-Protestant auxiliary police, the B Specials, from breaking our windows by tapping them with their batons as they walked past. Strangely enough, the Royal Ulster Constabulary men who walked the local beat from the station at Cullingtree Road were more favourably received. Many of them had strong Cork or Kerry brogues, having transferred into the RUC when the Royal Irish Constabulary was disbanded at the time of partition. Some of them were, of course, Catholics like ourselves and regular attenders at Sunday mass and other services.

The 1920s and 1930s, when I was growing up, were grim times in Belfast. There was little work for men. The great shipyards, then among the finest in the world, and the ancillary engineering firms in the Lagan Valley were all in chronic depression. World trade was in steep decline. No shipping orders were on the horizon. Belfast's other great industry, linen, was equally badly affected, with the mills either closing down or on half-time. One in four was out of work, and thousands of skilled and unskilled workers dug trenches in the streets for grocery chits of token value. There were no wages being earned and little actual cash around, so rent went unpaid. For a time the bailiffs were rampant, until the unemployed workers organised resistance to them.

In Britain in 1927 discretionary payments were introduced to alleviate poverty by replacing the poor law legislation with a new scheme operated through county and borough councils. Neville Chamberlain, the Health minister, was forced to change the law after a campaign by Labour councillors, led by George Lamsbury, to abolish the workhouses and the boards of guardians elected by local ratepayers.

In Northern Ireland wages were cut in line with the directions of the Westminster government, causing a rash of strikes in Belfast. Going into the thirties the unemployment and poverty worsened. The Belfast government, under Sir James Craig, hid the facts from the public gaze, believing that publishing them would expose the government to the criticism of Eamon de Valera and others in the Irish Free State.

The unionists also set out to deprive Catholic families and Labour supporters of any relief payments. Catholics were frequently humiliated by the prosperous Protestants who served as poor law guardians and disbursed the discretionary pittances that were payable. One of the worst was Mrs Lily Coleman, who remarked about the fathers of large families that there was clearly 'no poverty under the blankets'. The poor law inspectors, usually portly men with gold watch chains stretched across

5

their ample bellies, spread terror in the district when they arrived. Unfortunates who applied for relief were subjected to the public humiliation of having their names posted up on notices at street corners. In addition, the inspectors could order them to sell pieces of furniture, surplus blankets or other possessions to raise money. On occasion they were even forced to go to relatives and seek either food or cash handouts.

There was a poor law dispensary at Glengall Street in the city centre, next door to the headquarters of the all-powerful Unionist Party. As a boy I can remember going there with one of my aunts to get cough medicine. I watched fascinated as a little man with a greasy black apron dipped bottles into a large vat of medicine and filled them. It was the same medicine for all ailments, coughs, corns, removing warts or healing varicose veins. My aunt swore that the medicine must be better than Lourdes water for the number of conditions it could cure.

The unionists reckoned that their discriminatory parsimony would force many of their nationalist opponents to emigrate to the South or even further afield, while cushioning their own supporters until the world economy picked up again. But the length and depth of the depression drove even the favoured Protestant working class to despair. Matters came to a head in 1932 when the poor buried their religious differences and jointly challenged Craig's government on its failure to reform the system and make relief payments on a scale comparable with those in other major British cities. For the first time people from both the Falls and the Shankill areas made common cause. Indeed, nearly 60,000 people from both religions throughout the city marched by torchlight to the Custom House steps to protest. They were led by bands from both traditions, which played the tune 'Yes, we have no bananas' over and over again in case the traditional party tunes would give offence. But it was only after several days of serious rioting that the shaken government was finally forced to increase the relief payments by 50 per cent. Thereafter, payments were made in cash, instead of by the grocery chits from which unscrupulous shopkeepers siphoned off as much as 25 per cent of the value in commission.

Although we were far from being a wealthy family, we weathered the depression more comfortably than many of our friends and neighbours, thanks to the fact that my father had a war pension of fifteen shillings a week and a job with a modest regular wage of about thirty shillings a week. I can remember having his old army greatcoat over the bed in winter but we were much better off than other kids. We were never in our bare feet although our shoes leaked in heavy rain, and we had a set of Sunday-best clothes, unlike others who had to wear their single jersey and short pants every day until they wore out. My mother wouldn't let us go round the doors selling chopped sticks or papers, which most other kids had to do to eke out the small outdoor relief payments and help to pay the rent. Nevertheless, my mother's wedding ring and my father's Sunday suit were regularly in and out of the pawnbroker's as they struggled to make ends meet.

We ate well, if frugally by modern standards. Sunday was soup day, made with a big bone from the butcher, and that would have lasted another day or two by being augmented with rice. On a Wednesday, when my father collected his pension money, we would have a wee fry, although I can recall an egg being cut into three pieces and shared round the table. Other days we would have had stew with potatoes and vegetables in it and maybe a sausage and fried bread. The coal fire was very important, for it not only kept the place warm but provided a means of boiling water, and even of light, if there wasn't a penny for the gas. We made toast in front of the fire and sometimes baked potatoes in the hot coals. Now and again we would get tuppenny suppers, fish and chips, which again would be divided between us. Every morning we got fresh baps, with a bit of butter, which were delivered by horse and cart from Hughes' Bakery to my granny's house along the street.

Holidays were no more than day trips. I remember going to

Toomebridge with my aunts or on bus trips across the border to Omeath or Blackrock, something my mother loved to do but not my father. Once when we went to support Cavan against Kerry in the all-Ireland final in Dublin they halted our train at Goraghwood station for a search on the way back. We were held there all night and that put us off the idea of going to Dublin again for a match. Another yearly outing was the Joe Devlin excursion for schoolchildren, which went to Bangor, Portrush or Portstewart. Devlin collected money from wealthy Catholics and businessmen to pay for the trip, and provided lemonade, buns and a bag of fruit for each kid. Thousands used to go on the outing and there were often three train-loads of them. It must have been a real headache for the organisers and the stewards, unemployed men who went along to supervise the children. Efforts were made to march the children behind pipe bands, but they were conspicuously less successful than the Pied Piper of Hamelin. Every year they would run amok in the resort, stealing and shoplifting all round them, and because of overcrowding and insufficient stewarding there were times when children were even killed by falling or being pushed from the train on the way there and back.

These, of course, were the days before widespread electric light was available and although we had a radio, run from a wet battery, you were forced to make your own entertainment. There was no piano in our house but we had a wind-up His Master's Voice gramophone with a big horn. We used to play the records of Bing Crosby and John McCormack, which my mother bought in Woolworth's for the steep price of sixpence. On dark winter evenings we would all sit round the fire and sing along to them, joining in after my mother would start off the song. My father, who was a bit deaf, would just sit there. On Saturday nights other members of the family circle, who were good singers, would come down with bottles of stout and pig's feet and take part in the sing-songs. My sister Mary and I used to sit on the stairs and hope to be called for a song. One night during the Second World War, when they were having a sing-song, an American soldier with a few drinks on him knocked on the door and asked if he could come in and listen. He became a regular caller until he left to take part in D-Day in 1944. We never knew what happened to him afterwards.

My father was a small, quiet man who loved talking, but he could be hot-tempered. He was always great with the kids in the house though, pulling our legs and being very generous, giving us some money on a Wednesday when he got his war pension and on a Friday when he was paid his wages. Now and again he would take off and get drunk, but he gave most of his time to work and the family. He liked to read, cowboy stories and sporting magazines, but he had also been through Dickens and the like. If any of us were doing exams, for instance, he would always try to help. I read his magazines and also the *Irish News*, but although I read a lot, it was much later in my life before I got into serious reading material.

In the early 1900s my father, who had trained as a fitter, took off to Glasgow when he could find no work in Belfast. His brother, John, also left home because of the lack of jobs. He joined the Royal Irish Rifles and died of malaria after serving in India. When the Great War broke out in 1914 my father joined the military and was wounded in action. After that he went absent without leave for a time but eventually joined another regiment and was wounded again. He was awarded a pension for his first injury, but once, when he was out on a drinking binge, he sold it. In due course, with the help of my mother's father, who had himself served for thirty years in the British Army, he argued his claim at a tribunal and obtained a second pension of fifteen shillings a week. For years after that my mother always ribbed him about her father having to get the pension for him. He always teased her back for not being able to spell 'cabbage'.

My father, who worked in Andrews' flour mill, owed his job to a stroke of luck. His Uncle Peter was the driver for the

Andrews family, whose prosperity flowed from their flour and animal feed mill at Percy Street, which runs between the Falls and Shankill roads. His job was to drive members of the family in a horse-drawn carriage between the mill and their estate on the Glen Road. One day, soon after his return from the war, my father was standing at the corner of Alma Street when Peter waved at him as he pulled up at the watering trough for the horses.

When Sidney Andrews, the main director of the firm, heard that my father was Peter's nephew and was unemployed he called him over to his carriage and told him to come to the flour mill in Percy Street on the following morning. He immediately started work and stayed with the company for forty-two years. Years afterwards he told me that he later taught Sidney's son, David, future managing director of the family company, how to box because he was being bullied by bigger boys at school.

Boxing was one of the passions of my father's life, which he passed on to me. He brought me along to all the big fights at the Harps Hall and Grosvenor Park and I well remember him introducing me to Jimmy Warnock, my first boxing hero, who walked past our door every day on his way to and from his home on the Shankill. Jimmy was a famous fly-weight and the best known Irish boxer prior to Rinty Monaghan. He twice beat Benny Lynch, who was world champion, something no local boxer had ever done before.

My father bought me boxing gloves when I was about ten years old and taught me how to defend myself in the back yard. I invited other young people of my own age to box with me and often I got cracked on the nose for being so vigorous. I suppose I took advantage of some of the weaker boys. One father watching me spar with his son rushed out into his back yard to challenge me to fight him instead. I took the hint and changed over to football, another of my father's great interests. Indeed, he was known as 'Topper' Devlin, because I think there was a famous footballer of that name. He had played a bit of Gaelic football in his younger days before the war, but it was during his time in Glasgow that he became interested in Celtic with a fervour that was to last all his life. I once asked him why he supported a Catholic team and he told me that the Christian Brothers ran Celtic to get money to run the soup kitchens in Glasgow, which fed Catholics and Protestants alike. I suppose he had to go to the soup kitchens himself when he wasn't working and formed an attachment to the organisation through that. Whatever the reason, he developed an encyclopaedic knowledge of Celtic and for years afterwards he would enthuse about the great players and the great games.

From time to time he would get tickets for big local matches at Celtic Park in Belfast and I remember going there with him and later acting as ballboy. I became an avid street footballer. We played night, noon and morning with our own friends, then even with our Protestant neighbours. I actually became quite proficient at the game and played regularly afterwards with properly organised Shankill Road football teams. One of my heroes was Jimmy McAlinden, the George Best of his day. He was born in Lady Street and attended Milford Street school some years before me. He was the star of the school team and when he left at sixteen joined Belfast Celtic. In 1939, when he transferred to Portsmouth, I went down to the boat to see him off from Belfast. They won the FA Cup that year beating Wolverhampton Wanderers. He was a brilliant player, able to dribble the ball along the field and beat every challenger. My own aspirations to play football were heavily influenced by Jimmy, who remains an inspiration to me and a great friend.

I was also a keen swimmer and for years I swam every day at the Falls Baths; indeed I still have a cup I won in a swimming competition there when I was thirteen. For a time I was a member of the Cathal Brugha swimming club and played goal in their water polo team, but I eventually gave up the swimming in favour of football which interested me far more.

During his time in Glasgow my father also became interested

11

in socialist politics and trade unionism. His political views were firmly cast, however, when he returned from the Great War in 1918 to find that Lloyd George's promise of 'homes fit for heroes' was just empty rhetoric. Soon after he joined Andrews' he became a shop steward with the Irish Transport and General Workers' Union. This brought him into contact with the union leader, Billy McMullen, a Protestant from the Shankill Road, who was also involved with the Independent Labour Party. My father also joined the party and became a lifelong friend and supporter of McMullen.

This brought him into direct conflict with my mother, who had strong political views of her own and was a staunch supporter of the Irish Nationalist Party and of its leader, Joe Devlin, in particular. 'Wee Joe', as he was widely known (no relation of ours), was an MP who sat both at Westminster and in the Belfast parliament. A self-made man with no formal education, he had once been a barman in Kelly's Cellars, the famous old public house in the centre of Belfast. Though described as a nationalist, Devlin behaved more like a Labour MP and supported enlightened social policies, using socialist language in his speeches to the mill workers. He was an able orator and extremely popular with the 'shawlies', the Catholic and Protestant women who worked in the linen mills as spinners and doffers and took their name from the shawls they wore. They idolised Devlin because of his efforts to win them better conditions. Religion did not matter to him and he fought equally hard for all his constituents, whether from the Falls or the Shankill. He also had a seaside holiday home for the mill workers and their children at Bangor, which was very popular.

Now, come every election time my father would put a poster supporting Billy McMullen in the front window of our house. Each morning after he had gone to work at 6 a.m. my mother would replace it with a Joe Devlin photograph, which she removed shortly before my father returned about 6 p.m. One evening, however, when she forgot to make the switch, he was so enraged when he spotted Devlin in the window that he threw his tea can at it and broke the glass.

The rivalry between the Devlin nationalists and both the Irish republicans and the Labour supporters was intense. I can remember nationalists, armed with hurley sticks, preventing all but their own supporters voting at Slate Street school. My mother's fanatical support for her political hero was expressed in an even more tangible way, for she became heavily involved in what is politely called personation but actually amounts to vote stealing. Plugging votes was always a fact of life every polling day, and the rival parties posted someone at each voting point to deter all but the most determined pluggers. My mother was in that category and she stole votes all around her and cast them for Devlin. So it was that during one election my mother was challenged by a McMullen Labour man in the polling booth at Dunlewey Street school. 'I know you. You're Annie Devlin. You're not voting here,' he shouted. As he called the policeman (one was always posted to guard every ballot box) and made a grab at her to arrest her she hit him a whack with her handbag and knocked him down and ran. It must have been a hard blow for the bag was full of pennies and halfpennies she had collected around the doors for Devlin's election fund. Later, after the count, as they were carrying the victorious Devlin shoulder high along the Falls Road, my mother was also hoisted up by some of the crowd in recognition of her exploit.

She was a spirited, robust, sandy-haired woman with good looks but we never got on, probably because of our identical hot tempers. Once, after I brought her chocolates back from an excursion, she said she didn't want them. I threw them on the fire and stormed out. That was the flavour of our relationship. We never got on but I was very close to my father's two sisters, Maggie and Minnie, who were both spinners in the mills. They were very religious and spent a great deal of time collecting money for the training and ordination of Irish priests for the African missions. I often accompanied them to dances and concerts, held

13

to raise funds. They also made clerical garments for missionary priests to take with them, for those from working-class backgrounds had no resources of their own.

I frequently stayed with these aunts and was spoiled by their generosity. There was some friction between them and my mother, which I, unwittingly because of my youth, aggravated. They would say something about my mother and I would tell her. Then I would carry something back from my mother to them. The result was a tense relationship with my mother who regarded me as their Trojan Horse and would whack me at every given opportunity. I remember coming up the street and falling over a broken footpath and getting a thump. She would come and take me away from playing street football and give me a biffing, usually because I was wearing my boots or shoes. My enemies soon learned to go to her if they wanted me done.

By contrast I had a marvellous relationship with Paddy Lillis, my maternal grandfather. He was highly intelligent and self-educated. I think he was batman to a radical British Army officer, who encouraged him and helped him to better himself. By the time I knew him he was elderly and living a few doors from us in Conway Street. He was riddled with rheumatism and bedridden. He couldn't use his hands so I used to go in to him three times a day – at lunchtime, after school and in the evening – to fill and light his pipe. I can still smell the strong tobacco and see the curls of smoke drifting around the room as he talked to me about his life and experiences in South Africa, India and the Great War. He admired Sir Stafford Cripps as a great Labour lawyer and politician and he enthralled me with the story of the welfare schemes for workers at Port Sunlight. It was my grandfather who first told me about the formation of the co-operative movement in Rochdale and how the enterprise benefited the consumers themselves through their ownership of it. He was anti-boss and anti-war and it was from his lips that I first heard the word 'socialism'. He was bitterly resentful that the sectarian divisions in Belfast were so deep among the working class that they prevented the emergence of a labour movement.

My grandmother, Rosie, was oblivious to our conversations. She was a mean and quarrelsome woman who took our pocket money off us for biscuits. She often sent me down to Johnny McConville's in Albert Street to bring her up a half'un of Jameson's whiskey. When I was going in and out to my grandfather she would dismiss his 'old blarney'. 'I hope you're not listening to that oul' blether,' she would say.

While my grandfather, who always treated me as an adult, was a major influence on me and all that I did afterwards, I always reckoned that my own political activism was nurtured in the political squabbling that went on between my parents. My political instincts were most certainly inherited from both my father and my mother, although I tended to favour the Labour rather than the nationalist side, and therefore my father, when I joined in the arguments. Both were hot-tempered, especially where politics was concerned, but while my father was only angry in rare outbursts, my mother's fury seemed to smoulder away all the time, especially towards me. Nevertheless, my overall memory is of a generally happy, stable household and supportive family.

As our own immediate family expanded, the house in Lady Street became too small for us and we moved to Beechmount Parade, where the rent was a steep 12s.6d. a week. Meeting it was easier in the winter when my father had a bit of overtime. However, in the summer, when the cattle were out in the fields grazing, there was reduced demand for feed so the family budget suffered and my parents had trouble keeping their heads above water.

In 1931, when I was six, the situation eased very considerably when my mother decided to get a job as a spinner in Kennedy's mill in Conway Street, which she did with the help of my grandmother. Apart from her wages, the real attraction was that we also got a mill house in the street, with a rental of only four shillings or so a week. Having been used to seeing my mother in shoes, it came as a big shock to me when she started going across the street to work in her rubber apron and bare feet. All the mill workers went unshod, for the hot water coursing over the floors quickly rotted footwear, which they could not easily afford to replace.

My most vivid childhood memories relate to that house in Conway Street, one of three streets that formed an all-Catholic enclave on the Shankill Road side of the Falls. We were not really part of the Falls and by choice we were most definitely not part of the Shankill. Adjacent to the three streets was the 'back field', the traditional battleground for Catholics and Protestants. The area was one of Belfast's most dangerous sectarian flashpoints, and there was regular rioting even after what was called the 'big trouble' of the early 1920s had subsided. In my mind's eye I can still see the pockmarked pattern of bullet holes on the back wall of our bedroom. Apparently the man who lived there before us was a gunman who was always exchanging fire with the Protestants. At night when we were going to bed by candlelight you could clearly see the holes where the bullets fired at him had come in through the window and embedded themselves in the wall.

I recall one particular occasion around 12 July 1935 when an Orange mob came down from the Shankill to attack the Catholic residents at our end of the street. My father, who had just returned from refereeing a football match, was still in his football gear having his tea when my mother ran in to warn him that the rioters were approaching. 'Quick, Tommy,' she said. 'They're in on us.' At that time of the year, police in armoured and cage cars were frequently deployed between the two communities to keep them apart. That day there were no police about, so as the mob rapidly neared our house he grabbed his football whistle, put on his hard hat to protect his head from injury, and went towards the door. Before he went out he suddenly turned back and went to the jawbox where he took his false teeth out of a cup and put them with deliberation into his mouth. My mother was screaming at him: 'They are throwing bloody stones not sausage rolls, you ole fool ye.' He grabbed open the door and dashed out into the middle of the mob, whistle blowing and arms waving. They could not see him at the back but they heard the racket, stopped, then turned and ran. The leaders and those close to them at the front panicked and they too ran back up the street. It was as if they had seen an alien from another planet. My mother as usual derided him. 'You bloody ole idiot,' she said. 'Do you want to get us all killed?' But when the police arrived later they said it was a good thing for the Catholic residents that he had acted as he did. As ever, no one was arrested for the attack.

I had started school shortly before we moved to Conway Street, going first to Beechmount Parade and then St Paul's at Cavendish Square. My teacher there was 'Bonzo' McGonigal, a vicious, muscular, wee man with tight curls, and I was terrified of him. I first fell foul of him for trying to write with my left hand. In those days that was discouraged by beating, and he used to lash me across the hands and wrists with a bamboo cane. I got the same punishment every day for failing to come to grips with the meaning of the big words in the catechism, which you were expected to learn off as a rhyme. I became so scared that I decided not to go to school, but instead of 'mitching' I used to go and sit in St Paul's Church. It seemed that this would provide me with the excuse I needed. Inevitably I was discovered by my mother or the teacher and marched back into the classroom despite proclaiming that I needed mass more than the alphabet.

My ordeal at St Paul's ended when I transferred to Conway Street school after our house move. Now, the school was up at the Protestant end of the street and we regularly had to run a gauntlet of bricks and stones as we went there each morning or returned at the end of the day. One of the teachers, Billy McDermott, who was a well-known Gaelic and hurling player, was a particular target of the unionist mobs who often invaded the school looking to beat him up. I remember he used to have to fight them off. In 1935 the Orangemen even succeeded in burning the school down.

This created a serious problem for the parish, which was faced with finding the cost of rebuilding the school. In those days the Catholic church received limited public funding from the unionist government to provide or operate its own schools. In addition, the teachers' jobs were at risk if the school could not get going again with sufficient pupils on the roll. Father O'Neill, the parish priest, who wrote the song 'Foggy Dew,' came up with the solution of re-opening an old disused school at Milford Street, but there was strong opposition among the parents, for it meant we would all have to go across the Falls Road to the alternative premises. The priest was adamant, however, and he went round the doors of all the parents to persuade them to send us to Milford Street because we would get a better education there.

There were two masters and two teachers, who took eight classes of around forty pupils each. Our education was very basic, reading, writing and arithmetic, with catechism. Billy McDermott's sister used to come in and do singing with us, mainly stuff for the choir in the church. I found myself being singled out to distribute and collect books, crayons and all that sort of thing. They also sent me out to round up anybody who wasn't turning up in school. This was a reflection of the need to keep the roll numbers up or the class would have been closed down and the remaining pupils moved elsewhere. John McConnell, the principal, was a great nationalist and a close friend of Joe Devlin but remarkably enough, looking back on it, he didn't teach us very much Irish history or language.

To keep administration costs down senior pupils were required to wash the boys' and girls' schoolyards, a task for which I was in due course selected. One day we realised that certain girls were coming down to the lavatory while we were there. We pushed the door and they commenced to giggle. The doors opened and we were invited in. That was the beginning of a whole new series of experiences that led to us following the girls after school hours. We started to attend the Falls Road cinemas, like the Clonard and the Diamond, sometimes going further afield afterwards for more adventures.

By 1939, when I was fourteen, school for me was a bore. I had no interest in attending except to wash the schoolyards and meet the girls. No one was concerned about teaching me anything more. The principal knew that I was more interested in playing football or running his messages and that I had picked up as much as they could teach me. So, armed with a reference that said that I had been 'a hard working and respect-ful pupil' who 'passed through all classes with credit to himself and his teachers', I left in June that year and went off to look for my first job.

For about eighteen months before I actually left school I had been going into Samuel Bell's egg and poultry shop on the Falls Road to help the manager, Jimmy Burns, usually on Friday night and Saturday. My father knew them through football and he got me started. I began by doing messages and deliveries but before long I was able to clean rabbits and fowl, sort eggs and even handle the money. They were impressed enough by my ability to offer me a full-time job when I finally left school. Some days I was sent to work at Bell's other two shops in North Queen Street and Old Lodge Road, while Friday was normally spent at St George's Market. The wage of 4s.6d. a week was pretty miserable, so after a year or so my mother took a hand in things to find me a new job. After walking the length of the Antrim Road with her, going in and out of the various shops, asking if they wanted a message boy, we finally ended up in Walker's, a big double-fronted shop at Fortwilliam which sold fruit, vegetables and groceries. They had a vacancy, so, after my mother had negotiated a wage of eight shillings for me, I was sent down to the back of the shop to get a bicycle.

After wheeling it to the loading point, getting the delivery address and putting the orders into the basket at the front of the handlebars, the boss came over. 'Oh, by the way, what's your name?' he asked.

'Paddy,' said I.

'No, Percy,' he replied.

'Paddy,' I said again.

'No. Percy, Percy,' he repeated.

'Paddy,' said I emphatically. 'Fuck Percy.'

With that I walked out and headed home after less than one hour in the place. Although I had grown up in an atmosphere of sectarian confrontation, this was my first real brush with the insidious religious tensions which permeated and corroded every strand of life in Belfast. By calling myself 'Percy' instead of 'Paddy', none of the customers in the big houses around the Antrim Road would guess that a wee Catholic was delivering their foodstuffs.

Jimmy Burns thought I was a right fellow and he wrote a letter to Mackie's foundry on my behalf. I was called for interview, got the job and in due course reported for work in the moulding shop, a big hangar of a place with overhead cranes, piles of black sand, heavy iron moulds and more noise than I'd ever heard in my life before. The wages were good, about fourteen shillings a week, but the work was hard and demanding. It involved packing black sand very tightly into a mould and then clamping it down. Once it was shaped you began hammering it loose with two steel drumsticks. If it wasn't clamped down hard enough or broke when it was coming out, you had to throw it away and start again. I suffered agonies, for my hands were soft from working in the poultry shop and blistered at once, with the result that I could hardly hold the steel drumsticks, never mind beat out the mould.

Bad as my experience at the Antrim Road had been, I encountered what can only be described as naked sectarianism at Mackie's. Out of the three hundred workers in the shop, only three or four were Catholics and the Protestants used to constantly throw things at us. One fellow, from the Whiterock, could handle himself and he was spared the worst of the abuse but I was only a puny teenager of fifteen at the time and was always being singled out. They would leave heated tools and tell me to pick them up. I was physically grabbed and jostled by older men. Going to the toilet was a particular ordeal, for they would follow you in, beat the iron sides of the cubicles, shout vicious and frightening abuse and throw bits of iron and pieces of debris. 'Don't say anything. It will only get worse,' advised a workmate. 'What's worse?' I asked. When I was sacked and paid off after two weeks I was actually glad to go.

After a spell as a butcher's messenger boy, with Hugh Simpson of Albert Street, I was attracted to serving my time in the trade. He taught me about boning out meat and I learned about the machines for making mince and sausages, by cleaning them. However, at seventeen I wasn't able to get a formal apprenticeship so I abandoned the idea and started with Smyth's Musical, the gramophone record distributors, as a traveller and driver. They got a professional driver to teach me to drive an old Austin they had and soon afterwards I went on the road, driving throughout Northern Ireland, selling 78 r.p.m. records to music shops. I was accompanied by another member of the Smyth family, who sold saddles and bridles for horses and all that kind of thing. But the wages were low, less than twenty shillings a week, so I was interested in a newspaper advertisement from John Malcolm's, who were butchers in Holywood, Co. Down, for a delivery van driver. There were few staff and plenty of work to do, so, without any chance of a formal apprenticeship or learning a trade, I pushed myself forward to help with the butchery tasks. I stayed there for a year until my blossoming career was forcibly halted by my other, clandestine activities.

2

'A TOE UP THE ARSE'

Around about the time I was eleven I used to see groups of young men dressed in green berets, green tunics and black pants regularly marching around the local streets. One or two of them always had white lanyards and diagonal leather Sam Browne belts. These particularly attracted me. Boys who were not members seemed to have great respect for those who were, and from whispered enquiries I discovered that this was Na Fianna Éireann, the youth wing of the republican movement. It had been founded in Belfast in 1903 by Bulmer Hobson, one of the pioneers of Sinn Féin and the Irish Republican Army. Its aim was to train the youth of Ireland to play their part in the struggle for Irish independence. This was to be done by teaching Irish history and Irish language and by training them in military techniques. In truth, the Fianna was the breeding ground for the IRA.

Before long, I joined the Fianna myself. There was no great political passion or patriotic zeal behind this move. My motivation was simple: membership gave you a status among the rest of the eleven-year-olds. Those who were bigger and stronger might be able to fight more effectively, but for me, obviously an insecure boy at that time, joining the Fianna was the equaliser because you then had the backing of a greater power, and people were frightened of that.

My parents did not know of my joining up and what was to prove to be a momentous personal decision for me. When they found out a year or so later, my father didn't say anything but it became another reason for my mother to lash out at me. As we were always at loggerheads anyway, it was neither here nor there. Sometimes I smuggled my uniform into the house and hid it under the mattress, but usually I kept it at another house and changed there when we were going out marching. When I was fitted for my tunic I was initially disappointed to find that there was no Sam Browne belt, which was only worn by the officers. However, I was soon drilling and preening myself in the bedroom mirror at home. I took to marching up and down the streets saluting everybody, hoping that they would acknowledge they were witnessing someone very special. I also got a lot of fun later when I was recognised and brought to the attention of the detectives from the CID and the Special Branch, who rode round the Falls area on bicycles. We knew them all well – Detective Inspector Moffat, Inspector Fanning, Sergeant Norwood, Detective Gregg. I never thought that my enemy was other than these detectives. We never saw the military and indeed the ordinary uniformed policemen were quite benign. We did not like the B Specials, of course, but then we never did see them.

I was in the Frank Doherty Sluagh, or section, of the Fianna. It was located in the same area of the Falls that covered D Company of the IRA – the square bounded by Albert Street, Durham Street, Grosvenor Road and the Falls Road. I put my heart and soul into the Fianna work and soon I was promoted to section commander, responsible for the mobilisation of members for meetings or special duties, and the gathering of intelligence which was passed to the IRA. This was a period of calm, however, and the republican movement was not engaged in any violent activity, so our main preoccupation was preparing for the annual commemorative outing at the end of June to Bodenstown, Co. Kildare, where Wolfe Tone is buried.

Throughout the year we ran games of 'Housey', better known these days as Bingo, which was a real money-spinner, especially on summer nights when everybody used to sit outside their houses on stools and chairs and someone would walk up and down the street calling out the numbers. The proceeds enabled us to gather the funds for the outing. On the big day we would march through Dublin from one railway terminus to the other and if we could provoke a riot with the Garda Síochána, the southern Irish police force, that was the icing on the cake. We had a healthy respect for them, however, and always knew when to keep clear, for they had a reputation for taking no prisoners.

The content of the speeches on these occasions rarely interested us, but it was in the Fianna that my first serious interest in Irish history developed. I was captivated by the stories of the United Irishmen and the achievements of marvellous old philanthropic Belfast families like the McCrackens, the Joys and the McCabes who did so much for the benefit of the townsfolk. Their support for the building of two Catholic churches, the Charitable Institute, the Linen Hall Library, the first hospital and educational establishments and the Harbour Commission had been crucial to the development of Belfast. Perhaps their finest achievements related to the expulsion of the slave traders from the harbour, long before it was done elsewhere, and to our participation in the great debate on democracy in France and America at a time when debate in England was concerned with bolstering backward royalists. At weekly classes held in the houses of sympathisers and members we were lectured on Irish history right up to the present, and I became emotionally and romantically attached to what I saw then as the just and uncomplicated cause of freeing Ireland from British exploitation.

Another weekly chore was the Sunday morning drilling we carried out at the 'Hatchet Field', in the Falls Park. I can remember vividly our activities that fateful Sunday in September 1939 when the Second World War started. I left St Peter's after early mass that morning in a rush. I had to be on parade with the Fianna in fifteen minutes and as we had a new commanding officer with a tendency to bully I had no intention of becoming his victim by being late. Just as I reached the park, the adjutant called the parade to order and we started marching back and forwards, up and down, across the field. Suddenly there was a warning cry from one of the scouts, or look-outs, that had been posted in the trees around the area. 'Police coming. There's a lot of them,' he shouted.

The OC was unmoved. 'Let them get nearer,' he said. Such bravado was not unusual. Most Sundays we allowed the police to reach the edge of the field before we took flight, escaping through narrow gaps we had earlier bent in the railings around the field. Even if the portly, middle-aged policemen, who were not as fit or as fleet-footed as we were, could keep up with us, they were unable to follow us once we passed through the railings. That morning, however, as we fled, we were surprised to see several tenders loaded with policemen, not the usual half-hearted, half-dozen pursuers. We headed for the nearby city cemetery, where Protestants are buried, and moved furtively, taking cover behind the headstones. The police did not follow us into the cemetery for fear of giving offence to the mourners at the gravesides, as they represented the ruling class and the police knew better than to offend them. Having given the police the slip, we all set off for our homes wondering why they had made such a major bid to capture us.

Within minutes of my reaching the house, Lapsy Doran, who wore his coat and cap even in the heat of summer and who had been the scout in the trees, arrived to tell me to listen to the radio. The OC had sent an order to tune in because Neville Chamberlain, the British prime minister, was making an important broadcast. The atmosphere was electric as I settled down with my father and mother. As we waited my father talked about the air raid precautions and the use of gas masks that would become necessary if war was declared. Within a few moments we heard Chamberlain's historic words that war was indeed declared on Germany. We had little time for the British and were neutral about the Germans, as de Valera had advised us, so the Catholic community viewed the looming conflict with some detachment. Many young people of my age expected the German planes to arrive overhead at once and drop their bombs as we had seen pictures of them doing in Spain.

As soon as the broadcast was over, Lapsy arrived back at our front door. 'The OC wants you urgently in the back room of the Big Shot Billiard Hall,' he said. I followed him round and when we got there the OC called us to attention. 'I've just got word from Dublin. Great news. England's difficulty is Ireland's opportunity. They have fallen into our trap. Now they have Germany to face on the European front and ourselves lying in wait to attack their backs in a deadly pincer movement. They don't know that for years the Frank Doherty Sluagh of Na Fianna Éireann have been organising and getting themselves into a state of military fitness to battle it out with them to the death. The time has at last arrived to start our battle.'

The opening shots he ordered hardly matched such a grandiose build-up. We were ordered to get brushes and buckets and prepare whitewash to paint slogans on gable walls. I was not involved in the subsequent operation, but next morning on my way to work I saw the embarrassing results. 'England's difficulty is Ireland's opera tune' had been daubed on factory walls and gables all along the Falls Road. I prayed for rain.

At that time the IRA's D Company area in the Falls was effectively the heartland of the organisation in the northern part of the country, for the Belfast battalion and the northern command were both run from there. Although I did not appreciate the larger picture at the time, the IRA was in fact a ramshackle organisation, heavily penetrated by the police on both sides of the border. Thanks to the pressure they exerted through informers, constant house raids and searches, and pre-emptive action against IRA activity, the organisation had been reduced to all but a dedicated hard core of members. It had indeed been largely dormant for ten years, until the 1930s, when the trauma of partition and the subsequent civil war in the South had begun to subside. The beginning of a new campaign was compromised in 1936 when the RUC lifted virtually the entire northern leadership, who were conducting a court martial at a club in Crown Entry in Belfast. This led to their imprisonment and the subsequent killing of two men as informers. There followed some attacks on border customs posts, one set of which coincided with the visit to Northern Ireland of King George VI and Queen Elizabeth in July 1937.

A new leadership took over in the spring of 1938 and plans were laid for more attacks. Although internment without trial was reintroduced in December 1938, the organisation issued an ultimatum on 12 January 1939 telling the British Foreign Secretary to order withdrawal from the six 'occupied' counties. A series of explosions in Britain, the so-called S-Plan, then began, culminating with the bicycle bombing in Coventry on 25 August in which five people were killed. The declaration of the Second World War on 3 September completely eclipsed the campaign, which fizzled out on 6 February 1940, the day before the two Coventry bombers, Peter Barnes and James McCormick, were hanged at Winson Green Prison in Birmingham.

There was of course a close association between the Fianna boys and the IRA. The understanding was that when the boys reached sixteen years of age the suitable ones could join the IRA. By the time war broke out I was fifteen, and actively working to make the transition to the parent organisation. I had cultivated the Fianna OC and had progressed to officer rank, commanding a section. By lying about my real age, I had little difficulty manoeuvring my way into the IRA itself in early 1940.

My path into the IRA was easier than I had expected because the entire staff of D Company were arrested by the RUC and later sentenced to prison for seven years. They had been caught in a house in Getty Street, where lists of names had also been found, so the rest of the company volunteers were rounded up for internment. Those who were not at home when the raiding parties called mainly took off for jobs in England.

By the time I joined, therefore, the IRA was in some disarray although it was carrying out robberies to raise money for its activities and mounting sporadic attacks against the police and other targets. The IRA also began to collect 'royalties' from their local communities around this time. Social clubs and bookies at the race tracks were among the targets for contributions. It transpired that the payments were protection money against private enterprise 'hoods', who were beaten up in public view by the IRA. It was hoped that this would increase the IRA's popularity, but the public turned away. When the squad responsible for the beatings were eventually interned, they were ostracised by the other internees. Such conduct, including armed raids on private companies, was declared to be 'taboo' by the older republican leaders. Early in 1940, however, the move- ment scored a notable success by stealing one hundred rifles from the British Army barracks at Ballykinler, Co. Down.

I vividly remember my first gun lecture which took place in a small kitchen house in Balkan Street. Over twenty men had gathered in sweltering heat while an aggressive wee man at- tempted to drill us. He shouted commands at the top of his voice, revelling in his authority over us. Mercifully the punitive drilling stopped before I teetered over at the point of collapse, but the rest of the men suffered, for they were older and less fit than me. As we recovered painfully, he produced a Webley .45 from a cupboard. 'This is a Webley revolver, range sixty yards, accurate up to forty,' he said. 'It has three parts, a barrel, body and butt.' Thus I was initiated into the twilight world of guns.

One morning I was ordered to commandeer a car from a man who lived at the back of the Clonard monastery. Few people in the area had cars, and even fewer had petrol for them during the war, but this man worked in the aircraft factory and had a special ration. About 7.30 a.m., as he rushed from the house to go to work with a breakfast bap in his hand, I sidled alongside him and said: 'I want your car for the IRA.' Without a pause in his pace or his chewing, he swept me scornfully aside and said: 'Fuck off, you wee bastard, or I'll give you a toe up the arse!'

The unionist government in Belfast, always sensitive to the least hint of IRA activity, was, predictably, in a state of anxiety that the republicans were a fifth column in league with the Nazis. This feeling intensified as the pace of the war accelerated and precautions against bombing raids were introduced. There were also fears that the blackout would be infringed in the nationalist areas, guiding the bombers in. When the IRA organised the gathering and burning of the gas masks which were issued to everyone, these fears were aggravated. The RUC was ordered to act vigorously against the IRA, penetrating its ranks, observing its members and rounding up the most dangerous and active for internment without trial. The IRA was not popular with the Catholic community, and the police, who walked the beat and cycled around, were in close contact with people who passed on every scrap of information about our actions.

The round-ups were selective, reflecting clever police tactics. Volunteers who were physically conspicuous and easy to recognise because of their striking features, like size or hair colour, were allowed to remain at large. They were then followed by the police and those with whom they spoke or associated became suspects, who were, in turn, followed or arrested. Local people were also encouraged to inform, and membership gradually melted away. By this process I came to the notice of the police for the first time, resulting in a raid on our house in the middle of one night in May 1940.

It was clearly a fishing expedition, for at first they seemed to be more interested in my father, until they realised he was an ex-soldier and almost deaf. As I stood before them, they must have figured a mistake had been made when they looked at the walls festooned with the likeness and emblems of my mother's favourite politician, Wee Joe Devlin. She did not know that I had joined the IRA, so, with innocent conviction, she proceeded to lecture the raiding party on the merits of constitutional nationalism, of which her hero was the patron saint. 'My own father fought in the British Army for thirty years. If he knew you were in his eldest daughter's house, he would have you all court martialled,' she roared. It seemed to do the trick because they left the house without me. They were not deceived, however, and after sizing up the situation they soon came back again and took me away. I was held overnight in the lock-up at Musgrave Street and questioned before being released the next day.

Shortly after this episode the members of D Company were called to a meeting at which we were ordered to collect information about all strategic and military installations and report them back to the battalion staff. Other companies deployed their volunteers in the east, south and north of Belfast, while we operated in the area of the Lisburn and Malone roads. I remember hearing that low-flying planes had their numbers taken and the number of times they passed overhead, while a record was also made of the numbers of uniformed policemen patrolling the Falls and even how often they visited the betting shops. The locations of hospitals, industrial units and the sighting of soldiers of any type were also to be recorded. We were required to make written notes and draw maps of our observations, but most of our members were poorly educated and the necessary levels of literacy and drawing were well beyond them. At this time the republican leadership in Dublin was openly flirting with the Hitler regime, which maintained a diplomatic presence in the neutral Free State throughout the war.

Belfast's shipyards and aircraft factories became a prime target for the German bombers in 1941. On Easter Tuesday, the night of the worst attack, I was at a céilidh dance in the Ulster Hall and the air raid wardens came in to tell us that an attack was taking place; it was the first time we had seen them with their tin helmets on. Delia Murphy stayed on stage singing and we continued dancing and it was only when we were going home, well after the bombers had departed, that we realised how serious it had been. The night sky was lit up bright red by the intensity of the fires; 745 people had been killed, and thousands of homes destroyed.

From time to time I borrowed the car of my unionist employer, who often used to boast to me of their gun-running exploits with the UVF in 1914. I mainly used it to deliver republican newspapers around Co. Armagh and Co. Tyrone but there were other occasions, depending on the availability of the car, when I ferried northern command officers like Eoin McNamee and Brendan O'Boyle around rural areas of the north.

One day the Falls Road companies of the IRA were mobilised for an outdoor parade and we marched through the back streets of the area carrying hurling sticks. The press were alerted to what was no more than a publicity stunt, but the photographs published in the newspapers took the RUC and the government by surprise. As a result, the government ordered a crackdown and the level of police activity escalated. As I had already been in police hands, I had an inflated sense of my own importance and I was hooked on the romanticism of the struggle. Although I was very much on the fringes of the organisation and was never involved in any direct acts of armed violence, I thought loftily of myself becoming a martyr like Patrick Pearse or James Connolly, so I left home and went on the run for fear I would be picked up again by the police and detained. Being a 'fugitive' only slightly curtailed my habits; I still went to my work at the butchers every day and slipped in and out of my aunts' house in Lady Street for meals and a bed. I sometimes think I was on the run from my mother as well, for she hated the IRA, which she now realised I had joined, and made it clear how unwelcome I was at home. I was also playing water polo for the Cathal Brugha swimming club at the time, but I only played

31

matches for the team away from the Falls Baths, which the police had under regular surveillance.

Sometimes I slept in ARP posts or the fire brigade place in Hawthorn Street. For a time I even infiltrated the ARP organisation and went around at night in a uniform and tin hat with the ARP initials on it. Most of the time I stayed in houses in my local D Company area, taking care to get back in time to avoid the blackout, for the police knew our routes and waited for us in the dark. One night after being out late with a man called 'Josie the jigger', a flamboyant figure who always cut a dash with the ladies in the local dance halls or 'jigs', arrangements were made for me to stop in one of his houses. The woman of the house, an attractive blonde in her thirties whose husband was in the army stationed someplace in England, greeted us warmly and rearranged the livingroom chairs for us to sleep on. I was awakened around 2 a.m. by the lady telling Josie that there was some noise outside in the street. She invited him to come upstairs and check it out through the window to see if it was the police. He did so with alacrity while I settled down again on my makeshift bed and listened too. Instead of the supposed police raiding party, however, all I could hear was the creaking of the bedsprings from the room above.

Police effectiveness and internment in the early war years robbed the IRA of its most active members and leaders. Activity fell away so dramatically that several elderly republicans were drafted in in early 1942 to revive the organisation and its campaign against partition. At Easter an order was given to C Company, who operated in the Clonard area, to create a diversion while the 1916 Rising commemoration took place at Milltown cemetery in defiance of a government ban. They took up position on the Kashmir Road near an air raid shelter and waited for a suitable target. Shots were fired at a police car, and a policeman who got out and chased the unit was shot dead. Tom Williams, who was only nineteen, was wounded and was quickly arrested in a nearby house where he had taken refuge with the others. All were eventually sentenced to death for murder, but five were reprieved after Williams took responsibility. He was hanged at Crumlin Road prison in September 1942.

Williams, whose home at Bombay Street was close to ours in Conway Street, had been in the Fianna with me and we had joined the IRA together. He also swam in the Cathal Brugha water polo team. He was a quiet studious character and I still think he did not fire the fatal shot. Indeed, he may not even have been armed that day. I also knew the dead policeman, Constable Paddy Murphy, a pleasant family man who lived at Clowney Street. His son Martin regularly played football with me in the Falls Park. The policeman was well known to the entire community in the Falls and it was unusual for him to be in a motor vehicle. More often he was out on foot around the area, where he was very popular with the kids, always joking with them or pulling their legs. He almost certainly knew the IRA group involved because they were all locals.

As the date for Williams's execution neared, orders were given to the volunteers to get ready for a campaign to avenge it. The campaign depended on arms smuggled from the South to the North for the purpose. These had been collected and brought to four separate farms at Hannahstown and Budore in the hills above West Belfast. However, three days before the hanging the farms were raided by the police, who shot dead one of the IRA members guarding the arsenal and seized the entire contents. On the opening morning of the planned campaign volunteers were mobilised for certain meeting places at certain times. The police arrived almost simultaneously to arrest and intern them. Shortly afterwards they captured Hugh McAteer, the chief of staff, and uncovered a headquarters at Crumlin Road, where they seized weapons, documents and a radio transmitter. By the end of September 1942, 120 had been rounded up in Belfast and another 200 elsewhere in the North and there was nothing much left of the IRA after that. I knew in my heart it was only a matter of time before I too was apprehended and interned.

Late one evening towards the end of the month I left a dance in King Street with a group of male and female friends. We walked along Castle Street and into Divis Street, where we were stopped by a police patrol not far from Hastings Street police barracks. As we were all being asked questions one of the policemen shone his torch on my face and recognised me. I was promptly grabbed from behind and we were all frogmarched off to the nearby station. The officer who arrested me was actually the Cliftonville and Northern Ireland amateur goalkeeper, Fred McCorry, who knew me from my days as ballboy at Celtic Park. Our initial acquaintance was made during conversations when play was at the other end of the field. (I must say I never harboured any resentment against him and in later, happier times we met frequently and became close friends.)

Once inside the police station I was lodged in a cell with one of my companions, who was also in the IRA. The others, who were not involved, were released. I am convinced that he gave me away, indeed probably lured me into position for the police to apprehend me after the dance. We spent some time together in the cell, probably in the hope that I might say something useful or incriminating, before I was removed to the police lock-up in Chichester Street. The cells there looked big and cavernous, and the whitewashed walls were full of hand-written obscenities which I spent the night trying to read. Most of them referred to ladies who were either forgotten or appreciated. I recognised Constable McCormack, the jailer. He was a towering south of Ireland man, a veteran of the old RIC, who lived on the Springfield Road and was not far from retirement. I remembered seeing him on the beat. He had been a champion heavyweight boxer in his day, with a reputation of being quiet but someone to be left alone. As he was putting me into the cell he spoke to me in his customary kindly way, for he was a man who imposed the rule of law with soft tones and wise advice.

His was the only kindly voice I heard throughout the two days I remained there. Each morning he arranged for my breakfast from the Irish Temperance League café in Ann Street, and allowed me the latitude of exercising outside my cell and having a proper wash before I was handed over for interrogation to District Inspector Fanning, a Catholic member of the Special Branch. On the third day after my arrest I was taken to Assembly College, near Queen's University, for more questioning by District Inspector Albert Kennedy, who was later to become Inspector-General of the RUC. He had portraits of Joseph Stalin and Karl Marx hanging on the wall of his office, which I now recognise was a ploy to draw potential internees into conversation. Although I recognised Stalin, I had no idea who Marx was, and when Kennedy began to speak about their political philosophy it had no effect on me at all for I was still politically naïve. Despite this, the police had clearly marked me as an IRA activist and I soon found myself being escorted into a Black Maria for the short drive across Belfast to the Crumlin Road prison. The next few years proved to be the most formative of my life.

3

THE WHISTLING B-MAN

The police van backed up to the main gates and when the doors were opened I got my first view of the inside of Crumlin Road prison, whitewashed walls and tall, barred gates. I was hand-cuffed and taken through another gate, across a yard, then up steps into the reception hall, where I had my pockets emptied of three shillings in cash and four or five religious medals given to me by my aunts. After they were scrutinised I received them back again. The next stop was at what is called 'the circle', to wait on someone coming to assign me to a cell. The circle is the hub of the prison, from which the four wings of cells radiate like the spokes of a wheel. This enables the warders to see along each of the wings, which were designated by letters of the alphabet. The sentenced criminal prisoners accounted for the bulk of the inmates. A and D wings held the long-term political inmates, who were always referred to as 'the internees'.

Part of C wing was also occupied by detainees, who fell into two categories. There were those, like me, recently arrested and waiting the statutory twenty-one days for internment orders to be confirmed. The others were known as 'the signees'. They were long-term internees seeking release who had signed an application for a hearing by the appeal tribunal. It had power to free them if they co-operated with the police beforehand and signed an undertaking to sever their links with the IRA. They were ostracised by the main body of internees, who stubbornly refused to concede the legitimacy of the unionist administration by recognising the appeal mechanism. They were also regarded as traitors, for everybody knew they could not be released without giving the police information, such co-operation being evidence of their reformation. Despite accepting this stigma as informers, in the eyes of their comrades, the men, many of whom were forced by pressing family circumstances to sign for the tribunal, received little sympathy from the authorities. Once they applied for a hearing they immediately had to face interviews with detectives on their activities prior to internment. They were, of course, presumed to be active members of the IRA. It was not uncommon for them to be knocked back four or five times by the tribunal for failing to co-operate. Many of them spent a further eighteen months inside before regaining their freedom.

In the full rush of my naïve idealism I clashed with several of these angry and frustrated men during the earliest days of my own imprisonment. There was I, a cocky and inexperienced seventeen-year-old, telling these mature, married men, some with grown families and years in the IRA and jail behind them, that C wing was only purgatory before entering the paradise of full martyrdom for the republican cause. I became a fully-fledged internee on schedule after three weeks when my internment order was formally signed by Sir Dawson Bates, the notorious Minister of Home Affairs who once refused to use his official telephone because the switchboard operator at Stormont parliament building was a Catholic.

The permanent warder on the third floor of C wing, when I arrived, was a man called Moore. He was an outspoken bully with a fearsome reputation, who ruled his patch without compromise. I was intimidated from the first moment he looked at me, for I had heard on the prison grapevine that he was a member of the 'Beating-up' gang, a group of burly officers who amused themselves during the night by cruelly assaulting any prisoners who may have crossed them during the day. Stories of such beatings had a cautionary effect on the conduct of prisoners but it did not cow all of them.

This was especially true of Danny Trainor, a wee man with an enormous sense of humour. One morning he was in a black mood suffering from flu, so he waited outside his cell for the prison officers to say that the doctor was on the way. We all viewed the doctor as next to useless, for whatever your ailment, inside or outside, his sole remedy was M&B headache tablets. After a time the call came. 'D1, D2 and D3, the doctor is in,' shouted the principal officer.

Danny leaned over the landing railings and shouted down at the officer. 'Sure the doctor is only a fucker,' he said.

The officer was aghast and scanned the landings for the heckler. 'Up there, up there,' he said. 'Who called the doctor a fucker?'

'Down there, down there,' replied Danny. 'Who called the fucker a doctor?'

Though I did not worry about the privations and hardship of prison life at the time, in retrospect I can see it was a levelling experience. The day began with the degrading experience of 'slopping out', emptying the bucket which served as an overnight toilet in spartan cells devoid of all but a stool, a table and a bed. Food was brought to the cell by other prisoners. To please Moore, who supervised the process himself, they gave out larger portions to his 'blue-eyes'. It was a small concession, for the quality of the food was appalling. At breakfast time we got eight ounces of hard bread, a small and inadequate square of margarine and a tin beaker of tea. The main meal consisted of two large rotten potatoes and tasteless, unrecognisable vegetables. To stay alive you could not do without it, so I scoffed it, skins and all! The rest of the day was spent endlessly marching around the exercise yard.

After a time I was transferred to the 'paradise' of D wing, where I was shown to an allocated cell on the second of the three floors, not by a scowling warder but by another internee. D wing, surrounded by barbed wire, was set apart from the other wings with only one door through to the prison circle. An elected 'staff' of internees ran the wing. They decided who would be admitted and administered the allocation of all equipment and food to each internee. They even controlled a separate cookhouse. After a couple of months, when the staff realised I had been a butcher and could bone, roll and tie sides of beef, I was appointed to the cookhouse. This was a useful perk for there was milk and bread galore. Cookhouse staff soon grew fat and, as there was always pressure for the plum jobs there, I felt I did well in holding mine for nine months.

Good order and discipline in the wing were the responsibility of the internees, and the staff negotiated directly with the prison governor, an ex-army captain, on any points of dispute. One such conflict arose over a hunger strike in A wing. After two weeks getting nowhere and losing heart they sent a letter to our OC, Ernie Hillen, seeking support. I had known him ever since the time I had seen him in broad daylight, calmly walking away from a bank on the Falls Road with a Webley revolver and a sheaf of bank notes. He was interned soon afterwards and when I caught up with him again inside he was a bundle of tricks, always joking, with a thirst to be popular. This side of Ernie's nature caused him to promise support for the A wing protest and so we were ordered to commence a hunger strike one Monday morning. This meant staying in our cells and existing on hot water laced with salt and pepper. The governor boxed clever, saying that as there was no issue in D wing causing the strike, there would be no recognition or negotiation. A couple of days later, as I was out of the cell collecting water, I overheard a real barney going on between Hillen and some of the older internees. They told him the strike was ineffective and was just imposing unnecessary hardship. By the end of the week Hillen was outnumbered. The older internees concocted a face-saving way to throw in the towel, the strike was called off and he had fallen from grace.

The internees had much more latitude than convicted prisoners, such arrangements reflecting the fact that none of us had been charged, tried or sentenced for any offence. It also satisfied our own perception of ourselves as prisoners of war or political prisoners. We enjoyed social association from 7.30 a.m. until 8.30 p.m. each evening before lock-up for the night. The exercise yard was open three times each day except in winter. Outdoor sports like Gaelic football and general athletics were also on-going. Inside, in the dining areas where meals were eaten instead of in our cells, all sorts of recreation took place: Irish language classes, nightly rosary, meetings and parades, Sunday mass, concerts, sometimes choir practices, bridge and chess.

The warders, who were few and far between, were mainly concerned with keeping us in custody through a constant head-count of internees. There was longstanding official paranoia about escapes but, although some of the internees always sought the opportunity, by the time I arrived in 1942 all but the most dedicated had given up any thought of trying to break out. The majority were thoroughly bored of being in prison and were so completely fed up with each other's faces, habits and ideas that they had fragmented into disparate factions on the numerous issues of the day. Talks on strategy had been abandoned and gun lectures discontinued. These developments were clear evidence of low morale. At the time some of the men had been there for five years, since the start of the S-Plan bombing campaign in Britain in 1938. Others had been interned in 1939 on the outbreak of war. These were very long sentences for men who had never faced a judge or jury. Worse still was the likelihood of being kept in custody until the war was over. In 1942 that looked a very distant prospect. This was perhaps the most agonising aspect for us; you could not count the days to release because each of us was detained for an indefinite period.

I had met many of these men outside, some when I used my employer's vehicle to drive members of the leadership around.

I was bitterly disappointed when I arrived amongst them to find so many of my earlier heroes now disillusioned 'broken men', waiting for the opportunity or excuse to sign for the appeal tribunal. That was exceedingly difficult for me to live with but, having got a 'biff on the gob' earlier for arguing back with a 'signee' of mature years, I remembered the lesson and decided to keep my own views to myself. Nevertheless, my youthful ardour was heavily dampened by witnessing the leaders I had idolised criticising everything associated with the IRA.

In the months leading up to going on the run and being captured, I had moved on from simply enjoying the uniform, the excitement and the thrill of the chase. The real political purposes of the IRA were something I only vaguely understood, but I clearly recall beginning to feel a sense of Irishness. Catholic families in Belfast, especially from the working class, usually had forebears who had volunteered and served in the British Army, forced to join by the lack of alternative employment to keep their families at times of depression. Both sides of my family fitted this pattern, so I developed an aversion to what I regarded as British garrison dependency.

As my sense of being Irish developed, I stopped playing soccer, took up Gaelic football and started attending Irish dances and language classes. I began to use simple Irish salutations with my friends, such as 'Slán leat' – 'Good health be with you'. I loved Irish music, Irish dancing and John McCormack singing Irish songs. Traditional Irish music fired my spirit and stimulated my emotions.

Given this state of mind, the activities available to me when I arrived in prison were mouthwatering. I took to learning Irish properly, which had been an ambition for a number of years. With my rudimentary schooling and no knowledge of basic grammar, I had to do it the hard way, learning words, sentences, phrases and idioms off by heart. I started to carry books about with me at all times. When I had a free minute I would open the book at a page where I had my sentences written,

41

usually spelt phonetically. I would read aloud and memorise the sounds and the meaning of each word, a system of learning which I used in other contexts for years afterwards.

I learned words of salutation and words used in daily life in the prison and, picking out people with a more advanced knowledge of the language, I made it a point to walk round the exercise yard conversing with them to perfect my fluency. I was greatly encouraged when, after my first exam, I was allowed to wear a small green ring on my lapel. The second and main exam was not so easy, for it required an intimate acquaintance with the rules of Gaelic grammar. In time I was able to grasp them and win the gold *fáinne*, the badge which symbolised fluency in Irish. These badges were stamped out of an old jail bell, smuggled out of the prison, coated in gold, and then smuggled back in again. In doing so I had the enormous help of Liam McGrattan, a noted Gaelic scholar and writer, after I moved in to share his cell. Liam, a native of Portaferry in Co. Down and much older than me, developed his own talents by studying in his cell. He later became quite famous as a writer of short stories in Irish.

Football was still a major passion and there was plenty of time and opportunity to pursue it inside. Danny Moore, Harry O'Neill and Gerry O'Hare were all good players who shared my enthusiasm and we played virtually every day, except when extreme weather prevented it. The teams were drawn from town and country prisoners. These were absolute needle matches, keenly and often roughly fought, reflecting the rivalries amongst the internees, strengthened by the closeness of living together. The rivalry was exacerbated by the natural conflict that exists between urban and rural dwellers, their cultural differences and way of living. The strong religious ties of the rural dwellers, by contrast with those of the city people, set the pattern for the rugged individual clashes that took place in these games. I was delighted to play, usually as goalkeeper for the city side. The playing pitch was restricted, perhaps sixty-five yards by fifty, and as the goal area was narrow, I discovered that by positioning myself properly I could cut off all shots at the goal. I really wanted to play out on the field but the team would not allow it.

As well as my daily football and learning Irish, I extended my reading list. When I first went in I shared the popular taste for the sort of cheap paperbacks that my father used to bring me from the bookstalls in Smithfield market. These were of the thriller variety: detective mysteries and 'high-noon' cowboy shoot-outs. There was also a black market for 'blue' books. *No Orchids for Miss Blandish* was one such title that relieved the endless nights of boredom in lonely cells. Reading books was a major pastime in D wing. Classic novels went the rounds. More serious titles were identified and requested through reading book reviews in the newspapers, and were sent in from outside by relatives and organisations interested in internee welfare. Sandy McNabb, brother of the famous Father Vincent McNabb, a priest who regaled the crowds at Speakers' Corner in London, advised me on what to read to give me a better grasp of the English language. A highly educated man, and a great raconteur and humanitarian, he enabled me to benefit from internment by widening my reading and interests and know-ledge. I began to read political books so that I could take part in the daily debates and discussions that went on among the serious men. I read the works of James Connolly repeatedly until I understood his ideas. The discussions between 'Moscow' Jack Brady, Barney Boswell from Dockland, and Joe Rice and Danny Whelan from Ardoyne, were both instructive and fascinating. I learned new words and debating skills from them as they discussed the intricacies of religion, politics and economics.

Although we were all nominally republican and Catholic, some of us, like Barney Boswell, did not attend mass on Sun-days. Pressure was mounted by the wing leaders not to let the side down. We were told that each Sunday morning the warders would look into the cell to find who was still in bed while everyone else was attending mass.

'What will they say when they find you in your beds?' said one of the senior internees.

'What do you mean?' asked one of the non-practising Catholics.

'They'll say you're not a Catholic,' came the reply.

'Not a Catholic, eh! Well let them say "curse the pope" outside my cell door and they'll find out whether I'm a fucking Catholic or not.'

When I first went into D wing my cell was on the inside of the building overlooking the exercise yard which was deserted when darkness fell. With the blackout there was no security lighting, so B Specials arrived every night to patrol the yard to foil any internees trying to escape. One of these guards used to whistle as he patrolled. Every couple of weeks I used to hear this beautiful sound which echoed round the walls in the absolute silence that pervaded the jail through the night. As the months went by new tunes were added to the whistler's repertoire. After the 'Cuckoo Waltz' he moved on to Ravel's 'Bolero' and John McCormack's lovely 'Bantry Bay'. I was not alone in enjoying the performances, and we eagerly awaited the nights when we knew the whistler was on the guard rota. One night he began whistling 'Ireland Mother Ireland', which was a well-known McCormack recording, and one of my fellow inmates began duets with him, the two whistlers unseen by each other in the dark of the night. Suddenly he was gone. We never heard another tune. No matter how much whistling my friend did nightly from his window, our friend, the whistling B-man, never replied, but I still have the memory of him from the rare moonlit nights when there was a tall and a short B Special walking round the yard in step whistling lovely Irish airs. Only one of the two was the whistler. I never did find out which.

One day the single access door to D wing was thrown open and a tall stranger appeared at the top of the steps. He came down gingerly, looking around him. The staff member approached him, spoke a few words and then guided him to a remote cell well out of the way. The man was fed and took exercise alone, and no one bothered with him. 'That's strange,' said one of my friends. 'No one knows him. No one is bothering him. I wonder who he is?' We watched him walk round the yard and eventually engaged him in conversation. In time he told us that he was a former B Special who had become interested in Irish music and Irish history and then joined the IRA in Dungannon. The police found out and he was arrested and interned, which was deeply ironic, for he claimed that on a number of occasions he had done night-guard duty in D wing yard.

He was not the only controversial internee to arrive among us. We heard one morning that a man called Rory was in C wing as a detainee and would be coming to D wing as an internee. The Belfast internees had long regarded him as an informer and we did not want him with us, but the internee staff took the view that we could not stop it if the authorities put him in D wing. Some felt that if he came in he must be all right. If he was not, then he would hardly risk it and sign up for an appeal hearing. Stories about Rory's exploits as an informer had been going round the cells in D wing for months and he had earlier come under internal investigation by the army council as a result of these suspicions. The doubts about him centred on the fact that ever since internment had begun, Rory had remained unscathed as the officer in command of the Belfast battalion. Those who had served under him had either been charged and convicted or were interned. Others had left the organisation because of what they regarded as the inevitability of their arrest. Rory, they pointed out, was the sole remaining survivor of the battalion and must have been in league with the police. The only explanation for his immunity, they calculated, was that he acted as an informer.

It never seemed to occur to his accusers that Rory led a very lonely clandestine life, almost like a professional spy. He travelled from one part of Belfast to the other and lived in Protestant areas for cover. By avoiding Catholic areas and making his subordinates come to him in downtown Belfast or the Shankill Road, he avoided the intense police surveillance. His junior officers ran the risks instead of him. If he was guilty of anything it was that he did not share these risks equally, but then he insisted that, if there were to be arrests, others were more expendable than him.

The accusers were led by a heavily built, dogmatic man whose nickname was FP because of his constant reliance on what he called 'fundamental principles'. He never spoke on any subject, even the weather, without identifying the fundamental principle. When Rory first came under a cloud, word was sent out by FP and his cronies about the suspicions that Rory was a traitor. The message was transmitted to the army council in Dublin. Eventually a message was smuggled into the jail that Dublin were taking action and a team from there would arrive in Belfast forthwith. We heard that Rory had been arrested and taken to a house in south Derry for interrogation by the Dublin team. He denied everything. Unable to get a confession from him after prolonged interrogation, they decided he was guilty and prepared to shoot him. He was then made to dig his own grave in an isolated field. Getting out of the grave as night fell, he hit his guards with a spade and got away. We had heard nothing more of him until the news of his arrival in C wing.

When Rory arrived in D wing in 1943 he was very fortunate. Morale had hit rock bottom and the wing was no longer run on military lines or the men disciplined like a military force. Had it been, Rory would undoubtedly have faced an unpleasant court martial. His accusers remained exclusively the Belfast crowd, while the rural republicans offered him some comfort, though not explicitly at the beginning. The accusers could get no sign of support for their proposal to put him out of the wing, and when news of the pressuring from Belfast got out, the rural internees as well as other disinterested parties let their feelings be known about the unpopularity of the Belfast delegation.

Threats were issued by the Belfast men about what would happen to Rory if he was not put out of D wing. They told everybody within earshot that they would find lethal weapons to finish him off themselves. 'How do you know he is guilty?' they were asked. 'If he's an informer they would not place him in here among his accusers.'

'He ran away, didn't he?' countered his accusers.

'Wouldn't you run away if you were about to be shot?' was the retort.

Tension grew. The Belfast faction shouted through the cell windows at night. Threats were written up on the walls close to Rory's cell and on the lavatory walls. His cell door was hammered on the outside after he was locked up by the warders on night duty. I heard he faced his accusers several times on their own but they backed down. The football season started, and the threats began again after he registered to play. The Belfast crowd said their score would be settled on the football field. The two teams avoided each other until the end of the season, but came together in a crucial match for the championship title. The atmosphere was electric because everyone knew of FP's tough reputation. It turned out to be a one-sided match, with Rory's team well in front, and the two rivals never came near each other as both played in defensive positions.

Well into the second half, when the ball went out to the left wing, a foul was committed against Rory's team. FP shouted to get in on Rory.

A country voice replied: 'Do it yourself, big mouth.'

Accepting the challenge, he ran into the goalmouth as the ball came over. Rory caught the ball and brought it and his elbow downwards, right into FP's face. The blood spurted in all directions.

'The dirty bastard is trying to kill me. He's broken my nose,' he shouted to the crowd. 'Come on. Let's get the dirty bastard.'

'Shut up and take your beating like a man,' replied a rural voice. That shut FP up. He looked along the touchline for his friends but he was on his own. Rory got an easier ride after that. The threats died away and the graffiti disappeared, although he still preferred to make his lonely way round the exercise yard.

I have to say that I was not lonely during my time in prison. Although I was highly streetwise when I was first locked up, I was hopelessly idealistic, naïve and immature. Prison broadened and matured me in all sorts of ways. I enjoyed the football, the conversation with older, wiser men and the lasting education I received from the debates and reading. I adjusted entirely to the ordered rhythm of life behind bars and did not feel there was anything I was missing. If, for instance, you had to worry about your wife and kids outside, it was a terrible strain. If you were homesick and spent your time standing up at the cell window looking at those in freedom outside going up and down the Crumlin Road, you were going to go off your head and sign for the appeal tribunal. Many men did that and I learned to understand the pressures that drove them to it. I also realised the depths of conviction that motivated others to mask their personal emotions and endure their loss of freedom as martyrs for the republican cause. I didn't share either of those extreme positions and although I hoped to get out in due course I was not counting hours or days to possible release dates. In truth, I just enjoyed every moment of the time that I was in there and took each day and the experiences it presented as it came.

One morning in May 1945 we heard the war in Europe had ended. IRA activity had long fizzled out and when the new Labour government took over at Westminster the unionists at Stormont were ordered to abolish internment. Labour administrations were never comfortable with Northern Ireland's draconian special powers legislation. By early August the first batches of internees were being released.

In the second week of September my cell door was opened at 6 a.m. one morning and I was told to get ready for release. A few hours later I filed into the prison office to reclaim my personal belongings. Rory was there, too, and he acknowledged my nod. We were all emotional about the significance of the occasion as we were escorted to the outer gate and walked through it to freedom. I was behind Rory as he turned left to walk down the Crumlin Road past the Mater Hospital. He never looked back. I never saw or heard of him since.

As for me, the years of debates and exchanges forced me, for the first time, to understand and confront the issues raised by the IRA carrying on its activities in a so-called democracy. I was forced to consider the use of special powers, internment and the role of a politically manipulated police force, which acted in all but name as the armed wing of the Unionist Party. This led me to thinking about the democratic obligations of a majority government to respond to the rights and needs of minorities within its boundaries. Perhaps the most perplexing dilemmas I encountered arose when we debated how republicans acquired the moral right to wage war and take life, when they consistently received only a nominal vote at the ballot box and were therefore unrepresentative of the people. Over the years as the merits of the various arguments were rehearsed, I began to question, and finally reject, the violent republican ethos.

Discussions on the rights and wrongs of war were well to the fore. It was surprising to hear words of praise for Britain's part in fighting the fascist forces of Hitler and Mussolini. I began to understand better the reasons for the war, and to recognise that there were many admirable values in the British people. As I look back now, I realise that this period of my life forged attitudes and a personal style that governed my entire approach for years to come. I became competitive, confident and articulate to a high degree. It was as if I emerged from a tunnel of darkness. I learned to seek and understand the other side of each argument, a technique which later stood me in good stead. I had gone into the Crumlin Road jail a boy and come out a man.

4

CRUMLIN ROAD
TO CITY HALL

As I left Crumlin Road prison that morning in 1945 I found it hard to come to terms with the first whiff of my regained freedom. I was excited and apprehensive at the same time. I decided to savour the experience and adjust by walking home but the noise and pace of the early morning traffic frightened me and I waited for a break in the flow before I dashed across the Crumlin Road. At times I feared there might have been a mistake and that the warders or the police would come after me, so I had an urge to start running as I walked towards Agnes Street and then up the Shankill Road before turning into Conway Street and reaching home.

My turbulent relationship with my mother had slightly mellowed during my time in custody. Despite her aversion to republicanism and the IRA, she had been a frequent visitor to the jail and at times had joined in protests and representations to MPs to have internees released. My father, by contrast, kept a low profile on the issue and never raised the matter of my detention as he chatted to me quietly during his visits. When I stepped into the house my mother was overjoyed. She immediately put the teapot on and called in the neighbours. For the rest of the day I was the recipient of hugs, kisses and constant cups of tea. Despite all the unaccustomed attention, I was distinctly restless. I could not sit still and paced up and down, euphoric with happiness. This emotionally charged atmosphere lasted for a week until the usual cold reality of life asserted itself again. I had to to find work because there was no money coming into the house except for what my father earned. The loss of my income over the previous three years and the cost of sending parcels into the jail had been an added burden in my mother's constant struggle to feed, clothe and house the rest of the family.

I was keen to return to the butchery trade so I went back to the shop in Holywood where the owner had been impressed with my performance and, despite my detention, had spoken to others of my honesty and willingness to work. At first he told me there were no vacancies, as he had promised to reinstate former employees who were coming back when demobilised from the army and navy. In the end he relented and agreed to take me on for a month in the back of the shop, so that I could get acquainted with the knives again.

I travelled up and down to Holywood by train each day and frequently sat beside four young women travelling to their work as clerks at the Kinnegar Ordnance Depot. Invariably I wore my hard-won *fáinne*, prompting one or two of them to address me in Irish. Despite my new-found confidence, I was embarrassed by their attention and tried to avoid sitting with them. They obviously recognised this and, morning after morning, gleefully went out of their way to seek me out and discomfort me.

After the agreed month I left Holywood and cast around trying to get any job that was on offer. My chances were reduced by the stigma of my imprisonment, for there was a subtle mark on my identity and unemployment cards, a wavy line drawn under my name, that informed those who needed or wanted to know that I was politically undesirable.

After a short period of idleness, disappointment and frustration, a friend of mine, Peter Burns, also a former internee, arrived at my home and told me of a job as an apprentice butcher in a shop at the top of the Falls. It was first year apprentice wages, and if I did well I would earn more. I checked with the trade union official, who told me that if I passed the Trade Test I would be put on a higher rate of remuneration. I started work but learned within a few weeks why the owner wanted someone to assist him, for he was a man who could not get the doors closed quick enough to get into the local pub. There were other occasions when he stayed behind in the shop after luring young married women to come back at closing time.

The owner bought a milk run shortly afterwards and asked me to do it temporarily. I agreed, because it meant higher wages and running from house to house helped me to maintain fitness for my sporting activities. After life in jail, walking for three or four hours a day, playing football three times a week, with no drink and very little food, I was in better physical condition than if I had completed a course in one of these modern health farms.

In my first days of freedom I linked up again with the old Cathal Brugha crowd in the Falls Baths and resumed keeping goal for the senior water polo team. One practice night, I stood at the back of the pool to watch a strong swimmer being coached by an ex-internee named Frank Barnwell. When she came out of the water I recognised her as one of my tormentors from the Holywood train. A short time later I met her again at a gala night in Templemore Avenue Baths. She and her friends tried to embarrass me again by throwing paper boats, but this time I turned the situation to my advantage and used the occasion to 'chat her up'. Her name was Theresa Duffy and I ended up walking her home. That was the start of my relationship with the woman who was to play such a major part in the rest of my life. An operation for a nose complaint forced her to give up competitive swimming soon afterwards and we began to spend more and more of our time together.

My instinct to take charge and run things also began to assert itself about this time. I found myself taking initiatives in the organisations I was connected with, making suggestions on how to do things, running functions for local charities and writing letters to the press. My mother was elected secretary of the Hibs (Ancient Order of Hibernians) on the Falls Road and she pressured me into writing her minutes, another skill which proved very useful in subsequent years. I didn't like the Hibs, so I created a bit of mischief by writing long convoluted sentences where simple ones would have sufficed. I soon lost that job, much to my relief.

One of my major involvements was helping in the founding of a new football team. Prior to leaving the Crumlin, the town footballers decided to form a team when we got out which would be called the Sean Gaffneys, in memory of the popular Cavan man who had died in November 1940 while interned on the prison ship *Al Rawdah*, which was moored in Strangford Lough. Among those who ran the team with me was Seamus Twomey, who later became a founder and leader of the Provisional IRA. The team was full of good players and four of them later played for Antrim County.

In 1948 I hurt my shoulder in a match and was forced off work for six weeks. No one enquired how I was or showed concern about my loss of wages, which were pretty poor anyway. With the prospect of getting married, and well-paid jobs as scarce as ever, I decided to make a break with Belfast. Theresa's brother-in-law suggested I go over to join him in England where there was the chance of a job in Plymouth, so like many ambitious, unemployed and impoverished Irishmen and women over previous generations, I hit the emigration trail. On my first ever trip outside my native island, I travelled overnight by boat from Belfast to Heysham in Lancashire on the first stage of my journey. When we docked in the early hours of the morning, my identity card, with its tell-tale wavy line, led to me being the only passenger hauled away for questioning by the police, but I was allowed to travel on after a few innocuous questions and a short delay.

When I arrived in Plymouth the clerical work I had hoped for was not available. Men coming back after demobilisation from the forces had first call on the better jobs, but I was offered a vacancy as a scaffolder with a big building company which I promptly accepted. I was very lonely in Plymouth; I had little contact with the local people nor they with me. Digs were purely a money-making operation run by landladies, with only wet, sloppy meatless stew and toasted bread and cheese on offer day after day.

The sole consolation was that there was plenty of opportunity to play football. My observance of the Gaelic Athletic Association ban on playing 'foreign games' was quickly forgotten. I played soccer in the lunch break and in the parks on a Sunday and finally signed for a local team which gave me the right back position. Despite this outlet the loneliness of my life in Plymouth got me down, so I made contact with my Uncle Jimmy in Coventry. He caught on that I was unhappy but didn't really want to go back home to Belfast, so he sent a telegram saying he was ill, telling me to come to Coventry without delay. I left that same night. Coventry, like Plymouth, had no recognisable city centre. Both cities had been devastated by terrible bomb attacks during the war. The flattened sites and the marks of the craters left by the huge bombs were still to be seen. Most of the shops in the main streets were housed in Nissen huts.

Jimmy's family, my cousins, were slightly younger than me and they were well settled in Coventry with a wide circle of friends. His local watering hole was filled with Irish people, many of them from Belfast. Jimmy was also a keen footballer and he helped to get me a trial at Highfield Road with Coventry Football Club, where he was a prominent member of the supporters' club. Within days of my arrival, I was brought round there for a trial and given a football to kick against a goalkeeper using both my left foot and my right foot. They also gave me a heading test and then offered me the chance to play in a practice game that weekend. That led to my selection for the Coventry reserve team against West Bromwich Albion the following Wednesday night, which was the last match of that season.

54

After the game the manager wanted me to sign up on the spot for the 1949 season. At the same time I got a job with the Rootes Group in the city's fast-growing car industry. My task was to bring parts from the stores to the fitters, who attached them to the new cars taking shape as they moved along the assembly line in front of them. It was my first experience of night work, and I hated it. I could not sleep and my food tasted sour all the time.

My interest in politics, first fostered by my grandfather and parents and developed in prison, was now coming into play more and more. The Labour Party were in power at Westminster and radical legislation on health and education was being introduced. Nationalisation of the mines, gas, electricity, shipping, airlines and road transportation was effected to improve the economic infrastructure, making certain that the all-out effort to provide employment would not be hampered by the greed of private enterprise. I was impressed by how Britain was being transformed into a welfare state, well beyond that envisaged by Bismarck in Germany during the previous century.

I had enthused about this type of society during internment and far from being some mythical 'Shangri-la' it was now here and I was experiencing the benefits. This feeling encouraged me to join the Labour Party, so one night I went to the local Labour rooms which were, given the post-war desolation and short-ages, located in the inevitable Nissen hut. But when I got there and looked into the dimly lit room, sparsely furnished with a table and utility chairs, my nerve failed me and I couldn't enter. There were a number of people inside, standing in groups chat-ting. I stood outside in the rain for an hour without mustering the courage to go in. I went back again a second night and although the door was open no one was there. I was still keen to become involved, so I asked around my work place for a party member. Surprisingly I never found one, although I met a shop steward who brushed me aside like he was swatting a fly on the wall when I made an effort to engage him in conversation about Labour politics.

My Aunt Mary died in Belfast around this time and I decided to leave Coventry. Uncle Jimmy was understandably annoyed because he and his family had done so much for me. Theresa was certainly pleased at the prospect of my return, for we had kept in close touch while I was away and firmly intended to marry in due course.

Back home again I applied for a job with Kennedy's dairy as a milk roundsman but before I could start I had to lodge a deposit of £50 as a guarantee against bad debts. That sum of money represented almost twenty weeks' wages and raising it was no easy task. I approached an insurance company in Linenhall Street at the back of the City Hall for an insurance bond to cover me. I was told to wait while they must have made a telephone call somewhere about me. After a while they came back, laughed and told me I must be joking. I had no chance. Whether this was just a bit of basic anti-Catholic discrimination or particularly because of my own republican history, I still do not know. In the end I raised the money by borrowing from relatives and I deposited it.

At first I did a milk run around the Whiterock area of Belfast, then after a time they moved me to the Ardoyne area. It was a gruelling existence, getting up at five every morning, seven days a week, in all weathers. The greatest drawback came on Saturday afternoons, for I would have preferred to be playing football rather than going round the houses to collect the money. I was mad keen on the football and had high hopes of going places, having got games with Cliftonville Olympic and the Distillery Seconds. However, the struggle to play and keep the job proved to be too much and I reluctantly abandoned my footballing ambitions.

Ironically, in time, the job got beyond me too. With my socialist philosophy I was in principle sympathetic to the valiant efforts of the working-class families I served to make ends meet from their meagre wages. In reality, I was far too soft and was a sucker for every hard luck story I was told. The consequence was that every Saturday collection resulted in me spending the rest of the day in a vain struggle to balance my round book. After some two years of grappling with the problem I finally threw the towel in. My timing could not have been more disastrous, for there I was on the verge of being married with no job.

If I had been given the chance to select a mother-in-law from the whole world, I could have made no better selection than Theresa's mother. Liverpool-born and convent-educated, Mrs Mamie Duffy, widowed in 1946, was the mother of twelve children, of whom Theresa was the second youngest. My first encounter with Mrs Duffy took place when I arrived at her door one evening to take Theresa out for a walk. I was dressed in training gear, choker, rough coat and heavy boots and reeked of sweat. She asked Theresa: 'Who is that young man?'

'I met him at the swimming club,' she replied.

'Well, what does he do?'

'I'm not sure but I know he is just out of jail,' she said.

'What for?' asked Mrs Duffy, who must have been staggered at this damning aspect of my history.

'Oh, he was interned,' said Theresa, matter-of-factly.

'Well, bring him in and let me see him,' she said.

It was the start of a lasting and mutually respectful friendship, for she became a wise counsellor and a supportive influence on both of us until she died in 1977 at the age of eighty-seven. Other members of Theresa's family were not so impressed with my credentials. They saw me as a roughneck, without a steady job or prospects and therefore quite unsuitable to be with Theresa. She was put under pretty strong pressure by several members of her family to end our relationship, which she stoutly resisted, although for years after we had to endure a coolness towards me until they realised that their disapproving views of me did not affect the unbreakable bond between us.

57

Theresa and I married on 26 October 1950 in St Paul's Catholic Church on the Falls Road. Nerves took hold of her on the day and she could not reply to the question put to her by the priest, 'Do you take this man . . . ?' The priest interpreted her silence as consent. She did, however, sign the register in the right place, but now and again she reminds me that her silence leaves her free to go if I don't get into line!

After our wedding we moved in with Mrs Duffy, at 248 Grosvenor Road, but our married life had a bleak start, for although I looked everywhere in desperation for a job, there was nothing to hand or on the horizon. One day, when I was trekking round building sites looking for vacancies, out of the blue I met Stevie Devlin (no relation), an old swimmer who was the clerk of works for a new housing development at Riverdale in the Upper Falls. He started me on the spot as a labourer digging holes but after a time I got promoted to hod carrier, which paid much better wages. As work on the site neared completion I faced the prospect of unemployment again, so my father approached the management of Andrews' to get me a start there. Early in 1951 I reported for work and was assigned to pack animal feed into bags. I worked an eight-hour rotating shift system and the pay was reasonable but as my father had found years earlier, there was always plenty of overtime in the winter but only the flat rate wage in the summer, which I grew to dread.

The basic mills were at least a century old with some new badly designed parts tagged on. It was a very noisy process, with the iron milling rollers clattering incessantly twenty-four hours a day. There was also a very dry atmosphere, with conveyor belts running continuously through dusty tunnels, creating clouds of fine dust which dried up your mouth and nose and caused you to cough constantly. Today, workers have to wear ear defenders and hard hats and there is a maze of health and safety regulations to protect them from the harmful impact of such working conditions. My father, who had worked in the mill from 1919, had suffered from the constant clatter of the rollers and was badly affected by deafness. I wasn't long working there before I realised he was the butt of many jokes because of his poor hearing. I thought at the beginning it was a bit of innocent fun but when I realised how widespread and cruel it really was, I decided to stop it. I went round departments, locker rooms, waited on workers clocking in and out, even went to their homes and told them to stop or else. My efforts worked and he suffered no more ribbing until he retired ten years later.

In the early hours of one May morning in 1951, not long after I had joined Andrews', when I was on the night shift stacking bags of meal, I was suddenly poked in the back by a man with a revolver. He was a police district inspector, in plain clothes, wearing a hat and trenchcoat, and accompanied by two uniformed police constables. If he had been unarmed my response may not have been so muted. One of the constables grabbed me, twisted my arm up my back and I was frog-marched off at gunpoint before the astonished eyes of my workmates and father, ending up in the cells at Chichester Street police station. I found out later that they had earlier gone to the house looking for me and that Theresa, who was within a short time of giving birth to our first child, Anne, had been held for two hours in an unheated room by two other armed constables while they went to apprehend me at work.

I was kept in custody and spent a week back in the Crumlin Road, to foil what the authorities claimed was a 'dynamite plot' during a royal visit to Northern Ireland. A number of other republicans were also held. If there was something being planned, I knew nothing about it and intended to play no part, if asked. Frankly, I am sure there was no plot and that it was entirely a figment of the imagination of a bigoted politician, civil servant or Special Branch man. Such IRA 'plots' or 'scares' were regularly manufactured by the unionist government to keep their supporters in line.

Each election was fought on keeping the IRA at bay. In the run-up to each polling day the police stations would invariably be surrounded by sandbags and barbed wire, but, in a clear illustration of the hypocrisy of it all, there would be no fortifications at the rear of the stations. The object of these cosmetic scares was to get pictures in the local unionist newspapers, frighten the wits out of the Protestants that the IRA were coming down from the mountains to fight again for a united Ireland, and get them out to vote overwhelmingly for their unionist defenders. Such tactics enabled the Unionist Party to avoid fighting elections on their record of government or answering for their inactivity and heartlessness on the more relevant social and economic issues.

Despite government paranoia about the IRA, which the police parroted without question according to the Stormont script, the organisation had been virtually dormant since the middle of the war. When the internees were released at the end of the conflict they were too concerned with making up for their lost years inside to plot any violence. Certainly there was a hard core of republican families who kept the cause alive. An effort had been made to re-involve me in 1949, when I was called to a meeting. I listened to the guys in charge but they were far from clear or articulate about their aims and I was distinctly unimpressed. I formally resigned in writing soon afterwards, finally severing my links with the IRA, once and for all. The reasons I cited are still as relevant today, underlining the utterly futile and misguided paths the organisation, and its more recent adherents, have since followed. The modern IRA is, of course, far more ruthless and unprincipled than the republicans of my generation. We were more of a 'Dad's Army' by comparison.

At that time I had decided that physical force was not the way to solve the Irish problem and I was not prepared to sanction or support, much less participate in, any acts of violence designed to unite Ireland. Change, I recognised, could only come about peacefully through the ballot box. I was also concerned at the exclusively Catholic nature of the organisation and its lack of concern or policies for helping people get jobs and houses. The appalling discrimination practised by the unionists against Catholics was as nothing compared to their class bias, for the ordinary working-class Protestants were only a little better treated than their Catholic counterparts. I was convinced of the absolute necessity of embracing all members of the community in political action regardless of race or religion. This was the first time I had comprehensively articulated my political credo, which was to guide and dominate all my subsequent work. It formed the basis of my severing my links with the republican movement, and was clearly thought out and established in my own mind well before the police arrived at Andrews' mill to detain me.

My detention was only a temporary setback. Everyone who knew me recognised that I had not been involved in anything sinister. However, when I returned to the factory after my release some of my workmates held a protest meeting in the mill yard. To their credit, members of the Andrews family arrived to state that I had been guilty of nothing and would be resuming my job. After that, none of my workmates made any difficulties about the matter. Neither was it a setback to my growing interest and activism in the trade union movement, which I had taken to heart. I was convinced that trade unions were necessary to secure justice for workers. Without unions, employers could give whatever they felt they could comfortably spare, and they would not feel much compulsion to provide safe or decent working conditions. I knew that effective safeguards could only be provided by unions collectively bargaining for their members. I also reckoned that association with a Labour Party would keep down the prices of food and rents, and that lending rates and inflation had to be tied to stable conditions to keep the real value of wages and salaries. The lower the wages the workers earned, the more important it was that they had a strong trade union and labour movement to defend them.

My first campaign as a trade unionist had taken place at Kennedy's dairy, where the union organisation functioned in name only. This led to vast anomalies in what people were being paid for doing identical jobs. I found, for example, that my wages, a shade over £3 a week, were only a third or a half of what other milkmen were being paid. With many of my fellow workers also fighting the constant battle, I was having to get my money in and earn a living, the situation was crying out for a more favourable deal. I became the mainspring of a campaign and, after being forced to call a strike, we won a weekly increase of £2 per week. This success brought me into formal contact with the union movement and strengthened my interest in their activities. I subsequently went round the other milk distribution firms in Belfast and enrolled their workers in the Amalgamated Transport and General Workers' Union. At that time I discovered that some full-time union officials were simply time-servers, stopping members becoming active or too aggressive, because it created more work for them. Some officials were only active in the pub on a Friday evening, where they collected subscriptions and a drink from their members. I am afraid that this was an all too common feature of the movement and, in my view, seriously inhibited the unions' potential to bridge the sectarian divide and act as a cross-community labour organisation. If such a development had taken place it might well have helped to blunt the eruption of the dreadful events in the early 1970s.

By the time I moved to Andrews' mill I was already a committed trade union activist, and these views were reinforced by others I came into contact with in the firm. One of those who most influenced and encouraged me was Billy Hewitt, an ex-RAF warrant officer from the Shankill Road. Billy had been a Labour supporter all his life and his wife and family were all members of the Woodvale branch of the Northern Ireland Labour Party at the time. We were usually on the same shift, and during our tea-break conversations this widely read man introduced me to the arts, literature and socialist philosophy. In those days, before the advent of television, books were the most important learning tool one could use and I became a voracious reader. Billy once bought me a present of Joyce's *Ulysses*, which, like many readers before and since, I failed to understand although I tried hard several times. Other classic books he introduced me to fired my imagination and ambition to better myself by providing an insight into all manner of interesting lives and philosophies.

The impact of some of the books I read at that time has lasted all my life. *The Stars Look Down* by A.J. Cronin was an especially moving book, which introduced me to the unique life and drama of a mining community. Emile Zola's writings, especially *J'accuse*, his defence of Alfred Dreyfus, the French soldier falsely accused of being a traitor, and *Nana*, the story of a Paris prostitute, fascinated me. I remember many of the short stories by Guy de Maupassant, which led me on to enjoy the Irish short story writers like Liam O'Flaherty and Sean O'Faolain. The unique H.G. Wells also captivated me and converted me to the Fabian Society's view of rational politics. Another of the great masterpieces was the life of Peter Altgeld, the governor of Illinois at the beginning of this century who released the innocent men framed for the Haymarket bombing.

Altgeld's life led me to read about his great friend Clarence Darrow, one of the greatest United States lawyers around the turn of the century. He always defended labour against capital, the individual against state tyranny, the under-privileged against the privileged, and invariably won. I read and re-read all the accounts of his exploits in court with unabated delight.

It became one of my greatest pleasures to browse in the book stalls at Smithfield, the old second-hand market in the centre of Belfast which was a haven for bibliophiles and record collectors. Among the treasures I picked up there was an old copy of Victor Gollancz's *Red Book Club*, which had been published during the war, bringing socialists together in a movement 'to open the second front'. I was also heavily influenced by the writings of

G.D.H. Cole and Professor Harold Laski, of the Labour Party, in the early fifties. Their books were a great boon to me and others of a like mind, for they provided a vital theoretical input to our political views.

Billy Hewitt also had a finely honed sense of justice and he engaged me in his efforts to revive the moribund General Municipal Workers' Union as a means of promoting socialist values and getting a fair deal for the working classes. We gradually took it over and got it operating, which led to us attending union schools at Beatrice Webb House in Dorking, Surrey. I became a highly pro-active branch secretary, to the extent that the branch official used to run and hide when I went anywhere near the union office in North Street because he knew I would be confronting him with a pile of work. When I read the memoirs of Robert McElborough of Sandy Row, who had been a branch secretary in the same union at the beginning of the century, I was amused to find that he too had complained about the inactivity of the full-time union officials in his day.

Throughout these years our family was growing: after Anne came Moya, in 1956, Patricia in 1959 and the twins, Peter and Joe, in 1966. Theresa was entirely supportive as I developed my union activities, and my mother-in-law was also the source of much encouragement and wise advice on my self-improvement. They, too, motivated me to read and widen my vocabulary. I was helped to extract new words from the dictionary and put them in a small notebook which I carried everywhere in my coat pocket. When I got the chance I would study the words until I understood their meanings and could spell them. I was reluctant to speak in public because I feared my difficulties with pronunciation and grammar would cause people to mock or discount me. I was impatient to be an effective public speaker, to stop my usual dashing into a speech with an uncoordinated flow of jumbled words. I would go up to the attic at the top of the house and read books aloud to improve my diction and overcome my lack of confidence. I achieved that by convincing myself that I had more important things to say than those who normally dominated the meetings I attended, such as the regular meetings of the Belfast Trades Council.

During this period I never lost an opportunity to get my 'spoke' in to every discussion, in order to develop my confidence to speak in public. My grammar was poor and my pronunciation sloppy, and I eventually decided to disregard my worries about getting the pronunciation right as most people would understand what I was trying to say anyway. I came to think that as long as I persevered with it, the skill would come right in the end. The fact that I never reached the Churchillian heights of polished political oratory has never caused me concern, for over the years I have been able to speak in public and get my points across effectively. Indeed I frequently proved the telling effect of basic four-letter words, especially when there was a dash of menace or passion behind them.

The Workers Educational Association organised an economics course at Queen's University for which I enrolled. J.U. Stewart, the tutor, was a small, bald man, with a mischievous smile. He shocked us with his outspoken views, which were often argued well into the night when the class adjourned from the university to the Arts Club. He was a radical socialist whose views graphically articulated many of the social, economic and political values I was endeavouring to express. He encouraged me to write papers on current issues under his progressive eye, thereby helping me to work out the tenets of socialism which became my personal political manifesto. My writing ability also developed about this time, for I began to attend specialist classes organised by the National Council of Labour Colleges every Sunday morning. There was a large element of fiction writing involved, which did not attract me so much. More valuable was my work as branch secretary of the union, which involved me in preparing reports and drafting letters.

Perhaps the most valuable lessons in self-expression through the written word were gained by engaging in exchanges with a rainbow's width of correspondents through the letters columns of the various newspapers, for me, still, one of the best barometers of the ups and downs of public opinion on any issue. So, in the first serious writing I ever did, my imagined political enemies were bombarded with my views on the issues of the day. I criticised the policies of the Ulster Labour Unionist Association, the thugs, the thickies, the politicians and the bosses, and supported CND and the itinerants. Torrents of words calling for more jobs, less poverty and world peace poured from my pen, carving out and shaping the radical political views that were to become my stock in trade. The compelling logic of my position was that I should therefore build on my trade union activism by participating in mainstream politics.

5

ON THE MARBLE

By the 1950s, Northern Ireland and Belfast had changed very
little in the thirty years since partition. Sectarianism was still
assiduously fostered by the Unionist Party to maintain division.
Virtually all the political energy in the community was focused
on preserving or questioning Northern Ireland's position, a
futile obsession, for there was no real possibility of change.
London allowed the unionists to do what they wanted without
query. Dublin paid garrulous lip service to re-unification but, in
truth, was equally uninterested in the place. Pressing social and
economic issues were ignored, allowing poverty, squalor, unemployment and disadvantage to thrive. The resulting misery
was shared by the working class, without distinction, between
unionists and nationalists.

With unionist memories of the sacrifice at the Somme in the
Great War, and later of partition, still vivid, the reverberations
of the Second World War had only reinforced the community
division in the six northern counties. Churchill's praise for loyal
Ulster in the hours of danger for Britain was interpreted as a
strengthening of the union. His criticism of the Irish leader de
Valera, who maintained neutrality and denied Britain the use of
Irish ports to guard the sea approaches to the British Isles, was
music to the ears of the perpetually insecure unionists.

From the outset of their battles against Home Rule the

unionist men from the big houses, who pulled all the strings of influence, were determined to snuff out any trade unionism or labour politics, because they knew the solid unionist majority would be eroded and undermined. Within the counties of Northern Ireland a large proportion of this majority consisted of working-class Protestants bound into the unionist fabric by regular scares that the IRA was going to lead a rebellion and create a united Ireland which would deny them their breadline jobs and slum housing. They were lulled into a feeling of well-being through the Orange Order, which purported to 'look after them' by dispensing very limited patronage through its network of lodges. The few crumbs that were scattered among these uneducated and deceived people were stale and sparse.

The IRA's efforts to stir up the nationalist minority in the North had signally failed and they were effectively neutralised throughout the war, principally by internment. Afterwards, in December 1948, feeling even more isolated and abandoned, the Catholic community, which outside Belfast was essentially conservative and nationalist, welcomed the decision by the Irish parliament to declare a Republic and withdraw from the British Commonwealth, a club comprising the former members of the British Empire who had achieved independence. They hoped, in vain as it turned out, that this heralded a reopening of the national question which would lead to a determined campaign for reunification of the island.

The labour movement was also to be traumatised by the question of partition. The NILP had been formed out of Independent Labour in the early 1920s. It was mainly dominated by Harry Midgley, a Protestant trade unionist who later turned turtle and became a unionist cabinet minister, and Jack Beattie, who represented it in parliament. During the 1930s, however, they feuded first on the constitutional question, then on what view they should take of the Spanish Civil War and, finally, on Midgley's failure to stand up for the Catholics during the 1935 riots in Belfast. Midgley eventually led the party into abandoning the earlier anti-partition position that Beattie had consistently maintained. Midgley left after the war and formed the Commonwealth Labour Party which predictably foundered, and after a time he joined the Unionist Party.

The Midgley/Beattie rivalry actually carried on until the end of the decade, in 1949, when the British Labour government introduced the Ireland Act, giving the Northern Ireland parliament a constitutional guarantee that partition would not be ended without its consent. It was an effort to remove the issue of partition as an obstacle to securing a large labour vote from the Protestant working class but it infuriated many labour sympathisers and led to the defection of several prominent personalities. They formed Irish Labour Party branches in the North, effectively polarising the labour movement into Green and Orange factions.

By 1949 the national question, as it came to be known, was virtually set in concrete after the collapse of all hopes of building a broadly based, anti-sectarian labour movement. Those of a socialist disposition were divided by their attitude to partition, fatally weakening the real political influence that a united working class would have had. This development, I believe, was one of the seeds of future conflict and significantly contributed to our later Troubles. A unified working class, ultimately asserting conventional right–left politics, would have helped to steer us away from the rocks of nationalism, with which we inevitably collided.

It was a natural evolution for me to move from trade union activism to direct political action, a step already taken by many of my union associates by the time I was preparing to jump. My mentor was Jack MacGougan, an accountant by profession and a committed socialist, who was Irish regional secretary of the Tailor and Garment Workers' Union and a Belfast city councillor. From him I learned methods of research, and how to argue union members' cases before tribunals or other public bodies. I also picked up many debating tricks. My links with him began at union level, seeking new members for his union branches in Newry, Derry and around the many Belfast shirt factories. When we visited Newry, we always called at a restaurant owned by Charlie O'Donnell, a great old pioneer of the labour movement who had attended James Connolly's lectures in the Bounders College above Danny McDavitt's tailoring shop in Rosemary Street, Belfast. Charlie was a very well-read man with a vast repertoire of stories about the old Belfast socialists, which he would tell at the drop of a hat. His son, Turlough, who was also interested in the labour movement, went on to distinguish himself in the law profession, eventually reaching the highest ranks of the judiciary as a Lord Justice of Appeal in Northern Ireland.

At this time MacGougan persuaded me to join the Irish Labour Party, the rump end of what was left of the splits and faction fighting over partition which had sundered the labour movement in 1949. The party, which held seven Belfast Corporation seats in the Falls and Smithfield areas, was led in the council by Jack Beattie, a former shipyard worker and MP at Stormont from 1925 to 1949, who had held the West Belfast seat at Westminster twice: from 1943 to 1950 and again from 1950 to 1955. Beattie and the rest were still involved in bitter internal feuding, which had dogged them even after the split. It was soon apparent to me that they were 'defeated' men. By contrast I was new blood, heavily committed to the party, determined to be very active, learn the ropes and make my name. I found, as I had done earlier in the trade union movement, that there is always scope for the activist to advance quickly by moving into key positions for which there is little demand. Moribund or exhausted organisations, like the union and the labour movement at that time, were ripe for boarding by ambitious younger people like me. Within a short time, therefore, I was able to become secretary of the Belfast branch of the party and set my sights on eventually winning a council seat.

My chance came more quickly than I expected early in 1956

when I was thirty years old. A councillor resigned his seat to take up a position that barred him from elected office. At the ensuing by-election in the Falls ward I was nominated as the Irish Labour Party candidate, with MacGougan as my agent. The election was a straight fight between me and Gerry Fitt, who was then a young and unknown merchant seaman living at Beechmount and who fought the election as a Dock Labour Party candidate. It was, for both of us, the first experience of what turned out to be many electoral contests, although in all subsequent ones we were on the same side. I had the advantage that I was standing on my home ground, whereas Gerry, whose roots were in the Docks area, was regarded as a 'blow in'. We campaigned in cold wintry weather and, try as hard we did, it proved almost impossible to get people to come out and hear the speeches, never mind vote for two colourless nonentities. On polling day I was not surprised when fewer than 1,000 from a register of almost 20,000 people entitled to vote turned out. I beat Fitt by a decisive margin, the only election he lost until, like me, he was ultimately hounded from political life by the IRA in the early 1980s.

My first electoral success gave me passage into the splendour of Belfast's imposing City Hall. My initial impression was that it was nothing more than a club for old Unionist Party fogies. More real business seemed to be conducted in the plush, wood-panelled Members' Room, just beside the main entrance, than was ever done in the committee rooms or council chamber. The place was coming down with shopkeepers and estate agents, usually ponderous, dapper men with closed minds and little vision. Every morning they would gather in the comfortably fur-nished room, and as they sipped tea or coffee and nibbled digestive biscuits served by a uniformed steward, they trans-acted their business. The values by which they lived and boasted are best summed up as being loyalist and royalist, but all too often deals engineered at these sessions were later nodded through the council, regardless of conflicts of interest

71

that bordered on the corrupt. On the surface it was all very amiable. The hidden influence of the Masons and the Orange Order, and the rampant bigotry that motivated many of them, were carefully concealed.

Snobbery was also a factor, for the handful of working-class councillors were snubbed and excluded from the caucuses of power and influence. I soon learned that the way to work the council and push things through was to divide and rule, by getting alongside the working-class councillors, appealing to their class instincts and enlisting their support. They were all too often procedurally illiterate, and I had to help them draft motions and even write speeches so that an issue could be progressed. The key to achieving anything was to prevent the unionist group imposing a whip. If there was a free unionist vote and these councillors could be motivated, then, with Labour and other minority support, the designs and manipulations of the unionist establishment could often be frustrated.

Outside the Members' Room, 'on the marble' as we used to say, in the central hall under the ornately painted dome, City Hall was a busy place with constant rounds of lobbying and soliciting of councillors' votes by commercial and other interests. Groups of unionist councillors were constantly horse trading with such interest groups, and loggerheads often developed over planning consents and vesting orders for the opening of petrol stations or land for building developments. The estate agents, who were thicker in the council ranks than people from any other calling, were always in the forefront of such controversies.

One particular issue which caused special concern was a new by-law to prevent people keeping pigs in close proximity to dwellings. At the time raising pigs was a highly lucrative cottage industry throughout the city. The animals were kept in back yards and sheds and fed on 'slops' collected from houses in the locality by youngsters, who earned a couple of pence a bucket for their trouble. Apart from the smell, there were obvious risks to hygiene and health, so the proposal was to prohibit pigs being kept within twenty-five yards of housing occupied by humans. The lobbying against this legislation was quite intense. The angry pig keepers were 'on the marble' constantly in the run-up to the council decision, often dropping sizeable bribes into their supporters' pockets, but the new by-law was introduced, a small footnote in the social history of the city.

We created a major division in the Unionist Party when MacGougan swung a vote, consisting of ourselves and the working-class unionists, to vest land owned by a big unionist landlord in north Belfast for badly needed public sector housing. The landowner, a pillar of the unionist establishment who was connected with one of the local newspapers, was far from pleased and the councillors concerned were dropped from the Unionist Party team for the next election.

I served on three committees during my first spell in City Hall: Transport, Police and Education. In those days councils wielded real power and their decisions were important in moulding the lifestyle of the city. Inevitably what we were doing came under the closest scrutiny, not least from the Catholic establishment in Belfast, who regarded the trade union and labour movement as nothing more than a front for communism. Their silent hostility to us exploded into public criticism after we voted in favour of setting up a crematorium for the use of Belfast citizens. In those days Catholics could not be cremated, so letters appeared in the local Catholic paper, the *Irish News*, pointing this out and attacking our position. We were told we were not good Catholic representatives. We were not Catholic representatives, we replied. We were socialists representing wards in which Catholics lived. 'If you want Catholics in the City Hall then vote for them,' we said.

My presence on the Education Committee was a particular sore point. Although the schools system was, theoretically, open to all, it was, in practice, almost exclusively Protestant because the Catholics had opted out and operated their own education system, with help from public funds. The bishop sent me word to get off the committee as it undermined the Catholic school system to have me, a Catholic, on this committee, making teaching appointments and determining matters relating to so-called Protestant schools. I sent word to the bishop, saying that as he had no vote in my ward or in my party, I was taking no advice from him.

Councillors were also called upon, from time to time, to act as film censors. Although all films coming into local cinemas were viewed before release by a national film censorship board and classified as being suitable for either family or adult viewing, some controversial films often became the subject of local notoriety. When this happened the members of the Police Committee would attend a special showing and decide whether or not the good people of Belfast should see the movie. In truth, and especially by today's permissive standards, the films were entirely innocuous except to the sabbatarian Bible-thumpers who turned up at the showings to tut-tut and be shocked. We consistently adopted a liberal stance on such issues, bringing us into conflict with hardline Catholic opinion as well as the hardline Protestant viewpoints.

Despite our highmindedness where the unionists were concerned, the Irish Labour Party councillors in the City Hall had inherited a corrupt practice or two from the old nationalists who had played the 'patronage game'. Jobs which the councillors had a say in allocating were kept for 'the boys', their own personal friends or supporters. As a result, there were a group of flunkeys in our midst who butted in on our deliberations. I did not know they were there until one day I found myself unwittingly caught up in it. There were two middle-aged men who frequently attended our party meetings. One was small and meek, and the other, heavier, was quite aggressive. At party meetings he often complained about what the council was not doing for him. His name was Mick and he would kick his friend Johnny on the legs and say: 'Get you up and second that.'

Johnny of course would pop up like a jack-in-the-box and shout: 'I second that.' They were straightforward burlesque – a mirror image of Laurel and Hardy. Everything Mick said, Johnny would second regardless. On one occasion when Johnny sprang to his feet the chairman asked him what he was seconding.

'Mick's proposal,' said Johnny.

'But Mick did not propose anything, he said he was going to the lavatory,' pointed out the chairman.

'Well,' said Johnny, remembering his sore ankles, 'I second that motion as well.'

They both came to me one night after a party meeting. 'I want you to come to Raglan Street tomorrow, where we are digging a trench. The gaffer is victimising us for being Labour men,' Mick said.

'That's very serious,' I said. 'We will not stand for that. I'll be along about three o'clock.'

The next day I came into the street and walked alongside the trench speaking to several workers I recognised. Mick and Johnny were waiting on the kerb side with the gaffer. I immediately noticed they had clean hands, clean clothes and shiny spades. I feared the worst. They must have been sacked already, I thought to myself.

As I reached them Mick said: 'Want you to meet Danny O'Brien, the gaffer. He's a great man. If he wasn't here we would be crucified by these other yobs. We want you to get him a weekly bonus or a step up in rank. He deserves it for looking after the Labour party.'

My surprise rapidly turned to anger when he added: 'Hey. And another thing. Stop talking to those other pygmies. They're not in the party.'

It was obvious to me that they had the gaffer terrified and that our two boys did no work at all, leaving it to the other unfortunates. One of the workmen, whom I had recognised, confirmed my worst fears. Later that week I got notification of a party meeting at which a vote of censure was to be moved by

Mick against me. I briefed myself well and made sure that other councillors were on side. Then I called at Mick's door before the meeting to outline my evidence against him. I told him I was going to get him and his friend Johnny expelled from the party. We would have the story printed in the *Irish News*. Needless to say they did not turn up at the party meeting and I never saw them again.

By the time the next council elections came around in 1958 it was clear the Irish Labour Party was going to be confronted by a strong team of reactionary Catholics. Signs of a new militancy on their part were all around us. In the trade union sphere, Catholics were turning up for the first time at branch meetings to vote Catholics on to the branch committees and into union jobs. The inspiration for this came from the Catholic Action Movement, which had developed on the Continent in the wake of the Second World War. The idea infiltrated England and then Ireland, where it became a strong force amongst Catholics in Belfast and Dublin. The main brunt of the attack against the Irish Labour Party on the Falls came from the members of the Clonard confraternity, a large group of men who gathered at the monastery of that name in the Lower Falls once a week for a prayer meeting. They were largely motivated by the parish priests of St Mary's and St Peter's in the Lower Falls. Frank Hanna, a well-known Catholic solicitor, also played a prominent role in the campaign.

One night prior to the election, we decided to address the members of the confraternity as they were leaving Clonard monastery after their meeting. We were using our loudhailers to harangue them from the back of a lorry as they came out and they engaged us in heated debate over the usual issues of the crematorium and not banning blue films. When one wag shouted abuse at me, I immediately jumped over the side of the lorry to get at him but my way was blocked. Theresa, who was standing close by, stepped in on my behalf and, I am pleased to say, whacked him with her handbag.

Several days later I met one of these zealots on the street. I asked him why he was so anti-Labour.

'I am against communists,' he replied.

'But we are not communists,' I insisted.

'Well, you look like communists,' he said.

'How do communists look?' I enquired.

'Just like you do. That's how!' he said.

I walked away in frustration that such stupid prejudice existed.

All Catholic employers were canvassed to oppose us on the basis that we were anti-business and anti-Catholic. The Knights of Columbanus (the Catholic equivalent of the Freemasons) and other groups of prominent Catholics were all persuaded to join the anti-Labour party conspiracy. Monsignor Arthur Ryan, a senior but radical figure in the Down and Connor diocesan establishment, rang up Jack Beattie, with whom he was friendly, to tell him of the conspiracy and to apologise for not having the power to stop it. All the elements of the conspiracy were confirmed to me over the years by people who were in membership of these organisations but refused to support their interference in the election.

The unionists soon got wind of what was going on and decided to try and turn the situation further to their own advantage. They recruited the powerful Vintners' Association and the Licensed Bookmaking trade, both dominated by wealthy Catholics, to join the fight against us. Billy Douglas, the Unionist Party secretary, was sent to promise them favourable legislation later to benefit their already lucrative businesses.

In Belfast the outcome was predictable. Protestant trade union members saw the ploy and immediately started counter-activity to stop the 'take-over'. As a result a few good officials, not involved in this sectarian squabble, were lost to the movement. The situation was a heaven-sent one for Protestant extremists like Ian Paisley, who was then emerging into the public arena. On election day the Catholic businessmen and their allies turned out with their expensive cars and we were swamped at the polls. I lost my council seat after only two years in office. It was a bitter disappointment. I had worked hard throughout my term of office, I scrupulously attended both council and committee meetings and every day that I was not required in the City Hall I took up cases for people, representing them at dole and other tribunals. This was possible only by working a constant night-shift at Andrews' during those years.

The stories of the opposition campaign against us were hair-raising. I did not recognise myself from their description of me. I was particularly angry at a story I heard that the administrator of St Peter's parish, Father McAtamney, insulted Labour voters with his remarks outside the polls and had described me as a non-Catholic. When I heard about this I went down to the presbytery to challenge him. I said that he had known me long enough to be fully aware that I was a practising Catholic. Losing his temper, he lifted his cane to strike me but when I moved towards him he dropped it and ran for the door.

The outcome of the election proved to me that all but a hand-ful of my colleagues were the 'defeated' men I had initially suspected. Apart from Jack MacGougan, few even turned out to work in that election. During the inquest period afterwards I debated my personal problems with Billy Hewitt, who pointed out that the only party that filled my need was the NILP, which was then going from strength to strength. With active trade union backing it was climbing back into the natural position for a local Labour party: chief challenger of Unionist Party dominance.

With Billy's backing, I decided to join the Woodvale branch of the NILP, where the sitting MP Billy Boyd held sway. He drew strong support throughout the constituency for his 'surgery' work, looking after the social problems of the area. It has long been a fact of political life in Belfast that constituents turn to their elected representatives as a first resort when they hit a problem. British public representatives have always been amazed at the volume of constituency work we attract. Their people tend to turn to MPs for help only after they have failed to sort out their problems for themselves. The effective Northern Ireland politician therefore has to build his reputation on how quickly he can get the housing authorities to repair a broken window or a fractured spouting, or on how articulate an advocate he is at an industrial or social security tribunal. By this yardstick Boyd was judged a diligent constituency worker. As a dedicated lay preacher he could also conduct himself effectively as an advocate. He was no left-wing intellectual, though. His wife, Beatrice, a relation of Harry Midgley, was the real power behind him: she had the necessary political nous.

The Woodvale constituency, located at the head of the Shankill Road with only a tenth of the electorate Catholic, should have been a safe unionist seat, but years before, it had been captured from the mainstream party by a notorious zealot called John Nixon. He was a former RUC district inspector who had been thrown out of the force in the early 1920s for his anti-Catholic attitudes and involvement with sectarian murder gangs. As an Independent unionist, Nixon organised a large vote for himself from the working-class 'anti-fur-coat' brigade, in defiance of the party establishment which wanted to run Woodvale. These supporters remained in position after Nixon's death and Boyd pandered to their emotions and prejudices to secure a powerbase for himself. That was a risky strategy because such tactics, while winning Woodvale for Boyd, compromised the NILP vote in other constituencies where the Catholic vote was important. Consequently I was pushed into Catholic areas to canvass that vote, while Protestant members canvassed the Protestant areas. From the outset I was uneasy about the contradiction inherent in pandering to the ultra-Protestant bigotry of Nixon's policies. I knew that speeches in praise of the Orange Order had been made from NILP election platforms, and that members of the platform party had even worn Orange sashes.

These tactics paid off for the Woodvale branch on one or two occasions, but they backfired with disastrous consequences later in the 1960s when the Belfast Corporation was forced to defend its policy of chaining up the swings and keeping children's playgrounds locked on Sundays. Because of these local considerations the Woodvale councillors defied NILP policy and abstained on the vote, enabling the council to keep the playgrounds locked. Party policy on this matter, which Woodvale had supported, was for general Sunday opening of parks and playgrounds.

Despite convulsions like this one, the 1960s was a decade of great promise for the Labour party in Northern Ireland. For the first time in forty years there was a spirit of compromise in the air. People from the two communities were more prepared than ever before to live together in harmony, and the old shibboleths that had for so long been sources of division were being closely questioned. The NILP was in the forefront of this transition and new branches were being formed all over the place as a growing volume of members joined up. We were thus able to fight elections every time the opportunity arose. At the Westminster general election in 1964, we fought ten of the twelve seats and notched up a record total vote of 102,759. I had been elected chairman of the organisation committee by the party executive and took great pride in these successes. I was very much a 'hands-on' merchant, acting as election agent for local council contests, where we made unprecedented breakthroughs in places like Lisburn. I played a prominent part in another election at Ballynafeigh in south Belfast when Sam Hazzard ran against Major Ivan Neill, a senior unionist government minister.

I learned much from this particular election because it gave me an insight into precisely how the unionist election machine worked. I noticed that the machinery was supervised by little men in bowler hats, grey suits and waistcoats, from which gold chains and medals often hung. One of our election workers, Sammy Gardiner, a convener from the shipyard, knew many of them. 'They are the "hats" from the yard and they're Orange-men too. But don't be fooled. They are geniuses at the organisa-tion game. These guys sure know their stuff,' he told me. (Incidentally, they were known as the 'hats' because of the customary bowler hats they wore, giving better protection than the more usual flat cap if a rivet or piece of metal fell, or even was thrown, from a ship's staging during construction.)

The key election players were the 'number ones', the people directly in charge of the polling stations. Many were school teachers who were well known to the Unionist Party officers, if not actual members. Those who did not have official election posts manoeuvred themselves into favourable positions, often by bringing tea and sandwiches to the polling station staff, so that they could have the free run of the voting areas. This enabled them to glean vital information for other members in their party operating in the tally rooms outside under the com-mand of the 'hats', who could then accurately monitor which areas were slow or not turning out to vote. This information, coming from within the station, indicated the state of play hour by hour throughout every election day. The co-operation the unionists received from supposedly neutral election officials was often so detailed that they could work out which individual Labour people had not voted, enabling them to steal votes by having someone personate the voter.

Vote stealing was conducted on a wholesale basis. The union-ist battle plan for all elections was based on marking up the register of voters before each election. The list of voters in each street would be carefully coloured in blue for unionists, red for Labour and yellow for the others. Those who had died since the register was last compiled would also be highlighted; the per-sonators actually raced each other to claim the votes of the recently deceased. Registers used by tally workers at the polling stations were marked up to date again after canvassing to indi-cate who was voting and who was not. The votes of those who did not intend to turn out were invariably cast by someone else.

Unionists usually stole the Labour votes first and those of their own absentees afterwards. Many a person turned up to vote only to find their name crossed off the list and their vote already in the black ballot box. Our knowledge of the unionist election methods was confirmed when we found some registers in a hired caravan used at a council by-election in Clifton ward in the late 1960s. We brought them to the *Belfast Telegraph*, which published the story, giving the unionists much embarrassing publicity.

After my defeat in the council election I nursed my political powerbase by meeting people who needed help, at my home, 248 Grosvenor Road. I gave advice, wrote letters and represented people on national assistance, sickness benefit and unemployment benefit tribunals. I kept my name in the public eye by writing letters on topical issues and themes to the local newspapers. Whatever the subjects of the daily correspondence I always found something to say. At the same time I continued to better myself through education and I did courses on management principles and theory, industrial psychology and work-study at the Belfast Technical College. I was still working at Andrews' mill, where I was eventually promoted to shift foreman – a job that entailed looking after sixty men. It was a challenging job, for Andrews' premises at that time consisted of a dozen small buildings totally unsuited to storing grain and ground pig meal. The foreman had to improvise and use his initiative to deploy his men and get the full production totals ready for the following day's deliveries, especially as all material handling was done by hand and two-wheel trucks.

My mind was, however, more firmly focused on the prospects of winning the Falls seat in the Stormont parliament, which had been held by Harry Diamond since 1945. There had been no opposition to him for years; he was doing little work in the constituency and at Stormont he was only raising 'hardy annual' issues in a series of boring and repetitive speeches. He was largely silent on the closedown of the flax and textile mills in the area, and contributed little to the debate about the merits of the massive redevelopment scheme for the Lower Falls which was going to affect about 5,000 people. The civil rights campaign, which I took a leading part in from the start, was getting under way at this period and he completely ignored it. I reckoned the Falls needed something better and I was determined to offer it.

As a first step I decided to form an NILP branch on the Falls Road, where I had had a support base since my days with the Irish Labour Party. The response was more than warm. Trade unionists who lived there began to join. Some friends from my workplace became members. In the early days we met in a dingy room above a fruit shop at the corner of Colin Street on the Falls Road, but as we expanded we moved down to the office of the National Union of Seamen in Victoria Street. We started a weekly social to build up a fighting fund for future elections. These occasions became very popular and we often organised them on both Saturday and Sunday nights. Apart from the good entertainment we provided, with a number of fine singers including myself, we became famous for our hamburgers, an item never heard of on a menu in Belfast before that. They were made, to his own special recipe, by a Scottish fellow who was then the Belfast representative for the seamen's union.

In 1967 I was elected chairman of the party in succession to Charles Brett. Shortly afterwards the journalist Bud Bossence, an old friend, wrote a profile of me in his famous daily column 'As I See It' in the *News Letter*. He described me as 'a man with a mission'. I rather liked the article because it outlined my background, stressing that I had come into the trade union and labour movement from the Falls area, something of a phenomenon within labour circles. I always viewed that article as a landmark for me and the Labour Party in the Falls. It seemed to me that it directly encouraged labour and trade union sympathisers to join with me in a co-ordinated effort to win the parliamentary seat from Diamond. I decided that I would keep

83

the pressure on him throughout the year of my chairmanship until the general election ultimately took place.

By now I was thoroughly disillusioned with the Catholic church, and had ceased to attend mass and the sacraments. The church had opposed me politically and this encouraged doubts, and undermined my beliefs in the teaching of the church. In later years, I described myself as an agnostic.

My election campaign was carefully planned and prepared. I had my fellow workers out canvassing votes and marking registers. Thanks to the social evenings and the hamburgers we had also built up our funds to cover the expenses. A pool of eighty car owners, who would come out on the day to carry voters to the polls, was lined up and we enlisted almost three hundred workers to canvass, drive, and check votes in the polling booths and in the tally rooms. I had experienced captains in each polling district and, like the shipyard 'hard hats' who worked for the unionists, they knew their business and how to get the voters out. Captain Terence O'Neill, the unionist prime minister, finally called the election for 24 February 1969, reacting mainly to the impact of the civil rights movement.

The election campaign took a different form from what the electors expected or were used to. In the past the candidates tore each other apart in internecine warfare, outdoing each other in claims of just how Green or nationalist they were. My political philosophy broke that mould, for I concentrated on the 'bread and butter' issues, more jobs and modern houses. Far too many people were living in poverty, without basic amenities like indoor toilets, hot water and weatherproof homes. Their health was poor and children were being brought up in conditions that were intolerable. I was out to fight the bosses and the unionists for a fairer deal for the working classes.

Diamond said that it was indefensible for the NILP to be fighting the seat and contesting his 'long record' of service, but our canvass returns showed that people felt he hadn't delivered for them and indicated a clear trend in our favour. Our workers were so confident from the feedback that they slipped off quietly to back me to win. The bookmakers' information was not all that good, for Diamond was being tipped as the hot favourite and they were offering odds of six-to-one against me taking the seat.

On polling day I toured the polling stations but I nearly had a fit when I reached Slate Street school and discovered that a personation squad had been mustered to steal votes on my behalf.

'What the hell are you doing?' I asked an old personal friend, who was not a member of the party.

'This is the way you run elections,' he said. 'Everybody does it.'

'I am in politics to stop this racket,' I said. 'I am not going to stand for this. Stop it or I will have you arrested.'

That occasion set the seal on my attitude to stealing votes. I was dead against it and every one of my election workers knew it.

After the polling booths closed in the evening we all trooped down to the Presbyterian Hall in May Street, where the Falls boxes were to be counted. After a couple of nail-biting hours, close to midnight, I was declared duly elected by the returning officer. I polled 6,275 votes, a majority of 726 over Diamond, who got 5,549. One man who welcomed the result as much as me was my very good friend, the bookmaker Barney Eastwood. As the counts were being completed he and his wife, Frances, were on their knees on the floor of their house counting up the losses. If Diamond had won he would have had to pay out thousands. When my result came through he and Frances cheered and went off to bed content. About the same time we returned to our party rooms for a celebration, but little did I know that a crisis, of hurricane proportions, was already blowing up.

6

'WE SHALL OVERCOME'

When I got to Stormont I was brought down to earth by my first letter, from a former schoolmate, a bit of a tearaway, who was more interested in stealing and fighting than in lessons. I hadn't heard of him since he had left school at fourteen and taken off to England more than thirty years earlier. 'Imagine it. You an MP,' he wrote. 'What the fuck would I have been, had I stayed.'

Another bizarre introductory episode was enacted by one of my fellow MPs. He and his wife accosted myself and Theresa, offering advice about what to do when we went to Hillsborough Castle to meet the governor. Theresa could borrow the necessary long, white, over-the-elbow gloves and they would teach her how to curtsey. I told him in no uncertain terms that that would not be necessary, for we had no intention of going anywhere near the governor.

I was not able to attend the official opening of the new parliament because I was laid low with a bad bout of influenza. It was not surprising, for the election campaigning had been carried on in bitterly cold mid-winter weather. With a parliamentary salary assured, for a time anyway, I took the opportunity to sever my eighteen-year-long connection with Andrews'. As a leaving bonus, they sent me £100, but it was doubled after David Andrews intervened.

Still hoarse from the flu, I made my seven-minute maiden

speech on 12 March 1969 during the second reading of the Public Order bill. As is customary, I first paid tribute to Harry Diamond 'for his many years of faithful and diligent service on behalf of the people of the Falls constituency'.

I then told the House: 'In a democratic country a government must defend their citizens' rights to free assembly and free speech and in the context of this bill the right to peaceful protest and procession. I am a socialist and essentially my attitude must be to endeavour to widen the area of individual freedom under any type of legislation.'

I pointed out that over the years experience had shown that the unionist government had not tried to protect the right of the people to peaceful protest but wanted only to avoid disorder. 'The record has shown a consistently heavy-handed and oppressive attitude by successive ministers of Home Affairs. Too little effort and vigilance have been used to try to keep the individual's right to protest against what he does not like in society and the heavy-handed oppressive legislation that has been used to sweep away the individual's right of protest.'

I then queried some aspects of the bill in line with a brief that had been prepared for me by Martin McBirney, a Labour-minded lawyer who was later assassinated by the Provisional IRA.

The Public Order bill was the government's hardline response to the onset of the widespread rioting and disorder that marked the outbreak of what we call 'the Troubles'. Their tangled roots went back for years into the mists of Irish history, but their immediate origins could be traced to the emergence of the civil rights movement towards the end of the 1960s.

Inspired by the civil rights campaign to get justice and equality for blacks in the United States, a broadly based civil rights movement was emerging in Northern Ireland. There was a general feeling around that if the two communities in the North could bury their differences and live together on a basis of equality that, one day, they could jointly work out a solution to partition. I was involved in this process from the outset and at that time our objective was clearly and firmly to achieve a full measure of social justice and equality under the Stormont system by pressing for a series of specific reforms. The earliest meetings took place in the War Memorial Hall in Waring Street, Belfast, and at the International Hotel at Donegall Square South, at the back of the City Hall. The Stormont MPs Gerry Fitt and Austin Currie turned up and spoke at these gatherings. Although our reforming enthusiasm was spurred on by Gerry Fitt, who encouraged a number of British Labour MPs into making fact-finding visits and putting pressure on Harold Wilson (then in his first term of office as prime minister), the civil rights movement had a very slow start. The committee met on a regular basis but we had to try each other out. We did not know each other as individuals, for the political allegiances represented by the people around the room were wide and disparate. They ranged all the way across the political spectrum from labour and trade union people, like me, to some liberal unionists. We also had some local communists and members of the Wolfe Tone Societies, the Irish republican movement and nationalist groupings. We were an interesting bunch, some well-meaning, some with bleeding hearts and others who had their own agendas.

We held discussions on various subjects like housing, jobs, discrimination, policing and the travelling people. These discussions were fuelled by diligent research carried out by a range of organisations. For the first time we were debating the issues factually on a cross-community basis rather than exchanging generalities of prejudice across the political divide. We did nothing more worthwhile than talk, however, until Austin Currie, in an act of sheer desperation, occupied an empty new house at Caledon, Co. Tyrone, on 20 June 1968. Twenty-four hours earlier he had been ordered out of the chamber at Stormont during a rowdy adjournment debate about the issue. Austin was furious because a Catholic family with three very young children had been evicted after squatting in a council house while at the same time another house had been allocated to an unmarried, nineteen-year-old Protestant girl with influential unionist connections. According to Austin's research, this took place at a time when the Dungannon Rural District Council had 269 people on the waiting list for houses and only twelve dwellings under construction.

Austin was eventually manhandled from the house by a party of policemen and arrested. The incident galvanised the growing civil rights movement into direct action, and two months later, on 24 August, a large march was organised by a local committee. The intention was to take the demonstration from Coalisland into Dungannon, where a protest meeting was to be held. Gerry Fitt and Betty Sinclair, a communist who was involved in the trade union movement, were to address the meeting. Several thousand marchers turned up on the day but when they arrived at the outskirts of Dungannon they were stopped at a police cordon and prevented from marching into the town. The two speakers addressed the halted crowd at the police line and the rally broke up without serious incident, but the police action raised the new issue of the right to march. There was a strong feeling that as the civil rights marchers represented both traditions they should not be treated as lepers and be prevented from marching anywhere throughout the North. This feeling was all the more strongly held because the Orange Order was allowed to parade wherever it wanted whether or not there was local opposition to their presence. Accordingly arrangements were put in hand for a bigger, better organised demonstration. The chosen venue was Derry on 5 October 1968 and the parade was to cross from one side of the River Foyle to the other, symbolising that the marchers were not partisan. It turned out to be a decisive turning point in our history.

The week before the march I had to go to the British Labour Party conference in Blackpool as a fraternal delegate from the NILP. I met Gerry Fitt there. We both understood the significance of the coming march in Derry and suspected that it would end in trouble. We felt we needed some Labour MPs there as independent observers, especially as the British media had long turned a blind eye to Northern Ireland. On the rare occasions when they had ventured into what the mighty *Sunday Times* had once graphically described as 'John Bull's political slum', the Stormont crowd caused such earache for them back in London that they decided it was not worth all the bother. If there was a clash, therefore, we wanted the outside MPs, whose eyewitness accounts would be regarded as valid, to report back to parliament. The Wilson government was becoming increasingly hostile to the unionist hardliners; Wilson had actually said that Captain Terence O'Neill was being 'blackmailed by thugs', who were frustrating his undertakings to introduce fundamental and overdue reforms in Northern Ireland. During conference week we persuaded three MPs, John Ryan, and Russell and Ann Kerr to travel over. I already knew Russell Kerr from my trade union activities and I was pleased he agreed to come.

We collected the three MPs from Aldergrove airport on the Saturday morning, promising that we would get them back on the plane that evening for London. By then Bill Craig, the hardline Home Affairs minister in the O'Neill government, had banned the march from crossing the Foyle into the centre of Derry and had ordered the police to stop it. As we slipped into the city by back roads to avoid the police checkpoints, we knew that a confrontation was now inevitable. At the assembly point, the railway station, we lined up about ten abreast with Paddy Kennedy, Gerry Fitt and myself among those in the front row. Eddie McAteer, the leader of the Nationalist Party and MP for Derry, was also present. The atmosphere was electric as the march moved slowly off in the direction of the line of policemen and tenders drawn across Duke Street.

They were ready, as we knew they would be, and when we came face to face, the batons and blackthorn sticks, carried by the officers, came out and they started hitting us. Heads were split and groins were kneed as police and demonstrators engaged in running clashes. One of the first casualties was Gerry, who was covered in blood gushing down his face after a blow to the head. I was hit and then kneed by a policeman but he backed off before I biffed him back. The police then brought up a water cannon and I remember running away from the high-powered jets of water. The MPs, positioned behind the police, had a clear view of the events, which were also recorded for television by Gay O'Brien of Radio Telefís Éireann, the only cameraman present. He stood impassively in the middle of the clashes and water jets, graphically recording the action. His pictures were flashed round the world that evening and when Harold Wilson saw them in 10 Downing Street as he watched the evening news bulletins, he was appalled.

The unionists as usual did not comprehend the full implications of what was going on and fell into the trap of trying to suppress people seeking basic civil rights – a cause that dominated world events in the 1960s and attracted international sympathy, whether in the United States or behind the Iron Curtain of communism. By attacking the march the police force demonstrated that it was no more than the jackboot of the Unionist political party. Over the next few months the RUC's already controversial reputation plunged to zero as they consistently turned their backs on the civil rights marchers in a series of ugly confrontations throughout Northern Ireland. As far back as the disturbances in Divis Street, Belfast, during the 1964 general election, those with a critical eye on police capability had spotted that the force was under strength. They simply had not the reserve strength to cope with a sustained street challenge. As an economy measure Craig had presided over the closedown of several police stations as Minister of Home Affairs. The RUC strength, around 3,000, was the same as it had been in 1922 when the force was formed and over the years there had been virtually no investment in riot training, equipment and radios, weakening its capacity to deal with events like these. As the rioting worsened, the unionists were reluctant to call for help from the British Army for that would have been an admission that events were out of control.

Craig behaved more and more like an ass as the crisis deepened. He imposed bans on marches which the police were unable to enforce. He made repeated statements that the IRA was manipulating the civil rights movement and was therefore the cause of the trouble. This was completely wide of the mark. The intelligence gathered by the police at the time, upon which he partly based his inaccurate assessment of the situation, showed there was no grasp of the real causes of the discontent. The crunch came in early December 1968 after Craig had made repeated hardline public statements, stopping just short of a call for Ulster to 'go it alone' from Britain. O'Neill, who had vacillated as the disorder escalated, finally sacked Craig and produced a five-point reform package aimed at halting the continued civil rights marches and increasingly strident counter-demonstrations, usually with the booming figure of Ian Paisley at the front.

There was to be a new points system to ensure that public housing was allocated entirely on need and not through pull or favouritism. An ombudsman was to be appointed to investigate any individual grievances about the way the government and councils operated. The draconian Special Powers Act, the emergency legislation that had been introduced in the early 1920s and kept in force, was to be reviewed. 'One man, one vote', a central plank of the civil rights demands, was to be introduced through the abolition of the right of companies to vote in council elections. Finally, O'Neill announced that there would be a new Londonderry Development Commission to spearhead reform and regeneration in the city which had borne the brunt of the disorder until then.

There was an overwhelming groundswell of support and it appeared that feelings and relations between the unionist government and the people were about to be stabilised. Some civil rights activists were satisfied with the package and were prepared to heed O'Neill's call for the marching to stop to give the reforms time to take effect. But I was uneasy that they still did not go far enough to rectify the years of unionist abuse and misrule, and I favoured keeping up the pressure that had been created to achieve the fundamental and lasting changes in society that I knew in my bones were necessary.

In particular I was critical that the reform package did not address the question of electoral boundary reform. Gerrymandering – rigging electoral boundaries – on a grand scale was still rife in Derry, Tyrone and Fermanagh. It was unfair that equal voting rights for local government elections were denied poor families sharing the same house. There was also a strong case for abolishing the university franchise, which enabled graduates to elect MPs. O'Neill also failed to address the question of Catholics receiving a fair share of public appointments on merit.

People's Democracy, which had been started by students in Queen's University several months before, also took this view and amid much controversy announced plans for a four-day march from Belfast to Derry at the beginning of January 1969. I supported them. The march left from the front of Belfast City Hall on New Year's Day to go through Antrim, Knockloughrim, Dungiven and on to Derry. When I heard the organisers planning for many bars of chocolate to feed the marchers, I arranged for sandwiches and rolls to be delivered to them en route.

Before they reached the first overnight stop at Antrim the band of marchers had been harassed and harried by a gang of loyalist toughs, led by Major Ronald Bunting, one of Paisley's henchmen at the time. I had expected that such counter-demonstrations would be the order of the day. I linked up with the group early the next morning and noticed that even then their way forward was blocked by the flag-waving loyalist mob. There was just no way past, for they carried sticks and cudgels. Thinking of an alternative, I counted the marchers; there were forty. We had eleven cars at our disposal and there was a side road close to where we were standing that would bring us around the mob and on our way. I told the drivers to go and start their engines and wait with the car doors open. The marchers were told that after a set signal they should run for the cars and set off down the side road. The plan worked like a dream. We took the loyalists by surprise and they were left standing with their flags, singing their obscene songs. When they realised they had been outwitted they came after us in their cars but we gave them the slip again at Toomebridge. After two more days playing cat and mouse with the counter-demonstrators along the route, the marchers finally reached their final stopover at Claudy, late, and very exhausted, on the Friday night.

That night I set out for Derry with Brian Garrett, a solicitor and labour activist, to await their arrival. We hung about the City Hotel, where I remember meeting John Hume for the first time. He had played a prominent role in the civil rights agitation in the city. Given the events of the previous few days, I was anxious about the safety of the marchers, not least because my daughter, Anne, then a student at Coleraine, was among them. Hume was reassuring. He told me they would get through all right. Later that day when the marchers, by now numbering many hundreds, arrived in torrential rain, my worst fears were justified. They were literally 'walking wounded'. Scarcely one of them was left unhurt. They had walked into a vicious ambush, carefully laid by the loyalists at Burntollet Bridge, just north of Dungiven on the main Belfast–Derry road.

It later transpired that, the night before, loyalists had met in the Guildhall in Derry to plan a 'last ditch' operation to stop the march. Representatives from every loyalist area between Claudy and Derry were given instructions on what their role should be in the attacks. From early morning heavy quarry lorries carried loads of stones to the hilltops along the route into Derry. Groups of men, totalling some two hundred or more, and including members of the all-Protestant auxiliary police, the B Specials, gathered along the road. They were armed with sticks embedded with protruding six-inch nails, police batons and iron bars. Each man was told to wear an armband to identify himself to the other attackers. There seemed to have been some pre-arrangement with at least some elements of the RUC that they would take up positions away from the marchers at crucial points of the journey so as not to be caught in the crossfire with the attackers.

The confrontation at Burntollet Bridge was by far the worst. My daughter, Anne, was among the many casualties. Although she had been injured earlier in the march and was taken to the Royal Victoria Hospital in Belfast with a foot injury, she had insisted on rejoining the column. This time she was knocked unconscious from a blow on the head and fell into the river. She was rescued by other marchers and brought back to the bank. A photograph of this incident still remains one of the most telling images of the terror and brutality of the day. Anne was taken back to the hospital and kept in for observation, suffering from concussion.

The march, after several more attacks, particularly at Green Street Estate on the outskirts of Derry, came through eventually to the safety of the City Hotel. Outside, the police rampaged through the Catholic Bogside, conduct that was to become a major political issue and a great source of division between the force and the nationalist community for years to come.

These events helped to fuel more tension over another banned People's Democracy demonstration in Newry a week later. There the civil rights movement finally fell into the trap we, as leaders, had always warned against. The television cameras captured it all, as, for the first time, civil rights marchers went on the offensive and several police tenders were set on fire and rolled over into the canal. It signalled that our non-violent civil rights movement had gone up in smoke from that minute onwards. The London government was by now becoming visibly concerned as events appeared to be spiralling rapidly out of control. Very much at London's insistence, the Stormont government was forced within days to appoint a three-man commission, headed by the Scottish judge, Lord Cameron, to inquire into the causes of the violence. Brian Faulkner, the hardline but successful Minister of Commerce, who had his own leadership ambitions, resigned from the cabinet in protest. O'Neill decided to appeal over the heads of the extremists on both sides, as he naïvely saw it, by calling a general election for 24 February 1969. 'Ulster stands at the crossroads,' he had said earlier. 'What kind of Ulster do you want?'

The result of the election from O'Neill's point of view was not as decisive as he would have liked. It was my opinion that his days were numbered. Certainly, in spite of claims to the contrary, O'Neill had never had any heart for the reforms forced on him by the Labour government. In any case, they did not have much chance of helping him ride the storm. There was a marked lack of support within his own party and the civil rights reformers knew that he was on the run. In my view he should have stood up to the extremists on his own side and hammered them. This was, in reality, O'Neill's big weakness and because of his lack of guts he made it virtually impossible for those coming after him to lead the party.

As I began to learn the parliamentary ropes and come into daily contact with the unionists in the Stormont precincts, I had found them an arrogant lot. There were more commanders and majors and captains strutting about than you would have found in an officers' mess at Aldershot. Most were fairly low grade and undistinguished. They were sent along to vote without demur for unionism. When we scored debating points they did everything but threaten to use flamethrowers or launch grenades into Catholic areas. The Speaker and his deputy tended to allow quite a bit of latitude in these exchanges. We discovered one of the most noisy unionists had a house across the border in Donegal, so we used to refer to him as the honourable member for Burtonport, which usually shut him up. There were a few rare exceptions. Phelim O'Neill, the prime minister's cousin, was a courageous man, prepared to break the sterile sectarian mould. I much admired him for the occasion when he rebuked Lord Brookeborough during an economic debate. After the noble lord remarked that his heart bled for the unemployed, Phelim said: 'It's not bleeding hearts we want but bloody brains.' Brian Faulkner was a successful entrepreneur rather than a member of the landed gentry. In my view he was the most able parliamentarian around and I always believed that if he, rather than O'Neill, had succeeded Brookeborough and if he had become a liberal earlier, he might well have pre-empted the subsequent Troubles.

Robert (Bertie) Porter, a Queen's Counsel who held several ministerial posts, was one of my favourites amongst the unionists. He was a compassionate man and one of the handful who realised, as he often said, that 'unionism cannot stand still while the world was changing'. Dick Ferguson, another barrister and an excellent advocate, voted with us on several occasions when civil rights issues were at stake. Despite the fact that Des Boal was very closely involved with Ian Paisley, I developed a deep admiration for him, also a prominent and skilled barrister. There are few better orators and although he seldom attended Stormont, when he did, a hush fell over the building and people rushed to the chamber to listen. In stern tones, he delivered his speech, daring a heckler to intervene. Sometimes he even provoked his hecklers. On one occasion he looked across the floor at me and accused me of chewing gum. I protested to the Speaker that I had nothing in my mouth. Boal disregarded my protest and left the House smiling at me after his speech.

Nationalist MPs were regarded as the opposition in the pre-civil rights days, although they had never formally accepted the role. In the politics of demonology which the unionists pursued, the nationalists were portrayed as the enemy who represented the Catholic church, the IRA and the Catholic people. Ever since proportional representation had been abolished in 1929, the electorate voted on a purely Catholic and Protestant, nationalist and unionist, basis. In this type of election the Unionist Party, having a permanent two-to-one majority, was invincible. The minority was therefore unable to reverse or even share their political control, or to prevent the party in power setting the electoral boundaries and the form of the franchise with cold-blooded gerrymandering, keeping the Catholic voters locked into ghetto areas.

It was no wonder that members of the Nationalist Party were therefore a tired and lacklustre bunch. With the notable exceptions of Austin Currie, by far the most able and vigorous of them, James O'Reilly of Mourne and John Carron of Fermanagh, nothing for them had changed in forty years. They had suffered badly at the hands of the civil rights campaign, and by contrast with the new MPs like myself, John Hume, Paddy O'Hanlon and Ivan Cooper, who had come in as full-time parliamentarians, they were still part-time and poor attenders. I discovered that most of the nationalists, especially the senators, were closely linked to a chain of local newspapers. They would put the odd question down for a written answer, come in quietly and take the answer home to write banner headlines on their ingenuity at getting information to expose the evils of the Orange and unionist regime. It was a pitiful farce that the people reading Catholic newspapers had to put up with such tedious tactics for so many years.

The debates in the Stormont House of Commons, modelled in style and procedure on the British parliament, were invariably heated affairs, whether they were about housing allocations or warble-fly affecting cattle. Turning back over the pages of Hansard for my early days at Stormont I can vividly recall the rancorous, heated and often humorous exchanges across the floor of the House.

My first parliamentary campaign was fought over the Burntollet ambush. My aim was to use the democratic, parliamentary process to establish the facts about that brutal incident and force the authorities to deal with its implications. I wanted to ascertain just who the attackers were; if the police had colluded with them; and whether or not B Specials had been involved – on or off duty.

There had been considerable press interest in the entire march. Some reporters and photographers may even have known of the loyalists' intention to attack the students. During the course of the march thousands of photographs were taken. Once they had appeared in the papers of the following few days, these photographs were simply stored away in the various newspaper libraries. Vincent McCormack and Bowes Egan, both Queen's graduates who had been involved with People's Democracy, acquired large quantities of the photographs and then visited the areas in south Derry and east Tyrone from where the attacks on the march had been launched. Hundreds of homes, clubs and pubs were visited and a considerable number of the attackers were identified. A very high proportion of them were said to be B Specials. Having taken the exercise thus far, they approached me to seek more information by the use of parliamentary questions. All told I tabled 452 questions, most asking if a named person was a member of the RUC or the B Specials.

I was able to establish that the majority of the attackers were in the RUC or the B Specials, and to pinpoint their identities. In spite of the fact that hundreds of them were identified, only a handful were were ever charged with offences. I reckoned that more than a quarter of the replies I received were deliberately misleading and that those preparing the replies for the minister deliberately conspired to obstruct me. The cross-questioning exposed the fact that the Ministry of Home Affairs had far from efficient records of the membership of the B Specials.

I eventually raised the discrepancies in an adjournment debate on the floor of the House and gave notice of them a month beforehand. Yet when the minister, Bertie Porter, replied to my criticism, he said: 'The honourable member has submitted this House to a welter of questions split into over 400 parts. I am pointing out that since he gave me no prior information on the points he wished to raise that it would be unreasonable for anyone to expect me to deal with them this afternoon.'

The minister should have recognised what was happening and apologised to me and to parliament and then acted against the culprits in his department, but he never did. Neither, for that matter, did he take action against the police and Specials involved in the attack and those who carried out the half-hearted investigation into it afterwards. The minister said: 'I do not accept that there was anything improper or half-hearted in the carrying out of these investigations.'

Despite the attempts to obscure the facts of this extraordinary attack, I was encouraged that I was still able to get so much information through the parliamentary system. I learned that a determined member who has fully researched his case can compel co-operation in his pursuit of truth, however reluctant the administration. It gave me faith in democratic procedures but it was to be sorely tested over the next few months.

The acrimonious tone in the House intensified throughout the early months of 1969 when the new Public Order bill was the issue which dominated proceedings. New legislation was urgently needed for the current law both affected the right of people to march and prevented effective action being taken to curb counter-demonstrations. These could be organised by loyalists to prevent genuine demonstrations, and were often given police approval at the expense of the original demonstration. Police were also exceeding their authority and arresting people without due cause. The new bill, as drafted by the government, was much too draconian and failed to confront many specific issues we had identified. We had to make an impact on it, for every Catholic was waiting to see if parliament could be worked in the even-handed, democratic way that had been promised during the election campaign. When the House met to consider the bill on 19 March 1969, we had tabled about forty amendments, drawn up with the help of sympathetic lawyers and people from Queen's University. That day we kept the House in session until 3 a.m. the following morning, going through the small print in fine detail, and it certainly looked as if the government lawyers were debating the merits of the legislation with us in a constructive spirit, although we were consistently out-voted. I queried some aspects of the bill in line with a brief that had been prepared for me by Martin McBirney.

The pattern resumed the following afternoon when we met again to consider the bill, but after only three hours' discussion, Captain John Brooke, son of the former long-serving prime minister, who had taken no signficant interest in the exchanges, suddenly jumped to his feet and asked John Hume, who was speaking, to give way. When he did so, Brooke said: 'I beg to move that the question be now put.' Despite our most vigorous protests about this unparliamentary behaviour, the question was put and we lost the vote 26 to 10. At that point eight of us sat on the floor of the chamber and sang the civil rights anthem 'We shall overcome'. As the unionists panicked about what to do next I shouted: 'What would the Public Order Act say about this?'

The Speaker appealed to us to resume our seats but we refused and remained where we were. He then named us, which meant we were suspended from sittings of the House for a week, before adjourning for thirty minutes. When the session resumed we were still on the floor and he ordered the police to remove us. A sergeant was then called and we were escorted, one by one, into the corridor. We were astonished that some unionists would be so foolish on this fundamental issue as to guillotine the debate. Everyone, including O'Neill, felt the debate on the legislation was a good exercise for them. They had a chance to show that they were democrats, prepared to work parliament in a way that would demonstrate sensitivity to minority feelings.

Brooke's intervention reflected the infighting between the moderates and diehards within the Unionist Party hierarchy at the time. The moderates were prepared to introduce reforms, although not on the scale that we wanted, while the diehards resisted every demand. Craig, in political exile since his sacking, was making the running for them in belligerent speeches all over the place. The theme was that Ulster would not surrender its parliament without a fight. 'What we see today on the streets of our province will look like a Sunday school picnic if Westminster tries to take our parliament away.' O'Neill was coming under increasing pressure from both factions to stand down. His demise finally came on 28 April after events outside parliament took an even more sinister turn. During the month there were four explosions which seriously damaged water and electricity installations in the Belfast area. At first the authorities blamed the IRA, their usual knee-jerk reaction, but it soon became known that all were the work of the outlawed Ulster Volunteer Force.

O'Neill helped to manoeuvre Major James Chichester-Clark into the unionist leadership and prime ministerial post before bowing out. This 'landed gentry' fix was the end of the line as far as we were concerned. 'Chi-Chi', as he became known, was basically a decent man as unionists go but, as events all too rapidly proved, he was out of his depth and could not handle the disastrous pressures now coming at him from all directions.

That spring and summer were warm and dry, the perfect conditions for those who threatened communal peace. A trickle of Catholic families living in mixed areas began to leave their homes after threats or petrol bomb attacks. As sectarian tension stoked up, other Catholic families began to flock into the safety of West Belfast, mainly squatting in new houses that were being built in the Andersonstown area. Clashes between rival crowds became a nightly occurrence and the heavy-handed policing, by a force that was now overstretched and exhausted, did little to calm the trouble. There were few nights that I was not being called out to ease fears, oversee families fleeing their homes or plead with the outnumbered police for protection. One night at Hooker Street in the Crumlin Road area, which was one of the worst flashpoints, an elderly lady put out her Union Jack to celebrate the Twelfth of July. She had done it every year since she could remember without incident. Because of the tension in the street, which was religiously mixed, attempts were made to remove it. A great friend of mine at the time was Father Tony Marcellus, who was based at the Ardoyne monastery. He brought me up to try to reason with the local yahoos. No dice! I promised Tony I would come back that night to stand guard with him. That evening we positioned ourselves outside the house and were surrounded by a mob of hate-filled youngsters. One tried to lob a petrol bomb and Tony whacked him. They moved off up the street.

I now dreaded that if we didn't get the tension down the city would explode. I began to recall the cycle of vicious sectarian violence that had scarred the city's history for several hundred years. That summer the same combustible material that had sparked the earlier clashes was piling up with a vengeance. Tony suggested that if he could get the young people interested in the pop scene, they would come away from sectarian violence. We put our heads together and came up with the idea of a 'pop for peace' concert at the Minnowburn on the southern outskirts of the city. John Lennon had just written 'Give peace a chance', which provided a perfect anthem for our operation. The concert was a great success with several local bands attracting over 7,000 young people, who sang their hearts out. Loyalist 'tartan gangs' turned up but they were turned away by police before they could upset the atmosphere. As the clear-up was going on after the concert I turned on my small radio to listen to the news bulletin. In those tense days everybody listened to the news incessantly – morning, noon and night – to keep up to date with what was happening. 'Unity Flats attacked by Orangemen' was the headline. My heart sank. I now knew we were faced with serious sectarian trouble. I could not see how to avoid it.

The IRA read the tea leaves as well as the rest of us. They were still an unpopular body in Belfast, never having had much support in my time in the early 1940s or again during their so-called campaign in the late 1950s, when they could only operate from the southern side of the border. As a result of this lack of support they decided to change policy, going Marxist, following the liberation army concept to build up popular support by exploiting severe economic deprivation. The situation in Northern Ireland was easy for them to exploit with its blatant repression and injustice. The police and their unionist masters were playing into their hands. They calculated that the IRA was stirring up an armed uprising but they could not have been more wrong. At that time the IRA could only have mustered a couple of rusty handguns in Belfast.

July 1969 was a difficult month, with riots, fires and disturbances every night. I was in the thick of the crowds pleading for calm, trying to defuse the confrontations, but each night the crowds got bigger and tension reached new heights. Shops on the Falls Road were ransacked, looted and burned. Fire engines were attacked when they arrived to put out the fires. So too was the fire chief himself as he arrived to observe. He suffered appalling facial and body injuries when his car was petrol-bombed. District Inspector Frank Lagan, a very brave man, and one of the few Catholics in the senior ranks of the RUC, joined me in attempting to keep the crowds in check, but he was set upon himself. I got him away to hide in a house in Alma Street, off the Falls Road, until it was safe for him to leave the area. I was appalled at the disgraceful scenes, aware, as I was, that in the background of these attacks were Derry voices urging on the rioters.

As the trouble in Belfast got worse through the summer, so also did the agitation in Derry. I was a member of a group of MPs who visited Chichester-Clark to get the police withdrawn from the Bogside area of Derry, where a running battle between them and the residents had been going on for months without interruption. He refused and let this mad escapade by the police take its course. I saw nothing sensible about the regular charges into the Bogside except vindictiveness on the part of the police. Hostility to them reached new bounds with the death from coronary thrombosis on 17 July of Samuel Devenney, who had been badly beaten during one of these police rampages in April. Frustration was driving many of my colleagues to withdraw from parliament in protest at the lack of action, but I argued that each member of the opposition had a contribution to make and should stay in his place to make it. I was fed up with the walkout technique. I felt I was elected to say my piece and should do so.

The crunch came in Derry in mid-August when the government blindly refused to prevent the Apprentice Boys from holding their traditional march though the centre of the city, along the fringes of the Bogside. Within twenty-four hours the bedraggled police had lost control of the situation and the Belfast government mobilised the B Specials. But before they got into position the London government finally stepped in, deploying British soldiers in Derry to relieve the police and restore calm.

In Belfast, where British troops had not yet gone in, it was a terrible night. The police thought that a full-scale IRA-inspired uprising was under way and they put Shorland armoured cars, equipped with Browning heavy machine-guns, on to the streets. They fired hundreds of rounds throughout the night, killing two people at Divis Flats in the Lower Falls, including a nine-year-old boy. The crowds on the Shankill, frightened by the scenes on the Falls over the previous nights, feared for their lives. Crowds were organised early in the night and arms were brought in from rural areas in cars and given out to some of the men. Local people who knew the streets daubed whitewash marks on the doors or windows of Catholic homes. These homes were then emptied of people and burned. As far as I could tell around 650 Catholic families were burned out that night. Five people lost their lives in exchanges of sniper fire. Police in uniform, covered in civilian coats, were recognised amongst loyalist attackers in Dover Street and I myself saw police armoured cars in Conway Street, standing by as the mobs broke the windows of hastily abandoned Catholic houses before pouring petrol in to burn them. In scenes that had not been paralleled for nearly fifty years, I saw with my own eyes old people and former neighbours flocking out of Conway Street, where my grandparents had once lived at number 32 and my own mother and father at number 80.

Come daylight, the Falls Road was filled with heavily laden prams and handcarts carrying the household utensils and furniture of the unfortunate refugee families who had lost their homes. Schools and halls were thrown open as temporary accommodation and school meal-making facilities, idle because of the holidays, were reactivated. Bedding provided by charities and social services was erected in dormitory fashion. Old-age pensioners sat about in terror, holding hands and saying the rosary. As the day wore on, with no respite from the sniping and burning, other families from outlying mixed parts of the city converged on the Falls for safety. I rang the police several times throughout the day to ask for protection, only to be told by City Commissioner Graham Shillington that no men could be spared, as Donegall Pass and Tennent Street police stations were under attack by the IRA. I noticed, as I made my way to a friend's house for something to eat, that barricades were going up at many street corners.

I met my fellow MP Paddy Kennedy later that day and discussed what steps we should take to protect the Catholic population in Belfast, bearing in mind the refusal of the police to help. He too had called on them all night to come out and stop the 'slaughter of the innocent'. With troops on the streets in Derry, and Belfast in turmoil with no effective police presence, we decided to call for the military to step in. Paddy and I went into a house opposite the Falls Park, where we telephoned Home Secretary James Callaghan to give him a first-hand account of the dreadful situation that had developed and to plead with him for soldiers. We were also in touch with Gerry Fitt, who shared our view. He reinforced it in calls to both Callaghan and Harold Wilson, the prime minister. As we waited for news from them, we visited the expelled families from our constituencies.

When I arrived back on the streets that afternoon I was immediately besieged by families stranded by the awful violence of the night before. The stories were harrowing. They needed food, bedding and money. I got on to government agencies and was impressed by the speed with which help was provided. We got relief centres opened and the Department of Health and Social Services moved staff and resources in immediately. We were further heartened later in the day when troops, with fixed bayonets, moved in and established a 'peace line' with barbed wire chicanes along the boundary between the Catholic and Protestant areas. As the patrols of soldiers fanned out and occupied their positions along the Falls Road, to my horror they pointed their guns at the Catholic families who had been attacked the day before. We got on to Callaghan's office again to protest but it made no difference. The military had a drill for this sort of thing, already well practised in Cyprus, Hong Kong and other outposts of empire.

We stayed off the Falls that evening thinking that at least the attacks were at an end, but during the night we heard reports that Bombay Street, near the Clonard monastery, was under attack by the loyalists. The sky was red from the burning houses, torched while the military stood by, not raising a finger. By now both Paddy Kennedy and I were desperate as to what to do to contain the violence. The assistance that was available was nothing of the order required to meet the problem, which increasingly resembled scenes from the newsreels of the Second

107

World War. We decided that we might have to seek aid from Dublin. They were, after all, morally obliged to do something for those frightened people who, under the Irish constitution, were Irish too.

On the Saturday, 16 August, Paddy O'Hanlon joined us to review the situation and then we left together for Dublin. We hoped not only to obtain financial help for the many families who had lost their homes, but also temporary accommodation for them, even if it was only in a school or a military camp. More importantly, it was our intention to persuade the Irish government to pressure the British government into ensuring that its army would vigorously protect the Catholic areas. I knew that if this plea failed, the frightened Catholic community would turn to the IRA for defence, although people were at present taunting the IRA with the slogan 'I Ran Away'. More than most of my political contemporaries, I was acutely aware of the need to prevent the IRA gaining support.

When we arrived in Dublin that afternoon we planned to meet someone at the Department of Foreign Affairs in St Stephen's Green. We also hoped to meet Jack Lynch, the Taoiseach. Going down O'Connell Street, we saw a large crowd of excited people gathered at the General Post Office, scene of the 1916 Rising. They stopped our car and asked us to speak to them. It was a spontaneous meeting, with the crowd aroused by the reports getting through from the beleaguered Catholics in Belfast. I spoke about our helplessness. In response to a prompt from someone I said that we needed guns to protect our community, that the security forces were not carrying out their duty towards Catholics. These words were to haunt me and be used against me for years to come, but I have to say again that they were uttered in the heat of an emotional moment. I had long ago rejected the use of violence and severed my connections with the IRA. Furthermore, in the frustrating months beforehand, I had strained every muscle trying to achieve reform and justice through the democratic parliamentary process in the teeth of deep-seated unionist intransigence and violence. My remarks at the GPO did not accurately represent the thrust of my approach to the ongoing problem and I did not, of course, get any guns or take any steps to do so.

We left the GPO and continued our journey to Iveagh House, where we met Eamonn Gallagher, the senior civil servant in charge of Northern Ireland affairs. We listed our demands and he promised help and delivered on it. Within hours, frightened families were brought south and given lodgings in an army camp at Gormanston, north of Dublin. Financial aid was channelled through the Red Cross after meetings were arranged with the Irish Minister for Finance, Charles Haughey.

I sought out my good friend, Brendan Halligan, secretary of the Irish Labour Party. He helped us to meet people from the press and arranged for me to appeal for aid on RTE television at peak time viewing next day. Brendan helped me to prepare the appeal. I understand that the message stunned the population and the response was immediate. Aid committees were formed and private money was sent north in large amounts.

Meanwhile, the Irish Labour Party used its fraternal links with the British Labour Party to push for help to relieve the plight of the Catholic families in Belfast. When the news broke that I was in London for this consultation, the NILP were far from happy. Sam Napier, the party secretary, rang London and pleaded for them not to meet me with the Irish Labour Party. I felt this pettiness very bitterly. It was the beginning of the end of my hitherto constructive relationship with the NILP.

When I arrived back from the visit to Westminster, the Falls was in an uproar. Barricades were up at virtually every street corner, much to my horror, and self-appointed street leaders, vigilantes of all shapes and sizes, were exercising their authority, real and imagined, to dictate who came in and out of the street. The RUC were most firmly not allowed in: 'no-go' areas were being created.

I was most annoyed to see that good cars, which local people

109

had worked strenuously to borrow for or buy, had been com-andeered and thrown into the debris of the barricades. Local traders and businessmen, who provided employment, also found their vans and implements hijacked and added to the bar-riers. I knew that the situation, left to the devices of this regime, could only end in absolute disaster for my constituents. Things were as bad at home. Theresa told me that, in my absence, the young vigilantes had taken over my house. They sat around the floors demanding meals, tea and coffee, sleeping, plotting revolution and revenge, until in a temper, when more tried to get in the already overfilled house, she chased them all. For weeks afterwards we were still getting reverse-charge telephone calls, issuing threats at all times of the night and day, from out-posts throughout the city.

The Long Bar in Leeson Street, run by a very friendly man called Paddy Lenaghan, had been taken over as an unofficial headquarters by this new leadership. I felt it was important to get these citizens' defence committees under some sort of organised control. The committees had been set up by local priests like Canon Padraig Murphy as well as local businessmen like Tom Conaty, a fruit importer, and some IRA elements, such as Jim Sullivan.

We convened a meeting almost at once to clear the air and I was elected secretary with Jim Sullivan as chairman. Paddy Kennedy always attended the weekly meetings of the Central Citizens' Defence Committee but Gerry Fitt did not. With hind-sight I see he was right to keep his distance. The business usually concerned relationships with the security forces, both police and army, who were pressuring us to remove the bar-ricades and restore, as they saw it, normal law and order. We also handled relationships with City Hall, the housing author-ities, the dole and national assistance, and helped people with advice about how to take legal action to get compensation for the loss of cars, home and furniture. We prepared statements for press, TV and radio and gathered up general information to highlight our demands. Belfast, by now, had been invaded by the world's press, radio and television and much of our time was spent initiating them into the details of our plight.

The barricades were my main concern. I knew that as long as the barricades remained up, the self-appointed leaders would never go back into oblivion. They would trigger off silly and stupid activities that would be followed by the residents if I were not there to stop them. I couldn't always be there and, given the calibre of some of those involved, I feared that a lot of other sinister things could happen behind the barricades. Criminal elements were gradually emerging, charging 'royalties' to tradesmen for using the roadways and robbing vans of their contents if they did not pay. This money went into private pockets. Behind that again, the first machinations that led to the creation of the organisation known as the Provisional IRA had begun. These were the people, under the pretext of Catholic defence, who were giving gun-handling and bomb-making lectures.

The leadership was a mixture of older, right-wing members of the IRA, and other Catholics aroused by the recent attacks, many of them middle-class professionals never associated with the IRA before. I have always believed that a number of senior Catholic clergy encouraged their involvement with the emerging Provisionals in order to break the influence of the Marxists. It may well be that they identified a greater danger to the church through the 'Godless' having a more central role. There were first-division elements in the Fianna Fáil government in Dublin at the time who shared this assessment.

I privately campaigned for the barricades to be taken down, bearing in mind that as the Catholic people were now drowning the soldiers in tea, soup and sympathy, we could expect to be protected. Although publicly I maintained a hard line in this regard, to protect my credibility, my real objective was to remove the barricades and negotiate agreed terms for the RUC to resume their work in the area. Although I shared the doubts

111

about them, arising from their performance in the preceding months, I was at a loss to suggest a workable alternative. Better to reform them, I thought, than try to replace them with an untested and unknown alternative, but Billy McMillen, an influential republican just released from the Crumlin Road jail, said: 'When the barricades come down, we'll all be arrested. The Special Powers Act is still on the statute book.'

Meanwhile Dr William Philbin, the bishop of Down and Connor, was touring the streets in St Peter's and St Agnes's parishes in an effort to get the barricades down. I had to publicly oppose him because my belief was that if we got the people to act in unison we could bring all the barricades down as part of an agreed plan. His way of doing it, street by street, was enabling the yahoos to put the barricades back up again. I suggested therefore that I would approach Turlough O'Donnell QC, who knew the Minister of Home Affairs, Bertie Porter, and ask him to set up a meeting for us.

He instantly agreed to meet us at his home that night. Turlough explained our mission. I was anxious to reduce the political aspects of it all. We needed an assurance that the Special Powers Act would not be used against those who had built the barricades to protect the Catholic population. The lawyers debated their points as I sat listening. Eventually a formula was negotiated: 'There will be no special powers used but the ordinary civil law must take its course.' We left satisfied that we had what we needed to back the removal of the barricades.

We referred back to a number of the people we had been in discussion with earlier. They accepted what we had brought back from the minister and we left for home at 4 a.m. Turlough was due to go to court in Derry that morning and before he left, after the seven o'clock news bulletin, he rang to tell me the barricades were to stay up. It appeared that the CCDC had been overruled by a 'man from Dublin'. This mystery man had appeared on the Belfast scene several days earlier and was clearly throwing his weight about. News that the Protestant areas were now putting up barricades brought the matter to a head. This action was all the more provocative, for pirate radios on both the Falls and the Shankill were pumping out poison all day, keeping the people at fever pitch. They would broadcast calls for help at flashpoint areas and crowds from both sides would run there ready for battle.

The British Army now knew that if they did not get this under control, even greater trouble faced them. After consultation, in which I was involved, they decided to get the barricades down and silence the radios. They first moved against the barricades at Turf Lodge on a Saturday morning with heavy vehicles and large numbers of men. I had been promised that another two hundred soldiers would be deployed for protection duties on the Falls, so I set out for the major barricade at Albert Street and spoke from the top of it to the people gathered there. I suggested to them that as we had erected the barricades, we ourselves should take them down. We did, to tremendous cheering by the local people. All the main roads were cleared immediately, followed quickly by the side streets, thereby enabling coal lorries and milk vans to get through to the residents. As a safety precaution the army had agreed to curtail traffic at night, so the progress of doctors, ambulances and fire tenders was monitored by the soldiers. Although there were problems and further clashes in removing the barricades, the operation progressed steadily from there.

The discussions with the military had included clearance for them to build a so-called 'peace line' of corrugated iron and barbed wire at the flashpoint areas to separate both sides. It is to our shame that, almost a quarter of a century later, this line is still in existence, the rusting wire and iron having long since been replaced by more durable brick and concrete.

7

PROTEST AND PROVOS

On 11 September 1969, the day after the first barricades came down, I flew to London with three others from the CCDC to speak with Jim Callaghan in his Whitehall office. (At this time he was ringing my home on a regular basis. Invariably I was out and Theresa, who received the calls, had to repeatedly tell him he'd missed me. 'Get him to call me later. It doesn't matter how late,' he always said.) Callaghan most deeply interrogated us about our views of the RUC and B Specials. We were reassured to find that their future role was certainly uppermost in his mind.

On 10 October 1969 the report of Lord Hunt, whom Callaghan had appointed to examine the future role of the police, was published. The controversial, or as we saw them, the hated, B Specials were to be disbanded and it was recommended that a new part-time force called the Ulster Defence Regiment would be formed as a replacement. The RUC Inspector-General Anthony Peacocke resigned, to be replaced by Sir Arthur Young, a London 'bobby' with a brief to reform and modernise the RUC. Callaghan had struck as radically as I thought he would. Riots by protesting loyalists followed in the Shankill and Crumlin Road areas and, ironically and tragically, Constable Victor Arbuckle, the first policeman to die in the Troubles, was shot dead by loyalists.

I had met Jim Callaghan and Sir Arthur Young on the morning of 10 October in the Conway Hotel at Dunmurry. The civil rights MPs had been invited for breakfast. As we were leaving Callaghan gripped my arm and called Sir Arthur Young over. 'This is my man. I want you to look after Arthur. He should be in retirement but is staying on to sort out Ulster for me. He cannot do it without your help,' said Callaghan.

I decided to give this request from Jim my best shot. I realised that the cornerstone of any new consensus in Northern Ireland depended on having an effective and impartial police force. The appointment of Sir Arthur Young, with his experience and reputation, was a promising start. Events were already under way, however, that were to undermine this objective, and Young left in despair a year later having failed to break the grip of the hardline 'old-guard' in the upper echelons of the RUC who resented an outsider being imposed on them.

On 14 September 1969 a meeting had been held in Andersonstown by the right-wing old-timers of the IRA. There had been earlier meetings after the summer's events, where hostility to the IRA leadership in the Belfast area had been expressed. The meetings critically analysed the role of the IRA in the sixties, their departure from traditional republicanism and, most of all, why they failed to protect Catholic families in the Belfast area in the recent pogroms. The participants included Dublin businessmen and at least one top-drawer member of the Irish Army's intelligence unit. They significantly influenced the adoption of new policies that were to have a far-reaching effect on the IRA and future events in Northern Ireland. The northern IRA men were told by these powerful southern business and political interests that they would receive funds for arms providing they set up a new northern command, separate from the Marxist IRA faction, and undertake to confine all military and political operations to Northern Ireland.

On 22 September, after another meeting in Andersonstown, sixteen armed men went to Cyprus Street, where Billy McMillen was sitting alone. They accused him, as leader of the IRA in the North, of failing to protect the Catholic population, and ordered him to stand down. The coup was complete and the way was clear for the creation of the Provisional IRA who came into formal existence before the end of the year when the split with the Marxist elements was formalised.

I did not know of these matters at the time. It was only three months or so later that I learned the full detail of them, but I did suspect that there was turmoil in the background from the way things were going inside the CCDC. While recognising that at least some of the committee members were preparing the ground for a resurgence of IRA activity, my priority was to get things stabilised and the community back on a tranquil footing. I have to say, however, that I did become involved in events and transactions that, with hindsight, it would have been better to have avoided. I later gave a full, and frank, account of these matters to the Scarman Tribunal, the judicial investigation Callaghan appointed to chart the catastrophic course of events in 1969 and to analyse what lessons were to be learned from them.

The tribunal had opened on 22 September 1969. The elaborate and thorough hearings were conducted by Leslie Scarman, an English judge who went on to become one of the most distinguished legal figures of his generation. Over 168 days, the tribunal heard evidence from some 440 witnesses who were called and cross-examined by a large battery of lawyers. I spent two days in the witness box giving evidence and then undergoing searching cross-examination, which suited me, as I was determined to answer truthfully every question asked of me. My evidence ranged widely over what I saw during the riots, the action I had taken to get the police to do their duty and the background to the IRA split. I was also questioned about what I said at the Dublin meeting, but most interest was generated by my testimony about the bank accounts created to pay relief to the homeless refugees.

In the aftermath of the 1969 Troubles there was great hardship and distress throughout Belfast, but it was most acute in the Falls area. The mid-August expulsion of hundreds of families from mixed housing estates, who flocked into the area for safety, was bad enough, but each night afterwards brought more refugees with grim stories of losing their homes in east and south Belfast. Some of them came with just a few clothes and a bit of food pushed in a pram. Some of them had no food and only the clothes they stood up in. We got some schools open to shelter and feed them but there was terrible misery and poverty. The first figures collected by sociologists indicated that the communal upheaval in Belfast at the time was the largest enforced movement of population since the end of the Second World War. Research subsequently carried out for the Scarman Tribunal showed that between July and September 1969 alone 1,505 Catholic and 315 Protestant households were forcibly displaced from their homes. (Later, a more extensive survey by the Community Relations Commission calculated that between 1969 and 1974, 60,000 people, one in ten of the entire Belfast population, were forced to move home.)

We needed far more help than we were getting from the Northern Ireland government, so I travelled to Dublin to meet Charles Haughey. Jim Sullivan, a republican community activist, and Hugh Kennedy, a Belfastman who had been working for Bord Bainne, the Irish dairy marketing organisation, accompanied me. At the meeting, in Haughey's north Dublin home, we impressed on him the great need that existed and he indicated his willingness to help.

Not long afterwards I received a letter from Madame De Barra, president of the Irish Red Cross, setting out the terms on which help would be given, and giving the names of some people who had appealed for assistance. I was also told that £10,000 was available to be picked up at a bank in Baggot Street, Dublin, but, for convenience, the account was later transferred to Clones, a town in the Irish republic close to the border. My recollection is that we needed two out of three authorised signatures on every cheque. Those nominated were myself, Paddy Kennedy and a respected Belfast lawyer.

When these arrangements were made and I knew that funds were available, I contacted Paddy Kennedy, who set off with a signed cheque to collect the money and have it distributed amongst those in need. I gave him the Red Cross letter. I only ever signed three or four cheques and made just one pick-up myself on a day when Paddy couldn't go, but I passed the £2,000 cash on to him immediately afterwards. Some time later it was suggested to me by Paddy that the fund controllers wanted to change the signatories for the account. I did not demur. I was very busy and could not spare the time to go round and hand out the money. Anyway, knowing that people suffering hardship would get more regular aid from the social security system, I advised and helped them to claim, as was their right.

This was the limit of my involvement with this account. Its operation and the source of the funds later became matters of controversy in Dublin and were inconclusively investigated by a committee of the Irish parliament. I always thought the money had been raised by private donations from some of Haughey's wealthy friends, rather than coming from the Irish public purse. It was also alleged that at least some of the money had been diverted to buy guns and help in the setting up of the Provos. I do not know anything about that. As I told both the Scarman Tribunal and the Irish parliamentary committee, all the money that had passed through my hands went for genuine welfare purposes. Guns were never even mentioned.

At the beginning of 1970 I left Belfast for America with Ciaran O'Kane, a university lecturer. The trip was organised by a co-operative which had been set up specifically to rebuild and refurbish the houses in Bombay Street. A fund set up to help the civil rights leader, Bernadette Devlin, who had become an MP at Westminster, paid for our tickets. With the Northern Ireland civil rights office in New York as our headquarters, we were to visit New York, Boston and Philadelphia in a barnstorming tour to extract the £70,000 we needed from the Irish population of those cities. As it happened, the tour was extended to three weeks and included Chicago. We only managed to raise around £2,500, well short of our target. The affluent, elderly, narrow-minded, right-wing Irish-Americans we met did not like our idea of rebuilding the houses by forming a community co-operative. Indeed, some of them felt that the street should not be reconstructed at all but left as a monument to unionist hatred. At several of our public meetings we met potential donors who said they would give us virtually unlimited donations if we were to buy guns to use on the loyalists. I told them to stuff their money.

The tension fuelling the internal IRA faction-fighting in Ireland ran like a seam throughout our trip. The civil rights people we were working with supported the old guard Marxist faction in the IRA, soon to become better known as the Official IRA. The older Irish-Americans mainly took sides with the Provisional IRA. Some of its members were doing the American circuit at the same time, seeking money and guns, but we never actually met.

I obtained a copy of a lengthy unsigned letter setting out the case of the breakaway members, and this gave me further insight into the fundamental power struggle that was taking place. It claimed that the Marxists had taken over Sinn Féin by force in the early 1960s, converting the entire movement to communism. Names and incidents to back up the break-aways' cause were cited in support of the Provisional case. They said that they would fight 'the evil forces of Marxism on behalf of US Christianity' and take on the British invader as well. This language was highly appealing to the leaders and members of the various Irish societies who had emigrated to the US in the 1920s and were still dining out on highly dubious stories of how they escaped with the notorious Black and Tans in hot pursuit. Many of the hair-raising allegations made by the

Provos I knew to be untrue or overstated, but they were believed by many of the fanatical people we met.

The Official/Provisional strife caused one of our meetings in the New York area to be cancelled, though some money from the organisation was sent on later. We had a good meeting in Philadelphia, but Boston was a wipe-out because of heavy snowfalls, although there was compensation later when I got 2,000 US dollars for a speaker's fee at a big dinner which Hubert Humphries was unable to attend. I was also invited to speak in the City Hall by Mayor Kevin White, at a meeting to commemorate the murder of Martin Luther King. I was thrilled by the invitation and still have a film made of the occasion by a local TV company. Part of my thrill was the fact that I was speaking from the same spot where my great American hero, Mayor James Curley, held sway for many years. Curley, from Irish-American stock, was many times mayor of the city, governor of Massachusetts and a member of the United States House of Representatives. The Kennedys and the Fitzgeralds were kept in check for years because of the way he dominated city politics, a role well portrayed by Spencer Tracy in the film *The Last Hurrah*, based on the book written by Edwin O'Connor.

Our meetings in Chicago were a mixed bag. We were made most welcome in the university, but in the clubs, which were dominated by Boss Daley's men, we met outright resistance. When it was known that I was there, cronies of a crank lawyer named J.C. Heaney, who was tied in with the Provisional camp-followers in New York, turned up to heckle me but I was far too rumbustious for them in a toe-to-toe slanging match, so they stalked out of the meeting. Heaney was a trouble-maker who had nothing positive to contribute to solving our problems. At one stage he was working to stop US investment in Northern Ireland which would have provided badly needed jobs, and when I attacked him in the Stormont parliament he resented it very much.

I had already expressed reservations that Callaghan's autumn reform package was lacking in an important respect: there was no provision for increased spending capacity to create employment. Without a job, the unemployed would be vulnerable to those seeking to foster violence. I had deep forebodings that without jobs as a bulwark the violence would overcome any efforts to stay the tide. As I returned from the United States to face again the problems in Belfast and at Stormont, it was with a heavy heart.

While I was away in the United States the full story of the split in the IRA was published in the *Irish Press*. Seán Mac Stiofáin had emerged as chief of staff of what was known from then on as the Provisional IRA. They gave four reasons for their action in forcing a split in the organisation: the IRA's recognition of Westminster, Stormont and Dáil Éireann; their extreme socialist views; the failure to give maximum defence to the Catholic population of Belfast; and the campaign to reform the Stormont parliament instead of seeking its abolition.

I knew that life would be no bed of roses after this, both for me as an MP or for my constituents. I could only foresee these right-wingers getting embroiled in brute force from their ignorance. They were not politically aware of the distinction between the boss class of unionism and the Protestant working class. I knew they would be nakedly sectarian and probably end up attacking Protestants. I rightly feared that all the work we had done in the field of politics to close the gap between Catholics and Protestants, to remove the discord, distrust and ancient bitterness, would go for naught.

Up at Stormont, in spite of the best efforts of the non-unionist MPs to amend it, the Public Order (Amendment) Act passed all stages of parliamentary procedure and became law in February 1970. I felt the act was intended by the government to push civil rights demonstrations into the side streets of Catholic ghettos, while allowing absolute latitude to Orange marches to traverse their traditional 'coat-trailing' routes. It was an unmistakable signal to the politically restless Orangemen and Unionist Party backwoodsmen that their own people were still in charge. 'Nothing has changed' was the message. As the civil rights marchers took to the streets again, the growing Provisionals were provided with an opportunity to give their fledgling recruits experience in street hostilities.

The Provisionals were increasingly taking the initiative away from the Marxist IRA. Their appeal to the frightened Catholic community was simple – they would defend them at all cost. The Marxists were against the Catholic religion anyway, they argued, therefore, why would they defend Catholics? It was said they failed in 1969 because they had sold their guns to the so-called Free Wales Army. The Official IRA could not counter this dubious propaganda because it was carried so quickly by word of mouth through the tightly-knit Catholic communities that even the most blatant lies and rumours took on the force of a biblical message to an evangelist. The ordinary folk in the Catholic areas, who could not understand the complexities of Marxist theory anyway, were satisfied with the reassurance of Catholic defence. Few understood the wickedness that the Provisionals were fostering, and those who did kept their counsel.

A telling factor in the emergence of the Provisionals was the stance of the Catholic church. Traditionally it had refused to recognise the need to allow politics to develop along party or class lines. Its interest, it assumed, was better served by blocking Catholics from supporting left-wing politics, even though, by doing so, it was keeping in power a political party that existed solely on its capacity to divide society by its anti-Catholic character and propaganda. Elements in the church had long been concerned about the activities of the Marxist IRA and, after the events of 1969, were happy to move by stealth, taking advantage of the situation that had arisen, to undermine the organisation. But to out-manoeuvre them the church had to find allies in other forces, compatible with its own views. The Provisionals were ideal for this purpose and, for a time, until the ugliness and immorality of what the Provisionals really stood for became clear, they were actively promoted by the church and enabled to take over in Catholic areas. It was to be many years before the church recognised its error and condemned the beneficiaries of it.

In the early months of 1970, therefore, the split between both factions of the IRA hardened. Personality clashes of the earlier years added to the aggravation. The majority took the Provisionals' side, with entire areas like Ardoyne, Short Strand, Clonard and Andersonstown going over. Other areas like Lower Falls broke about even. That Easter came the first evidence of just how vicious the split had been, with the Provisionals clearly out for trouble. They needed to create activity to fulfil the promises given to their new members in the early weeks of 1970, when they were recruiting at an alarming rate. Up to this time a single service with an agreed speaker marked the Easter commemoration of the IRA dead at the republican plot in Milltown cemetery. Now both organisations decided to have their own service. The Provisionals arranged an early service, timed so that they would be leaving the cemetery and could cause maximum disturbance just when the Officials would be gathering for its service. To distinguish their supporters the Provisionals made their own cardboard Easter lilies, held in place by pins. They were promptly christened the 'pinheads', a nickname which never stuck. The Marxists printed Easter lilies on adhesive labels. They were henceforth nicknamed the 'stickies', a label which is still used. Efforts were made by myself and the CCDC to avoid any trouble at Milltown cemetery. In the event there was none of any significance, mainly because cool heads among the Officials prevented a full-blooded collision.

But the Provos soon found a more appropriate outlet for their aggression. After the gains accrued by the civil rights movement in the previous year, hardline unionists were increasingly disenchanted with their leaders. Easter traditionally marks the start of their annual marching season and that year there was an extra spring in their step as they resolved to show that the Catholics must be kept in their place. The CCDC committee feared that the high level of community tension that had survived the winter could all too easily be fanned into fresh flames with only the slightest provocation. Consequently we had implored the military and police authorities to divert one of the new season's Orange marches away from the Lower Grosvenor and the Upper Springfield roads, which over recent years had become almost exclusively populated by Catholic residents.

The local chief superintendent of the RUC was sympathetic to our point of view, but with the army running things and the unionists still in control of the Ministry of Home Affairs, his influence was decidedly limited. The authorities decided to push the marchers through the Catholic areas, as they did not want to lose the goodwill of the Orangemen. Tampering with the right to march on what the Orangemen called the 'Queen's highway' could well be curtains for any unionist politicians who got involved, given the great turbulence inside the party. For their part, the military, who must have felt that they were sinking helplessly into a quicksand, clearly had no intention of facing the IRA in a confrontation while an alienated Orange majority took them on from the rear.

Faced with this situation, Cardinal William Conway, the head of the Catholic church in Ireland, and his local clergy backed the CCDC in appealing to Catholics to tolerate the march over what after all was a traditional route. Events that Easter Tuesday were, however, quickly exploited by the Provisionals, who steamed up local feelings and organised a mob of stone-throwing youths, who laid an ambush for the Orangemen as they returned in the evening. The army promptly responded and full-blooded rioting ensued, the first contact between the Provos and the British Army in an unremitting campaign that none of us then imagined would last so long or plumb such depths of savagery.

I have always believed that the military were delighted with this development because they were spoiling to take on the Provos. I was in the Ballymurphy area across the road from the New Barnsley enclave, where the few remaining Protestants lived, when the marchers were attacked. The military came in hard on the stone-throwers, employing their 'snatch squad' tactics for the first time. Soldiers would line up in company strength across the main roads, providing a target to lure the stone-throwers towards them. Then they would suddenly break ranks to allow runners in light gym shoes to dash through and arrest the main culprits, who would be dragged back and put in a military wagon.

But the plan fell apart in the courthouse the next morning when the military sprinters were put in the witness box to explain their reasons for making a 'citizen's arrest'. All simply stated that their sergeants had given them orders to apprehend persons pointed out to them. As the sergeants were not in court the magistrates had to release the prisoners, who returned to the streets freshly aggrieved after a night's sleep in custody.

Over the next few nights the clashes progressively escalated and although the regimental sergeant major appeared in the witness box to read out the names and evidence of arrest, sloppy evidence led to repeated acquittals. The officer had no explanation when it was pointed out to him by the magistrate that the arresting soldiers often seemed to be simultaneously at three different spots on the Springfield Road.

I found the military tactics extremely badly planned for dealing with a situation which was easily containable. On the second night of the riots the soldiers had their faces and hands blackened and played a tom-tom beat with batons on their shields. Their equipment and numbers were overpowering, bearing in mind they were dealing with a handful of stone-throwers. Resentment at their behaviour brought youths from all over the West Belfast area like moths to a flame and the military then introduced CS gas, which saturated the entire Ballymurphy area.

Fear of the Catholic stone-throwers and more direct intimidation led to the organised removal of the unfortunate Protestant families from New Barnsley. On the first night of the riots I had stood with other members of the CCDC to protect the road to the New Barnsley houses, but within twenty-four hours there was yet again the sickening sight of lorries and vans being hastily loaded with furniture, as families abandoned their homes.

During that spring of 1970, Provisional-IRA-inspired rioting spread through the Flax Street, Tiger's Bay, Lower North Street and Clonard areas like an epidemic. The trouble usually started with stone-throwing and ended up with petrol bombs being brought into play. The army threatened to shoot the petrol-bombers on sight but although they killed one young man the trouble did not abate. Several other factors made matters worse. Brigadier Frank Kitson appeared on the scene to replace Brigadier Peter Hudson. Kitson, famous for his efforts to suppress the Mau Mau in Kenya, was an expert on combating terrorism and was brought to Belfast purely because of his expertise and skills. In my view his appointment was clear evidence that the military were going on the attack.

The political go-ahead followed a change of government at Westminster, when the Conservatives, headed by Edward Heath, replaced the Labour administration after a general election in June 1970. Labour's policy had been one of containment, playing for the hearts and minds of the people. The Conservative approach was one of outright suppression of the violence, which was only one symptom of the Troubles. The impact of this explicit change of policy was very much a reality from the earliest days after the election. In Catholic areas military patrols began to interrogate and knock young people about. The Provisionals no longer needed to incite young people to attack the military. The young people now did it to get their own back on the ever more aggressive foot patrols. Many young people were beaten up and humiliated in front of friends, girlfriends and members of their own families. After some of the worst episodes, queues of young people, boys and girls, formed outside the houses of the leading Provisionals, all seeking to join up.

Local police who knew the form and could have advised on better tactics were distrusted and ignored by the military. On occasion they were directly humiliated by the soldiers. One night, in a bid to draw people away from a clash with the army, I persuaded a folk band to come out from one of the pubs and play in Leeson Street. The ploy worked and most of the crowds of young people drifted away from attacking the local police/army post and began to take part in the sing-song around the group. But before long soldiers charged down the street and arrested the band members for playing their instruments in the street. Chief Superintendent Paddy McAndrew, a brave RUC officer who refused to let the army boss him around, refused to charge them and told them to go and play on – as long as the neighbours did not object.

The situation worsened all summer and the military appeared to be doing what they liked as long as the Catholics were at the receiving end. At the end of June, after the first gun battles between the army and the Provos, the Home Secretary, Reginald Maudling, who had replaced Callaghan, arrived at Stormont to interview the political parties. I was part of the delegation that met him and I took the opportunity to hit out at the military tactics which I strongly believed were making a bad situation worse. One of the British tabloid papers had run a story that morning predicting that internment without trial was being considered, in a bid to contain the worsening situation. Given my own experiences, this was complete anathema to me and when Maudling, who was plainly out of his depth and bored rigid, denied the story, I threw the newspaper at him in anger. No wonder that when he got on the plane to return to London that evening he exclaimed: 'For God's sake bring me a large Scotch. What a bloody awful country.' My attack on him had a lasting effect. During the rest of his tenure as Home Secretary he refused to meet any delegations with me as a member.

One afternoon in early July a large force of soldiers arrived to search for arms at a house in Balkan Street on the Falls Road. It was a most remarkable situation for the military to raid for arms at 4 p.m. on a Friday afternoon. All arms raids took place discreetly at 4 a.m. – never in daylight or at a time when some local males would be fired up, drinking in the pubs.

As word spread about the ongoing raid hundreds of youths quickly gathered around Balkan Street. Predictably, stones were thrown from both ends of the street, as the captured guns were removed from the house in full public view. I arrived on the scene with a number of clergy from the adjacent Catholic church and together we persuaded the stone-throwers to stop, although they remained in the vicinity. Unknown to us, however, there was a major force of troops mustered on the corner of nearby Durham Street and Divis Street. Hundreds of men were deployed in lines of lorries and armoured vehicles. It was clear the arms raid was only the trigger for a major, well-planned confrontation.

The Lower Falls area was an acknowledged stronghold of the Official IRA and I calculated that this was clearly a punitive raid on the entire district because Jim Sullivan, one of the stalwarts of the Officials, had recently criticised army policy and Lieutenant-General Sir Ian Freeland, who was directing it. Indeed, Sullivan had issued a warning a fortnight earlier stating he was not to come onto his patch without his approval. The army clearly believed that there were many arms hidden there and that after the violence of the previous weeks (mainly by the Provisionals) a deliberate confrontation with these challengers was called for. As violent clashes developed and intensified throughout the evening CS gas canisters were lobbed into the area by the military. A helicopter, with an underslung loudspeaker, descended to virtual roof level and a voice announced that the area was under curfew and anyone on the streets after the warning would be shot.

The Officials, who now saw themselves being disarmed by this planned search, feared they would lose the little face they had left and be vulnerable to future attack from the Provisionals or loyalists if they did not take the army on. As the first shots rang out and the curfew deadline loomed I headed for the CCDC headquarters to establish a contact post, where some journalists joined me.

The shooting increased in tempo as darkness fell. The high-pitched whine of the armoured cars as they manoeuvred round the narrow streets and the occasional burst of heavy calibre fire filled me with dread. The shooting only stopped at dawn. The CCDC headquarters was on the main Falls Road, at the boundary of the curfewed area, and we spent the night listening to the battle, fortified by tea, coffee and soup laid in for just such an emergency. During the thirty-four-hour curfew, the phone rang constantly, giving us first-hand accounts of what was going on. The military no doubt had the line bugged in the hope that some IRA chief would use it to talk to his men.

Daylight brought the follow-up search by the military. They axed doors down that could as easily have been opened, ripped up floorboards, broke furniture unnecessarily and tipped the contents of drawers and cupboards all over the place. Residents later complained bitterly about the Black Watch, a Scottish regiment, which seemed to give most of its attention to breaking religious objects and symbols of the Glasgow Celtic football club, which enjoyed huge support among Belfast Catholics. Hundreds of assorted illegal weapons were found in the house-to-house searches and taken away to Springfield Road barracks, where they were piled up and exhibited to newspaper and television cameramen.

The strict curfew caused great hardship to those caught in its restrictions. This was a working-class area where poverty was rife and housing conditions dreadful. Many people ran out of food because they could not go for their normal Saturday shopping trips. In the afternoon, in response to telephone calls from affected relatives and families, about 1,000 women from the Andersonstown area loaded their prams with milk and bread and set out to break the siege. The army relented for a period to allow the delivery and then reimposed the curfew again. During the two-hour interval I was on hand to get information from my constituents about the hardships they were being forced to endure.

While standing at the corner of Osman Street and Sultan Street, noting complaints from constituents, including two elderly women whose shop had been looted, I was accosted by several soldiers from the Devon and Dorset Regiment. They told me to move on but I said I would only do so when I was finished. A major told me I was under arrest and ordered his men to detain me. Holding me at gunpoint they said they would 'blow my brains out' if I didn't shut up. I was grabbed by the arm and taken to Plevna Street, where they told me to stand facing a wall and threatened to shoot me if I turned round. Then I was ordered into one of the armoured troop carriers and forced down on the floor while they put their feet on me. 'Take him up to Springfield,' the driver was told, but the vehicle had only travelled a short distance when I was released after the intervention of two senior police officers who knew me well. When I got out of the military vehicle one of the officers said I was not arrested. I replied: 'Read the *Irish News* in the morning and you'll see whether I was arrested or not.'

After discussions with the police and a more senior army officer, who said I was free to go and that his men had had 'a trying time', I realised there was great doubt about the legality of the entire search and curfew operation. When I got away I immediately contacted Father Padraig Murphy and other members of the CCDC to arrange a quick meeting to decide what to do. I also rounded up a number of people to take detailed statements about the military excesses. Gerry Fitt rang me to arrange an immediate visit to Westminster, where he had arranged to see Lord Carrington, the Minister of Defence, who was responsible for the army, and Maudling, the man who was directly responsible for Northern Ireland matters.

When we got to London, Maudling would not allow me in, but later we pushed Carrington for an independent inquiry into the army's extreme behaviour. I gave him a detailed account of incidents which I had witnessed and other reports we had received. We later apprised the Labour MPs of what had happened in the hope they would support us, but the majority were no more than lukewarm about the request. I was disappointed to realise that Westminster MPs, of whatever party, did not like their army criticised, even when the criticism was true. This was the reality of a colonial empire in action – 'our boys – right or wrong'.

Three civilians were killed and many people injured during the Falls Road curfew but there was never an official casualty count, for the victims were too frightened to go to hospital where the military were waiting to arrest them. Hundreds of people, including journalists, were arrested and brought to court, but the charges were later dropped when it was declared in court that the curfew was indeed illegally imposed. I broke with the CCDC shortly afterwards when I noticed the name of Dickie Glenholmes, a republican street leader, included in a delegation which I was to lead to meet the security forces. 'I am not going if that fellow is to be present,' I said. I had no intention of adding credibility to anyone sailing under a 'flag of convenience', so I left the headquarters and never returned.

Throughout that turbulent summer and autumn of 1970, when my hands were more than full as secretary of the CCDC, my contacts with the NILP had inevitably lapsed. I had of course noticed the deafening silence emanating from the organisation, no statements condemning the horrors of the summer, no assertion of the non-sectarian socialist principles we had tried to promote. It is an understatement of the most extreme kind to say that I was bitterly disappointed. Bearing in mind the experiences of the social democratic and socialist parties in both

Germany under Hitler and Italy under Mussolini, I felt that I had a duty to stand up to fascist mobs. In doing so I assumed that standing at my shoulder would be my Labour comrades. But when it came to the crunch they weren't there. I was left on my own.

Despite its apparent socialist and liberal credentials, the NILP in fact tended to disregard the existence of the civil rights movement and more frequently reacted with what I can only call unionist instincts. The dilemmas the movement raised for the Protestants in the NILP were uncomfortable. The executive had issued a series of statements which were later incorporated into articles for the Manchester *Guardian*, but they were more pious than practical. A couple of years earlier Tom Boyd of the NI committee of the Irish Congress of Trade Unions had asked for a meeting with Terence O'Neill and trade union executives came along to support us. The issues on the agenda were entirely those concerned with the lack of justice for the Catholic people of the North, all contained in a memorandum which we later published for all to see. At that time of great opportunity the parliamentary Labour Party was widely judged to have inadequately responded to the civil rights campaign, despite the fact that many prominent members of the labour and trade union movement were very publicly involved. When the Nationalist Party, taking its duties at Stormont seriously for perhaps the first time ever, moved a bill to establish electoral equality – one man, one vote – the NILP, to its eternal shame, refused to support the proposals.

The failure of the parliamentary NILP to follow up on other civil rights issues outside of the electoral equality bill was equally scandalous. A set of new legislation to tackle job and housing discrimination was passed by the Westminster parliament and later brought into Northern Ireland because of the agitation, yet the NILP was virtually indifferent.

The failure to act on these basic issues was to prove costly in time. An early intervention by the NILP working with the nationalists in the first half of the 1960s, when there was a distinct whiff of cross-community compromise, could have reduced the sectarian gap, thereby exposing the real intransigents, the unionists. Moreover, it would have more effectively drawn the attention of the British Labour government to the plight of the Catholic minority, encouraging intervention long before it was forced by the events of 1969.

My drift from the NILP could be said to have really begun during the summer of 1969. When I went to Dublin, seeking help for the 'beleaguered refugees', Sam Napier, the party secretary, issued a pointed statement affirming that I was acting on my own behalf, not that of the NILP. A month later they publicly reprimanded me again for temporarily boycotting Stormont because of the inadequacy of the unionist government responses to the crisis. I clashed with the party hierarchy again early in 1970 when a special conference was convened at Transport House in Belfast to discuss a special motion to merge with the British Labour Party. This had been suggested by the secretary of the British Labour Party. It had been tried before, but this time around I knew that Jim Callaghan and George Brown would not wear it. Anyway, I was completely opposed to the idea in principle, as were the members of the Falls branch of the party. The branch delegates were Turlough O'Donnell, my daughter Anne and myself. I spoke against the proposal, saying that such a merger was in reality a move to consolidate Lord Castlereagh's Act of Union in 1801, which had removed industry from Ireland and left us only with land to graze cattle for English consumption.

I also feared that it would leave us with 'single issue' politics – unity with London or Dublin rather than the fraternal links with the British and Irish labour movements that I favoured. Other vital issues like jobs, houses, economic growth, human rights and electoral reform would go to the wall in an exclusively British link-up. At the end of the meeting we suffered an overwhelming defeat. The time-honoured card vote by the trade unions passed the motion by a grandiose 20,000 majority when there were in fact only a handful of people present. As I well knew, the size of the vote did not matter anyway. However, the proposed merger came to nothing.

Looking back on events now, the Falls curfew of July 1970 turned out to be the most significant turning point in the early stages of the Troubles. It represented a major policy change by the British, brought even more recruits to the Provisionals and bolstered their credibility, while it also triggered the formation of what was to be an important and lasting political realignment.

The military, cock-a-hoop with their illegal takeover of the Falls, proceeded to put the boot in with a vengeance. Cars were stopped and the occupants ordered out to be humiliated or searched in a most degrading way. Homes were raided and ransacked at random. Pedestrians were halted and questioned as they walked innocently along the streets. The measures intensified as more and more troops were poured in. Everybody in the Falls was subject to this unjustifiable repression, no one was immune. Even as an MP, I was subjected to constant harassment and suspicion by the military. Overnight the population turned from neutral or even sympathetic support for the military to outright hatred of everything related to the security forces. As the self-styled generals and godfathers took over in the face of this regime, Gerry Fitt and I witnessed voters and workers in the Dock and Falls constituencies turn against us to join the Provisionals. Even some of our most dedicated workers and supporters, who had helped us through thick and thin at election times, turned against us. Many of them would indeed later viciously attack members of our families and our homes, eventually driving us out. As we contemplated this sorry scenario and the escalation of violence, which we rightly feared was going to plunge Northern Ireland into even deeper turmoil, we knew we had to do something to meet the deepening crisis.

The political opposition in Stormont at the time was fragmented and lacked any co-ordination. The nationalists were the main opposition party but they had neither the stomach nor the drive for a real fight. The Labour Party, as I have said, was inadequate for the task, while the other MPs, elected on the civil rights ticket, were mainly acting as independents. I recognised there was little effective work we could do in parliament if we continued to act in this way. We needed to form a broad-based labour party that would attract wide support from all over the North and provide an alternative political platform. Only that way could we hope to head off the headlong charge towards tribal confrontation which was being consciously fostered by the Provos and steadily aggravated by the behaviour of the military.

The Provisionals' bombing campaign was now under way and although at least one of their members was killed in a premature explosion, they were steadily perfecting both gelignite devices and others made from agricultural fertiliser. The viciousness of the emerging Provisionals shocked me when I learned of the murder of two men from the Whiterock area who were fixing a car in broad daylight. It seemed that they had been accosted the night before by several Provisionals and being tough men – one was a well-known ballroom bouncer – they retaliated with their fists. They were shot dead the next day as a warning to others that the Provos would tolerate no challengers.

In Stormont during the heated debates at this time the only NILP comrade who could be described as supportive was Vivian Simpson. He was a notably conscientious man but not a natural civil rights supporter, turning up on some issues but leaving others severely alone. My natural allies more and more appeared to be the civil rights members, John Hume, Ivan Cooper, Paddy O'Hanlon and of course the one and only Gerry Fitt. Austin Currie, alone among the nationalists, joined in our deliberations. We appeared to complement one another and we found ourselves working together more and more, planning our strategy for debates, dominating the chamber and providing tough and searching opposition for the increasingly shell-shocked unionists who had never been confronted so effectively before.

Our opening common ground existed in the area of civil rights. Gerry Fitt, Austin Currie and myself had worked with the organisation from the outset, were present for every demonstration and made civil rights issues the main planks of our election programmes. Fitt and Currie were seasoned parliamentary performers, knew the ropes as far as the rituals and routines were concerned and were very good at throwing unionist speakers off their stride by heckling. In recent years Gerry has been much maligned, and it is all too often forgotten that his enormous and historic achievement was to force the abuses of unionism and the plight of nationalists on to the political agenda at Westminster, where there had been a scandalous convention to ignore them for the forty years after partition. Moreover, in speeches throughout his political career he consistently advocated a democratic solution to our problems, never encouraged the gunman or bomber and fearlessly spoke out against them. He was among the first to realise that civil rights reforms would mean that the traditional 'place of the gun' in Northern Ireland politics could no longer be justified.

Austin Currie was a bright young university graduate who was positioned closely alongside Fitt rather than the Nationalist Party to which he belonged. His performances in the House were of a high standard, with speeches well thought out, cleverly delivered and timed to allow even the slowest-witted unionists to challenge him on his material. He was always well prepared with figures and background and scored constantly as they rose to the bait. Both men were incessantly attacked by unionist MPs for promoting violence, but it is quite easy to follow in their speeches, as recorded in the Stormont Hansard, that they were actually campaigning for the causes of violence to be removed.

Ivan Cooper, whose early background was as a unionist businessman before transferring to the NILP and the civil rights movement, was the best outdoor orator I ever heard. He was a splendid phrase-maker, with a strong, resonant voice which carried a long distance from public platforms. In parliament he was equally good, making points that were always relevant and succinct. He was a kindly man of great intelligence, courage and mental strength, and had a gift for mimicry. Although I am told I was regularly one of his subjects and he recounted wicked stories about me behind my back, he became my best political friend in those days and I still hold him in the highest affection.

Paddy O'Hanlon was another young civil rights personality with an irrepressible sense of humour who irreverently impersonated the most dour of the unionists and got us singing Irish ballads in the Members' Bar at Stormont when the sessions ended in the House. Despite this frivolity, Paddy's contributions to the debates were distinctively his own. It was Paddy's interpretation of constitutional parameters that there were in fact three states in Ireland: one to the south, centred on Dublin; one in the North around Belfast; and one in south Armagh, around his native Mullaghbawn. One notable thing about him was his utter reliability. He was always there. Regardless of hardship, sacrifice or hazard, Paddy would never let you down. He is now a learned barrister, and I am pleased to count him as a wise friend.

Last but notably not least in our group was the Derryman John Hume, a one-time student for the priesthood and former school teacher. He had come to initial prominence through setting up the Credit Union movement in Ireland, a beneficial loans and saving system for small communities, which enables them to by-pass the Shylock-like grip of the mainstream banking system and the moneylenders. John was a deeply complex man and probably the most intellectually able among us. His mind could grasp the strategic elements of each issue, articulate complex statements and write up the material in concise language. From the outset of our relationship I had misgivings about his motives and doubted the strength of his loyalty to us as a group. He had a tendency to identify the most powerful and influential people among those we encountered and go off into corner-huddles

with these pace-setters and opinion-formers. Editors of important newspapers and TV programmes were those most regularly
endowed with these special briefings, which laid the ground-
stones for his later reputation as a political visionary and fixer
extraordinaire.

For John nothing ever stood still. He was always moving,
pushing for change, usually on the constitutional position.
Unionists in particular and Protestants in general never seemed
to trust him in those early days and indeed still don't. He only
wanted to work the system when it was going his way. As our
cohesion developed he led our group away from Stormont on
several occasions. I allowed myself to be dragged into these
boycotts and walk-outs, sometimes reluctantly, for reasons of
unity, but deep down I harboured doubts because I believed
that outside parliament is no place for a democrat. That's the
posture that gunmen thrive on, interpreting it as a mandate,
and in the descent into chaos that was enveloping us at that time
I calculated it was a dangerous posture. It showed me that,
despite his apparent radicalism, Hume was cast from the stuff
that old nationalists were made of. That appears to me still to
be his biggest weakness and although he is by far the best
nationalist politician since Wee Joe Devlin, his potential has
been blighted by this defect.

We were hopeful of bringing John Carron and James O'Reilly
from the Nationalist Party along with us. The rest of them were
stuck in a time-warp and, in our unanimous view, would not
have fitted in with the new consensus. Paddy Kennedy, one of
Gerry Fitt's allies, who had trained as an accountant, unfortunately tended to steer away from us, appearing to have different priorities and allegiances we did not share. Even Gerry,
his party leader, avoided meetings with him, thus widening the
gulf.

In no time we were meeting together virtually each day. We
noted what was happening in Dáil Éireann and at Westminster
and plotted tactics accordingly. Question time was a boon to us

and we plotted queries on topical issues and organised supplementary questions that all but overpowered unionist
ministers unused to being given a tough time. Our next target
was the departmental financial estimates and we began to rake
the ministers over the coals on the most obscure details. We
soon found out that some of the ministers did not even read,
and that many could not understand, their own estimates. We
found Fabian Society pamphlets to be a great source of inspiration, not least because the unionists would never have read
them and been alert to the issues we pursued.

Our burgeoning relationship was not all peaches and cream,
however. A Labour-held senate seat came up for grabs. We
needed only four votes to elect a Labour man to the senate, so
Vivian Simpson and I nominated John D. Stewart, a retired
colonial civil servant, who had chaired the inaugural meeting of
the Northern Ireland Civil Rights Association. Gerry Fitt and
Paddy Kennedy, whose votes were canvassed behind my back,
committed themselves to the moderate Protestant lawyer
Claude Wilton, as did John Hume, instead of debating the matter openly in the group. In a vigorous public statement I condemned the stealth and the disruptiveness to our compact.

With the overwhelming need for real, not sectarian, politics,
the growing inevitability of our position was that we should
form a new broad-based labour party with a portfolio of reforming policies based on the civil rights demands. The more we
worked together the more I felt alienated from what I now
regarded as a timid NILP. As we made no secret of our alliance,
and the growing co-operation between us was ever more evident, the political grapevine was buzzing with rumours that we
were indeed going to form a new grouping. As these reports
reached a crescendo, the NILP made a pre-emptive strike on 19
August 1970 with a public statement that they had terminated
my membership on the grounds that I was actively engaged in
discussions with other MPs to start a new political party. I refused to comment, for at the same time I was tipped off about

activities of John Hume which threatened to undermine the principles on which I thought any new party must be constructed.

What I had learned from a friendly Catholic lawyer was that John Hume had been at a weekend meeting in Donegal designed to form a Catholic political party. I found this very surprising because Hume was heavily involved in the talks the civil rights grouping were having with a view to a broad-based party. What surprised me most was that none of our group were invited to come to the meeting or were even informed of it, which, we heard later, had been attended by middle-class Catholics, mainly from Derry. I could smell that the Knights of Columbanus were probably involved.

We were angry with Hume, for it was not the first time we had felt he was pursuing his own agenda. In the June election he had supported the nomination of Eddie McAteer, the leader of the Nationalist Party, against the nomination of Claude Wilton for the Derry seat at Westminster. We believed that McAteer had no chance but that Wilton had. He was a popular figure in Derry, completely non-sectarian and generously liberal in outlook, and respected by all sides. He was likely to get the Catholic vote and many Protestant votes, just the sort of cross-community support we were aiming to attract as the political bedrock of our new party.

The more I thought about it the more I saw Hume's action that weekend as not only divisive but probably primarily aimed at stopping us from organising just such a cross-community party. There was likely to have been a bit of self-interest on Hume's part as well. In such a Catholic party he would have been the undisputed leader, whereas Gerry Fitt, as the most experienced and senior politician among us, with a seat at Westminster, was the obvious leader of our intended party. I was of course completely hostile to the church dabbling in party-making and politics anyway. After all, it was their misguided meddling which had enabled the Provos to get started, and I was highly

140

critical of how elements of the church and priesthood, over the years, had played a conservative, anti-socialist role, supporting the status quo and opposing any attempt at a radical rethink or restructuring of society. Poorly thought-out and irrelevant sermons delivered from Sunday pulpits signally failed to address the issues of equality or morality that mattered to ordinary people. There was no reference to the issues of deprivation, the lack of jobs, poor housing, extortionate mortgage rates, excessive rents or the wave of violence, robbery, social security fiddling and corruption that the Provos ultimately unleashed.

Austin Currie must have received the same word from the Donegal meeting as I did, for we independently issued separate statements that Monday morning, saying that we were forming a new political party immediately and that Gerry Fitt would be leader of it. As events turned out we were quite right to protect the momentum of our initiative and head off any alternative plan by Hume, for we soon learned that he had also met the National Democratic Party and members of the Nationalist Party, with a view to getting them to join his own political party. Gerry Fitt and I were conscious that Hume and his Derry group portrayed us as difficult socialist politicians, and used us as ogres to influence voters against our stances on political issues. Hume's efforts were easily defused after Austin Currie, Ivan Cooper and Paddy O'Hanlon all sided with me and Gerry. It has always seemed to me that Hume's work in trying to get a Catholic party established was influenced by Cardinal Conway who, though he was broad-minded in many ways, was deeply conservative, and recognised the need for something more effective to replace the demoralised nationalists but safer and more predictable than the sort of radical agenda we envisaged.

Hume had undoubtedly developed a big reputation in church circles, building the Credit Union throughout Ireland, something the Knights of Columbanus had simultaneously claimed credit for. He was also a leading member of the Derry Catholic middle class and must have seen 'revolutionaries' from black

Belfast, like Gerry and me, as some sort of potential plague. It is interesting to look back and see how these flawed strands, pragmatically built into the structure of the new party at the time, ultimately buckled and led to our departure. But at that time Hume quickly realised that we had pre-empted him, abandoned his own moves and immersed himself in the ongoing situation. The full creed for the new party had still not been finalised and meetings went on behind closed doors for another period until a full statement of the aims and objectives of the organisation could be agreed.

One of the thorniest issues was just what the name of the new party should be. Currie and Hume felt it should be called the Social and Democratic Party, but Fitt and I held out for the word 'Labour' to be included. As far as we were concerned, this was vital, for, apart from our commitment to socialism, the description was necessary to attract voters in Belfast where nationalist issues had taken second place to social ones since 1942. I further pointed out that the word 'Labour' should come after 'Democratic' rather than before 'Social' to prevent us from being called the LSD Party – I knew what the punters and our future political enemies could do with that variation.

The basic party philosophy was to be socialist and democratic, and work for the unity of Ireland by consent. When the Social Democratic and Labour Party held its first press conference on 21 August 1970, the following statement was issued: 'The SDLP's aim is to promote co-operation, friendship and understanding between North and South with a view to the eventual re-unification of Ireland through the consent of the majority of the people in the North and in the South.'

Gerry Fitt added: 'We support the maintenance of Stormont at the present time as it is the only institution which can bring about the reforms we desire . . . we do not believe that Ireland can be united by violence.'

8

'OUR BOYS –
RIGHT OR WRONG'

The announcement of the forming of the SDLP was greeted positively by the entire community. To my delight many on the unionist side recognised that we were committed to work at Stormont for equality and reconciliation in the community, using the democratic outlets to seek the changes we wanted. Top of the list of my priorities were measures for the betterment of the workers, the poor and the disadvantaged, whatever their religious or political background. From day one I always intended that the new party should develop and work in a way that would enable people from both sides of the community to join us. With the hard-won reforms to the electoral system in place, we were able to compete for a vote from every point in the community, to break down sectarian divisions and effect change by the ballot box. We heard very early after membership applications had been issued that some Protestants had joined. I was excited that we at last appeared to be on our way to creating genuine community partnership. The vexed question of a united Ireland could go on the back-burner; time enough to consider it when we had healed our internal problems in the North.

We opened a party headquarters at 20 College Square North, on the edge of Belfast city centre. There were a couple of rooms upstairs on the first floor which were big enough to hold meetings in, while downstairs there were a couple of smaller offices and a kitchen. Senator Paddy Wilson, Gerry Fitt's right-hand man and election agent, was installed to look after the office. Before long Paddy was overwhelmed with work and as I was the most accessible Belfast-based member of the party, with Gerry in London most of the week, I started coming into the office every day to look after affairs. In those early days we were fortunate to have the services of Mary Gordon, who laid the administrative foundations for the party and kept the kettle on the boil for the streams of callers we attracted.

We built up files and records to give us the research material to bolster our contributions in parliament and sustain our presence on TV and radio. We issued daily statements about the current topics and events for use in the news bulletins and next day's newspapers. We had attracted positive attention and were determined to keep it, with fresh, hard-hitting statements. We also adopted virtual open house for not only the local journalists but increasingly those from the national and international press, who had based themselves in the Europa Hotel a few minutes' walk away. A cadre of them turned up every morning for their coffee and stories. The trick was never to let them down and we never did, capturing much favourable publicity for the new party and its policies of hope.

Party meetings were held every week but sometimes more often when an urgent need arose. We usually held these gatherings in a small ground floor room which was located at the side of the entrance hall. People outside the window could have listened to our conversations, so I started to park my car on the pavement outside to prevent any eavesdropping. At first we were not very security conscious but as the violence steadily worsened and the political stakes became progressively higher, we became more and more concerned to protect our confidences and debates. We were tipped off by contacts in the post office that our mail was being screened. We knew from sources in the telephone service that widespread interception of calls was going on and we became circumspect and often paranoid about the lack of privacy.

At times people who lived adjacent to the party office would come to the door to tell us our meeting was coming over their telephones. We didn't believe it at first — who ever heard of bugs for telephones in 1970? We rang up and had the telephone people check the line. It was in order, they said. But there was strong, if circumstantial, evidence that we were indeed being monitored. The military invariably turned up around the office just as soon as we gathered for a meeting. I remember sometime later going to see Prime Minister Edward Heath about seeking an end to internment without trial. We had discussed our negotiating tactics beforehand at a meeting in the room at head-quarters and afterwards I was sure that a grimly smiling Heath had anticipated every move we made, every suggestion we put to him, because he was well briefed on our plans as a result of the eavesdropping. From what we have learned since, it is more than likely that we were indeed under sophisticated surveil-lance. Both the authorities and the Provos, who have done their own share of bugging, would have wanted to know what we were planning.

Raising money to pay for our ambitious plans was of course a major initial priority. Begging letters were sent out from the office to potential donors and members. In the early days we made several lucrative trips to Dublin, where a support group of sym-pathetic business and professional people, some of whom were exiles from the North, handed over generous sums of money. Noel Pearson, the impresario, was an indefatigable worker and organised cabarets and concerts for our cause, which were very generously supported. One night the writer Ulick O'Connor spoke about us on RTE television at peak viewing time. After-wards we were inundated with people anxious to help us and soon we had support groups all over the South which organised Sunday 'chapel gate collections' throughout the country, in the time-honoured way of raising money in Irish politics.

These collections filled me with dread, however. Remembering the effect the Anti-Partition League's 'chapel gate collections' had had on the unionist population in 1949, when the
greatest ever unionist vote was recorded to repudiate those who
had organised the collection, I feared that if word got out we
would be smeared as just a nationalist party and suffer the consequences accordingly. In the event that did not happen, and
the funds gathered that year and the next gave us sufficient
financial security to develop a professional party organisation.
At the end of December 1970 I gave an interview to the *Irish
Independent* in which I said that the forming of the SDLP was the
most important event of that year. Everything in the North had
changed beyond recognition. 'Until now, through the Orange
Lodges and a very elaborate and well maintained political
machine, the Unionists have been able to persuade the Shankill
Road working man that his interests and those of the landed
gentry, who control the Unionist Party, were one and the same,'
I said. Because of the policies of the Conservative government,
especially the cuts in social welfare, I said I detected the begin-
nings of disillusionment with Britain among the Protestant
working class. 'We intend to show the Protestant working man
that the real purpose of business is not to make profits for
wealthy people but to employ people, spread wealth in the community and break the centuries-old grip of a handful of landed
gentry on this part of Ireland.' The myth that unionism would
never change was well and truly shattered, I thought, but
events in 1971 were to prove me horribly wrong and my views
all too idealistic and premature.

Living at Shaw's Road in Andersonstown, as the family now
were, left us directly in the eye of the gathering storm as the
conflict between the Provos and the military steadily intensified.
Each day took on a more demanding pattern as the newly
aroused Catholic population, who once would have suffered
ignominy in silence, began to complain in full voice and demand
redress and justice.

The telephone calls usually began at 4.30 a.m., immediately after the military dawn raiding parties had pulled the latest IRA suspects from their beds. Anxious relatives demanded that I do something but all that was in my power was to complain to the local police and army posts. Most of those lifted were released fairly quickly but some of the people detained and charged came from good, respectable families and, as friendly RUC officers advised me privately of their criminal activities, the scale of the cancer that was spreading in our community filled me with horror. It was predictable that people associated with the traditional republican families would be turned over, but this time the net was being trawled more widely. More often I was downright angry at the mindless harassment, degrading obstruction and casual brutality the soldiers meted out to all who came in their path. I spent hours boiling over in anger and frustration, incoherent with rage, complaining to arrogant, overbearing British officers who failed to see the damage they were doing, the way they were walking into the trap the ruthless Provos had laid for them and how they were only acting as recruiting sergeants for the Provos.

Also, the quality of the military intelligence was appalling. They failed to understand that many families shared common surnames but were not related in any way. And even within families, more times than I could count, they arrested fathers when they wanted the sons and the sons when they were after the fathers. Innocent teenage schoolboys and old men thus found themselves held at the point of a British rifle, and many people I dealt with then were so alienated by the experience that they joined the Provos and later became notorious terrorists. I got a reputation among the soldiers for being difficult and found myself halted and delayed at the road checks, which became a formidable daily obstacle to moving around Belfast.

On one occasion they tried to smear me by leaking a story to the Sunday tabloids that a politician named 'Big Paddy' had been pillow-talking in a massage parlour, in fact a brothel run

147

by military intelligence, and had given vital information about the Provos. There was, of course, not a scintilla of truth in the story and I successfully sued for libel.

Breakfast time each day brought the first of the constituency callers and others from across the city. It was an endless tale of woe: people being intimidated at work, forced from their jobs or houses; people sick with fear and worry; relatives of the latest victims of the violence; not to mention the usual procession of people with problems over social security, rent, house repairs and debt. Most mornings they would be queued in the living-room, shuffling round from the sofa to the chair to the table where I sat taking copious notes of the cases to follow up with the relevant departments. By mid-morning I would often have to leave to go to the party office or a meeting where, invariably, there would be another queue. The telephone would have been going constantly at home and in the office with more complaints to be sorted out as well as messages from my party colleagues and journalists seeking a chat.

The afternoons at Stormont brought a respite, and in between stints in the chamber there was a chance to get on the phone to follow up some of the morning cases and return other calls. By the time I would get home in early evening the house would again be packed. I usually had to eat in the kitchen to get some privacy while Theresa and the kids kept the kettle and the teapot going, as they had already done in the morning, to com-fort and console the often tearful and distressed people who called. After tea, while the phone again kept ringing, there would be more cases to write down and a new workload to be handled the next day. When the last callers had been dealt with there was still no respite from the phone, which often continued until the early hours.

Over the years Theresa and the children put up with an awful lot, supporting me as I tried to do my best for the people I represented. The privacy of the family home was non-existent. They could not sit down and watch the television uninterrupted, their meals were eaten under the gaze of the stream of daily visitors and were often shared by them with people who pleaded poverty and hunger. On a regular basis the family retreated upstairs to their bedrooms but even there their tranquillity was not guaranteed. At times of real crisis the queues of people often overflowed from the livingroom, up the stairs and into the bedrooms, where they sat on the beds waiting their turn to see me. On one memorable occasion, I had a group of Provo sympathisers in the kitchen, two policemen in a bedroom and other callers in the livingroom, none of whom wanted to see each other. It was like a theatrical farce moving the people around and distracting them in order to prevent some of them meeting each other.

Some of my callers were there to lecture me or hector me on what I should be doing or saying. These were quickly shown the door and, on occasion, forcefully. The unadulterated tribal propaganda they expected from me as the local MP was not on, although I had no reservations about the endless illustrations I received of army violence and reacted stridently against it. At this time I calculated there were some 2,000 soldiers billeted in my constituency, one for every ten voters. On a single Saturday night I counted thirty armoured vehicles cruising around the network of narrow streets and housing estates of the Falls. The police were invisible and the streets were patrolled by soldiers deployed in groups up to two dozen strong who marched in single file along both sides of a street. Most of the time the military blandly denied every allegation made against them, causing journalists, who had seen their excesses at first hand on the streets, to describe their press office at the headquarters as the 'Lisburn lie machine'.

I scored one or two direct hits against the military at this time. In 1971 the GOC, the man in charge of the army in Northern Ireland, was Harry Tuzo. One morning he attended a meeting of unionist MPs at Stormont during which he told an unflattering joke about me. Ian Paisley informed me that this had happened and tipped me off that the general was still on the premises, attending a sherry reception in the Members' Dining Room. I went up to the room on the first floor of the building and established he was there. Then I went to the opposite end of it and shouted out, 'Hey, Tuzo. Where the fuck are you?' The general and a couple of his aides promptly dived out into the corridor and scarpered. Two days later I got a handwritten note from him. 'Without reservation I apologise for having retailed that rather bad joke about you. It was a silly thing to do and I'm sorry I did it. Unfortunately, one so often wishes and cannot eat one's words. So far from this lapse being some indication of my opinion of the opposition MPs you should know that my hope is to enjoy good relations with all MPs – not least yourself.'

After a raid on a house at Riverdale, in the Andersonstown area, an officer dropped a booklet, classified 'staff in confidence', which had been prepared by army intelligence for briefing soldiers about why they were in Northern Ireland. It was quickly brought to me and its contents were so hair-raising and inaccurate that I raised the issue in parliament. I was stopped from directly quoting it by the Unionist Party hack who occupied the chair, but this problem was quickly overcome by leaking photocopies to the local journalists who saw that its idiocies were well publicised. Before I was stopped I had been able to read into the parliamentary record an oath which it claimed was sworn by members of Sinn Féin. 'I swear by almighty God, by all in Heaven and upon earth, by the Holy and Blessed Prayer Book of our church, by the Blessed Virgin Mary and Mother of God, by her sorrowings and sufferings at the foot of the cross, by her tears and wailings, by St Patrick, by the Blessed and Adorable Host, by the Blessed rosary and holy beads, by the Blessed Church in all ages, and by our Holy national martyrs, to fight until we die, wading in the fields of red gore of the Saxon tyrants and murderers in the glorious cause of Nationality.' The rest of the material in the book was just as sick and inaccurate. The Siege of Derry three hundred years earlier was, for instance, described as though it had taken place only the previous year. It was said that Clan na Gael operated a secret code. The word 'Irishman' became 'JSJTIMZO', supposedly reached by substituting for each letter the one following it in the alphabet. I said I had been thrown out of first class at school for failing to master that code. Apart from feeding such bilge to its officers, the army's partiality was exposed, for there was little mention of the UVF or any other loyalist paramilitary organisations, even though they accounted for a significant proportion of the violence at this time.

While the Provisional sympathisers welcomed my attacks on the military as music to their ears, they were far from happy at me uttering public statements which put a labour view of events. They brought me and my family much grief and abuse. My car's tyres were slashed, its wiring was ripped out, its lights and windows were broken and vandalised, and the car itself was daubed in red paint with slogans like 'Chairman Mao' and 'Paddy the Red'. The children suffered too. Patricia was so badly treated at school that we had to take her away and send her to another across the city, which, for her protection, she attended under a false name. The twins, Peter and Joe, were regularly picked on, bullied and assaulted. They were urinated on and rubbed with excreta by their fellow pupils. Theresa, of course, had to take the nasty phone calls when I was not at home, and when she was out and about she also suffered threats and insults. She was always getting pushed and jostled on the steps at the chapel or women would run into her legs and feet with trolleys at the supermarket. Some of the people who did these things were well known to us. They included neighbours and many people I had helped or would have regarded as friends.

We all kept quiet at the time because we refused to let any of them see they had hurt us. I knew what to expect, and it was therefore not too frightening for me, but it must have been terrible for the innocent family. The most serious incident took place at Leeson Street on the night of 8 March 1971. I had called down to Jimmy Sullivan's house to bring himself and Mary, his wife, out for a birthday drink. We went to a local pub and while we were there gunmen arrived and put us out before setting the place alight. They were local Provos and this incident was the beginning of a violent feud between them and the Officials. The Provo strategy, evolved that year, was to kill off the Officials as a rival force in the Catholic community and to turn the Catholic areas into strongholds for their anti-British campaign. I drove Jim and Mary back home to Leeson Street and went into their home for a cup of tea. While I was there my parked car was raked with machine-gun fire. The gunmen had been waiting for us but didn't open fire because of the woman present. The next day I obtained a firearms licence from the police and bought myself a Browning 9 mm pistol, which was to be my constant companion for many years.

Forty-eight hours after that shooting, on 10 March there took place an incident of great political significance which shocked the community to its core. Three off-duty members of a Scottish regiment were abducted from a city centre bar in Belfast with the lure of going to a party. Instead they were taken to the hills overlooking the city where they were shot in the head at point-blank range while they were urinating at the side of a lonely road. Two of them were aged only seventeen and eighteen, the third was twenty-five. The level of Provisional violence had been worsening throughout the early part of the year but Protestant reaction to the brutality of the three soldiers' deaths was heightened by the fact that they came from Scotland, which enjoyed close links with the Belfast loyalists through support for Glasgow Rangers and the Orange Order.

In a show of anger against the ineffectiveness of security policy, on 12 March some 4,000 workers downed tools at the shipyard and walked to a protest rally outside Belfast City Hall. This was the most visible sign that the final heave had begun in-side the unionist establishment to overthrow the Stormont prime minister, Major James Chichester-Clark. He had proved equally impotent in halting the slide into chaos and disorder and was plagued by the hardliners in his own ranks who saw any reforms as concessions and obstructed them. By the end of March the coup was complete and Brian Faulkner, a tough-talking man who had a reputation for getting things done, found himself in the hot seat. Although he had taken care to cultivate the back-woodsmen, I had long regarded Brian Faulkner as the most able individual among the overwhelmingly dour unionists and, looking back, I feel that the real tragedy was that he got his chance to solve our problems too late, when the sands of time had almost run out. If he had replaced Brookeborough in 1963, after the years of stagnation, with his ability, energy and vision he would undoubtedly have managed reform, the need for which he recognised, in a way sufficiently effective to have headed off the crisis that subsequently en-gulfed us.

From our point of view Faulkner made a brisk and encourag-ing start. He immediately announced a new cabinet which included, for the first time in the history of the Stormont administration in peacetime, a non-unionist minister. David Bleakley, a member of the NILP, was appointed to the important and sensitive post of Minister for Community Relations. Faulkner also announced a nine-day arms amnesty in a bid to get guns and ammunition out of the wrong hands. The outcome was quite successful, with some 1,618 weapons and almost 100,000 rounds of ammunition, 85 per cent of them illegally held, being handed over to the police. During one of his first public speeches he assured us that there was not going to be a crackdown on Catholics. 'My administration will be scrupu-lously fair to everyone under the law,' he promised.

In June, coinciding with the fiftieth anniversary of the opening of the Northern Ireland parliament, Faulkner made a dramatic proposal in a serious attempt to widen the role of the opposition at Stormont. In addition to the Public Accounts Committee there were to be three new, nine-strong committees, to deal with social, environmental and industrial services. They were to be consultative and review rather than executive bodies, but they provided a long overdue outlet for the permanently out-voted opposition, particularly as it was envisaged that two of the four salaried posts for chairmen would go to our side of the House.

My reaction was one of surprise. As I said in the House, I had thought that Faulkner, like a lot of other people, had become discouraged but I welcomed the initiative which I described, in a widely reported remark, as showing 'plenty of imagination, his finest hour since I came into the House'. We all respected Faulkner's ability and we agreed to give the new proposals a chance to work, recognising that the alternative was no alter-native. However, the shine was taken off the gesture a couple of days later when Faulkner and some of his senior ministers very publicly trooped off for talks with Orange leaders about the forthcoming marching season. We were shocked at this. It seemed to us, since we were not informed, that the government had gone off to get permission for the reforms. We, of course, could not tolerate being seen to be 'bossed' by the Orange Order, but for the precariously positioned Faulkner, on the other hand, it made political sense. He needed their support to stay in power and he was able to defuse our attacks by pointing out that he had persuaded them to cut the number of marches for the tense Twelfth of July period that year. Looking back I can see the logic of his position and, of course, if he had been able to wring more concessions out of the order the possibility is that we could have stopped much of the worst violence that follow-ed. These matters were aired during a meeting between Faulkner and the opposition parties at Stormont on 7 July. Afterwards we assented when he said that 'nothing of this sort involving private and completely frank exchanges has been at-tempted before'.

The meeting was to be the first of a series to hammer out the framework for the formation of the new select committees but events outside parliament, overwhelmingly the mounting toll of Provo violence, were actually writing the political agenda. Bombs were going off constantly and street rioting seemed to go on for ever. Life was spent rushing from one flashpoint to another in increasingly vain bids to calm people, reassure them or persuade them to go home, but the blood was boiling that summer and one had to recognise that the ancient hatreds had now been fully aroused on all sides. Matters came to a head on 8 July when the army shot dead Seamus Cusack and Desmond Beattie during the fourth consecutive day of rioting in Derry. The separate shootings provoked the usual controversy, with the army claiming that both men were engaged in rioting and John Hume taking a strong stand to the contrary. In the aftermath of the deaths members of our group, but not myself or Gerry Fitt, met and decided that unless there was an independent inquiry into the killings, the party would withdraw from Stormont. Gerry and I were livid with anger. Just at a time when there were signs that we might be getting somewhere, the old nationalist knee-jerk of abstention was brought into play. We were already steaming because the threat to leave Stormont had previously fallen from some lips within our group. Gerry and I told the other party members that we would not follow the move if they made it but we agreed to discuss it further at a meeting in Belfast two days later.

The Stormont parliament was due to adjourn for the summer recess on 8 July and just after 6 p.m. that evening, in what turned out to be my final contribution to the historically turbulent Stormont parliament, I engaged in bitter exchanges with Faulkner about a shooting incident at Ballymurphy in my own constituency involving the army, and the latest reports from Derry where the violence was still continuing.

Gerry Fitt and I made it clear from the outset that becoming absentionists was going to leave the way clear for the Provos; indeed, we believed the party had fallen for a Provo trap. When it was clear we were getting somewhere with the unionists on democratic advancement, the Provos increased violence with the aim of turning us back, forcing us to leave parliament and put them into the driving seat. Gerry and I refused to support the earlier statement on the Derry shootings but, bearing in mind the potential for SDLP success if we remained together, we tried to get some accommodation with the others on the matter of withdrawal. Gerry used all his contacts at Westminster to make sure they understood the gravity of the situation but, as I found before, it was again a case of 'our boys – right or wrong' and he came away empty-handed.

Faced with British unwillingness to give us some face-saving formula, although the holding of the inquests was accelerated, Gerry and I were unwillingly sucked along with the majority feeling, which was emotional rather than practical. Unable to maintain our opposition we agreed to withdraw from parliament, for all the wrong reasons, although there was no hint of that in the lengthy public statement, drafted by Hume and myself, which was published on 16 July 1971, setting out the reasons for withdrawal. Attempts were made to disrupt our press conference when bomb warning calls were phoned to the Belfast hotel, but we decided to ignore them and carry on.

Our statement made the point that, as responsible public representatives unable to secure action on an issue which had outraged our constituents, we felt no role was left for us in the present parliamentary system. If British troops had shot dead civilians in a riot in Birmingham, what would have been the reaction of the British public? Would there have been any inquiry? Our statement continued: 'The action by both the British government and the army on this issue confirms our increasing suspicions about the role of the army in the NI situation. These suspicions date from the arrival of the army in power in the local administration. It was instanced by the military curfew in Lower Falls in 1970 and instanced again by the unquestioning acceptance of army statements covering the various actions of the military, the virtual disappearance of due process of law and democratic checks on army excesses.'

While the army was the butt of our criticism, it was now starkly clear to me that the inherent instability of the Northern Ireland political system itself could not produce the basis for peace, justice and stability. Reform, without a change of heart, was not going to be enough. We had discussed the dangers inherent in our withdrawal. We knew that the vacuum created by our departure from Stormont would be filled by gunmen. We therefore had to get ourselves a new and effective forum, keep up a political output to the media and maintain leadership of our constituents.

Ivan Cooper was given the task of getting an alternative forum organised, while we arranged party meetings throughout the North to keep a high leadership profile that was crucial to our existence and survival. As the violence continued to escalate and the confrontations between the army and the community intensified, the word 'internment' was on everybody's lips, especially when the army launched a major series of dawn raids on Catholic areas at the end of July. I could see that they were dry-runs and that it was only a matter of time before they sprang the real thing. From my contacts I learned they had visited a number of IRA homes, including those of sympathisers, and brought these people in for interrogation, clearly in the hope of building up files. The police at that time had no good information on the new generation that had joined the IRA. The old Catholic informers had disappeared once the Catholic community had been attacked, and the 'no-go areas' behind the barricades, which excluded the police, killed off any hopes they had of cultivating new sources. None of this inhibited the great body of unionists who believed that internment, as it had been in the 1930s, 1940s and 1950s, was the best answer to the growing IRA problem. Prominent among them was, of course, Faulkner, who had had first-hand experience of the matter when he was Minister of Home Affairs in the latter stages of the

1956–62 IRA border campaign. It had then been very effective in combating IRA activity because it was in use on both sides of the border. This time it would be applied only on the northern side. Given my own experiences of internment and the hostile way it would be greeted by our constituents, I knew in my bones we were on the verge of utter disaster.

Early on the morning of Saturday 7 August I received a telephone call from Springfield Road RUC station. A senior officer asked me to come down at once for something serious had happened. I scrambled out of bed, got dressed and hurried to the station not daring to think just what was wrong. There I was told that a man had been shot dead by a soldier. Hearing a van backfire, the soldier, who was on sentry duty outside, thought he was under attack, opened fire and shot the driver dead. The driver and his passenger, who was uninjured, were both building workers from south Armagh, so we rang Paddy O'Hanlon who also came to the station.

The senior police officers in the station were very distressed. They obviously feared a renewal of attacks on the station, where a soldier had already been killed in an explosion some time before, but seemed to me to be genuinely concerned about the circumstances of the shooting. Riots, as expected, broke out shortly afterwards as news of the incident spread and by the afternoon there was widespread turmoil in Belfast, south Armagh and other parts of the North.

The rioting that weekend clearly forced the hand of the Faulkner government. We know now, from subsequent reports, that Ted Heath, for months reluctant to agree to internment, finally relented and gave Faulkner and the army the go-ahead for the long planned swoop. Early on Monday morning, 9 August, I was wakened by small stones being thrown at my bedroom window. I was told by the thrower that the military were arresting everyone in sight. 'There are thousands of them every place,' he said. I learned gradually throughout the morning that large numbers of people had been lifted, and when the introduction of internment was finally announced by Faulkner it was revealed that 342 men had been arrested. Given that Faulkner had promised to be even-handed, I was incensed to find that all the internees were taken from Catholic areas and that but for the intervention of the local police, myself and Paddy Kennedy, who were on the military's list, would have been among them. This was Faulkner's most fundamental mistake. After all that had happened up to that time, and the clear evidence of loyalist as well as republican responsibility for violence, there was no excuse, other than bigotry, for directing the swoops against only one side. Faulkner could have defended an even-handed approach, and we would not have been cast even further into the political wilderness.

As I went out and about that morning, pondering the implications, I found the Falls Road was in an awful state. Burning buses, cars, vans and lorries blocked the road and littered the side streets. It was the same picture throughout the city and rioting spread to Newry, Strabane, Armagh and Derry. Faulkner said the swoops had taken place to smash the IRA and protect life and property but within an hour it was clear that they had only unleashed even worse violence. His policy was seen to be in total ruins when the IRA 'leadership' appeared at a clandestine news conference and boasted that the army had missed most of the people they were after. Within four days twenty-two people had been killed in rioting and gun battles, well over two hundred houses had been ransacked and burned in fresh sectarian upheaval and 7,000 people had fled the North, taking refuge in Irish army camps in the republic. Far from halting the violence, internment had provoked a level of destruction which was far worse than anything experienced to date and, as I was soon to discover, even more sinister things had been sanctioned by the authorities.

Mrs Hannaway, from Clonard, was a member of one of the best-known republican families in the city and, not surprisingly, her three sons had been arrested in the main internment swoop. Over the next week she had been refused permission to visit them in Crumlin Road prison and she was worried at not having heard from any of the sons by letter or message. Some of the detainees had been released within this time. After she contacted me I applied for a visit to see them. What I saw and heard when they were brought out to the visiting hall staggered me. Their eyes were bulging in their heads as they tried to tell me of their ordeal after arrest. There had been the predictable assaults, kicks, punches and so on by the soldiers, but there was a worrying new dimension to what they told me. At one stage, after being blindfolded, they were brought up in a helicopter and then thrown through the door. The aircraft was actually only a few feet off the ground but the terror felt by prisoners being treated in this way was unspeakable. The most disturbing information, however, concerned the next stage of detention when they were taken by helicopter, still blindfolded, to another place where they were made to stand in the same position for hours on end without food and water while being subjected to 'white noise' – a terrible high-pitched, screeching, disorientating sound. I instantly recognised that this was more than just humiliating treatment. It was nothing but pure torture which was certainly immoral and, I suspected, probably illegal.

Over the next few weeks we gathered up much more evidence from the relatives of internees, who had been in to visit them. There was a clear pattern to their stories and some of the victims had been seriously affected by their experiences. We decided to present our dossier to John Whale and the influential *Sunday Times* Insight Team. On 17 October, after making their own checks, they published a major article about the brainwashing techniques practised on internees. The British government would only set up a private inquiry, not a public one, to investigate this most serious development, so we asked Jack Lynch, the Irish prime minister, to have the matter raised at the European Court of Human Rights. He shared our concern and immediately agreed to take formal steps to collect the necessary evidence to mount a case. Sean Donlon, a young Irish diplomat who later became Irish ambassador to the United States, and John Murray, a barrister, travelled to our office in Belfast where we gave them facilities to interview witnesses.

We decided to await the publication of the British government investigation into the situation before taking our next step. The Compton report, published on 16 November, confirmed that detainees had been subjected to hooding, the use of continuous noise, deprivation of sleep, being forced to stand against a wall, and a bread and water diet. This amounted to ill-treatment but not brutality, the report concluded. As far as I was concerned this amounted to a blatant cover-up. None of the internees that I named had even been asked for a statement. Exactly a month later the Irish government lodged a formal complaint in Strasbourg, containing detailed allegations that Britain had violated six articles of the European Convention on Human Rights. The case, which turned out to be a major irritant in Anglo-Irish relations for many years, was nevertheless vigorously pursued by successive Dublin governments until January 1978 when the European Court finally ruled that Britain had been guilty of ill-treatment, but not torture.

In the immediate aftermath of internment our days were occupied, as they had been in 1969, with trying to reduce the hardship of the many people affected by the consequences. The one-sided nature of the operation and subsequent military harassment of the Catholic community closed off any chance that we would or could go back into Stormont. All respect for our position as elected representatives seemed to have gone to the wall anyway. On 15 August we were holding a meeting at the Greenan Lodge Hotel in Belfast when troops surrounded the building and pointed guns at us through the window of the room we were gathered in. When we left a short time later our cars were singled out and we were detained for more than fifteen minutes, 'on orders', an officer told us. Feeling utterly powerless, the SDLP threw its weight behind a call for a major campaign of peaceful civil disobedience by the nationalist community. Accordingly we advised our supporters not to pay their rent or rates as a protest until internment was ended. Meetings were held throughout the country in an effort to get momentum into the campaign.

However, the authorities showed little concern for our worries; military repression intensified and a new purpose-built internment centre was opened on the site of a wartime airfield at Long Kesh, ten miles from Belfast. A request by us to visit the camp was granted but we had to run the gauntlet of a crowd of local loyalists throwing stones. Bearing in mind my own experiences of internment in the Crumlin Road prison, some thirty years earlier, I could see little that was radically wrong. I ate a meal with the prisoners which was well above the standard of anything I had seen in prison before, but the food did get cold being conveyed from the kitchen to the various Nissen huts. I made representations about this after the visit and improvements were made, but a deep sense of injustice that people were being held indefinitely, on suspicion alone, without the chance of a trial was to gnaw away at my conscience until the last internees got out in 1975.

Although we made the ending of internment a precondition for any political progress, the real priority we faced in the autumn of 1971 was to halt the violence and create the conditions for a lasting political settlement. We convened our grandiose Assembly of the Northern Irish People at Dungiven on 26 October, but it was only a talking shop which did not have any potential to seriously influence events. I believed that the most effective way to get the British government's attention on our agenda was to encourage the Lynch administration in Dublin to work more closely with them, providing a counter-balance to the traditional, but strained, links between the Conservative government and the unionists at Stormont.

Both the British and the Irish governments, shocked at the ever deteriorating turn of events in Northern Ireland, had already begun to consider the way ahead at a two-day prime ministerial summit at Chequers on 6 and 7 September. This meeting turned out to have a significance that we never suspected at the time. Indeed I do not think that Jack Lynch has ever had proper acknowledgement for successfully persuading Heath to adopt a major change of policy. Until then Heath had listened almost exclusively to Faulkner, who sold him the line that internment would solve the IRA problem, halt the violence and make everything else fall neatly into place. After the Chequers summit things changed and Faulkner was called to tripartite talks with Heath and Lynch. Faulkner's analysis of the problems was challenged by Heath, who told him that a political solution was needed, not military oppression. Faulkner seems to have disregarded the importance of what Heath said to him, feeling that his position in charge of Northern Ireland affairs was invincible and that Heath and Lynch were inconsequential. As things turned out, Faulkner was actually at the 'last ditch' and didn't know it.

Heath contacted Harold Wilson and asked him to use his influence within the SDLP to lock us into a round of political negotiations about the future governance of the North. Before the Westminster parliament was recalled at the end of September to discuss the events of our long hot summer, Wilson had put forward an interesting twelve-point plan in what he said was a constructive attempt to restore balance in Northern Ireland. It provided for a minister of cabinet rank to be stationed in Belfast, reporting to government and parliament, and for proportional representation to be introduced for all local elections, thus providing for fairer minority representation. He sent Jim Callaghan and Tony Benn over to talk with us, something which I was pleased about. Not knowing of Heath's change of heart I felt the British Labour Party, which was then in opposition, had a more sympathetic understanding of the need for root and branch reform than the Conservatives had.

Gerry Fitt, John Duffy and myself met Callaghan and Benn at the Dunadry Inn, a hotel near Belfast airport, on 11 November 1971. Callaghan immediately wanted to know if we would join an administration that would include unionists, in order, he said, to bring Northern Ireland and its people back from the brink of anarchy. Gerry replied that we would be willing to negotiate such a settlement – the first time anyone had formally proposed power-sharing to us – but we also outlined the formidable obstacles in the way of any settlement, not least the continuation of internment, the heavy-handedness of the army and our doubts whether control of security policy should remain with what we now regarded as a completely discredited Faulkner administration.

Callaghan, who seemed to be of the opinion that there was enough give in our position for talks to begin, reported back to Wilson, who came to Ireland himself in November for an extensive four-day visit to both north and south. He tried out a number of ideas on those he met, all encompassed in a fifteen-year transition plan to a united Ireland. He questioned internment procedures, when and how the military should leave the North and whether security responsibility should be left with Stormont or transferred to London. These concerted moves by the Labour Party, at the highest level, were structured to get us back to the table, as we were still boycotting Stormont. We saw the advantage of our position with so much wooing going on and decided it would be senseless to throw it away for too little. So we stuck to our demands – we needed something on internment, the role of the army and the responsibility for security. Any political talks, regardless of who they were with, had to follow concession on these matters.

During his visit Wilson had a long session with Catholic leaders in Belfast and kept us waiting for nearly three hours. I suspected he wanted to get something from them with which to pressurise us. His staff made sure there were lashings of drink in our waiting room to while away the delay, but we were well used to that ploy. Despite an unyielding attitude on our part, Wilson did not give up hope and invited us to further meetings, but we knew in our hearts that Heath, who was after all actually prime minister, could deliver far more if we kept up the pressure. We did so during a short pre-Christmas visit Heath made to Belfast. By the end of 1971, with over 200 people dead since 1969 and violence raging all around us, we felt that we were making an effective case and that 1972 would see progress. It did, but as things turned out, at an awful price.

Life at that time was a nightmare for all of us in Northern Ireland. Between January and July 1971, before internment, there had been thirty deaths attributable to the violence. By the end of the year, after internment was supposed to have dealt with the gunmen and bombers, the human toll had soared by another 143. In July there had been 78 explosions but after the fiasco of internment there were 131 in August, 196 in September and 117 in October. Bomb scares and security searches had disrupted life on an unimagined scale. In Belfast, Derry and virtually every other town and village, bombs and incendiaries had laid waste offices, shops and public buildings. Many jobs had been lost and the economic damage was incalculable. Fear forced people to stay indoors at night, for pubs were particularly singled out for attack and people were being abducted off the streets at night by sectarian murder gangs.

It is not an exaggeration to say that the six of us, who comprised the SDLP front line, lived under the constant threat of assassination. Austin Currie's house at Donaghmore, near Dungannon, was fired on so often by both sides he lost count. His wife, Anita, bore the brunt of one attack when loyalists broke in and carved the letters 'UVF' on her chest. Ivan Cooper's house in Derry was damaged by a bomb and a shot was fired through his window. Once, he had to fire shots in the air to prevent a mob attacking his house. On another occasion he was on the telephone checking the authenticity of a call asking him to go to hospital to visit a friend, apparently hurt in a road traffic accident, when a fifteen-pound bomb went off underneath his car outside the house. If he hadn't checked out the call he would have certainly perished in the explosion. At least one plot to assassinate John Hume was exposed; loyalists from the Burntollet area were discovered watching him as he travelled through the area at night returning to Derry from Belfast.

One day at Belfast airport, when John Hume and I were travelling to the House of Commons in London to brief MPs for a debate on Northern Ireland affairs, we were being escorted by two plainclothes RUC officers. As we were sitting in the lounge waiting for the flight to be called, a wild-eyed man approached, with his hand inside his bomber jacket. As he drew a gun from inside the jacket, one of our policemen struck him on the side of his face and knocked him down. As he fell the gun went spinning along the floor. The policeman restrained him in an arm lock while the other collected the gun before he was handed over to the airport police. Needless to say we were relieved and thankful at the decisive action taken by the policemen but before we went through to the aircraft one of them drew me to the side and pleaded that his name should not be given to the newspapers. 'Don't give my name, for Christ's sake,' he said. 'If some of my relatives up in Londonderry hear that I saved you and Hume, I'll never be able to go back home again.'

I had to go into the Mater hospital for a time in the latter half of 1971 to have an operation on an old football injury to my ankle. I was pretty apprehensive about the stay and a police guard was provided for me. My anxieties were not allayed by their presence, however, for they seemed more interested in pursuing the shapely young nurses along the corridors than in looking after me. When Gerry Fitt came to visit I told him this and, acting on his advice, I rang up the police headquarters to have them taken away. Bill Wilson, from Andersonstown police station, then came over to say that he would do the duty and from then on he and another selfless man, Bob Colhoun, took charge of my safety and arranged all protection when necessary. On one occasion, after a Police Federation spokesman criticised politicians for not supporting the police while taking their protection, the two of them actually offered to accompany me in their own time. I was deeply moved that two policemen would so bravely offer to protect me, at great risk to themselves and potential loss to their own families, for I was very much a target at the time.

One night, after a very heated exchange with the Orange Order leader, the Reverend Martin Smyth, in the Ulster Television studios on the Ormeau Road, I was warned that my car was under surveillance by a number of men. The police arranged to slip me out the back in a police car while one of them would take my car to the Ormeau embankment, where it would be handed over to me. We met as arranged and my companion, Andy McKenna, and I changed over and drove off leaving the police behind. When we turned on to the Malone Road, we noticed a car coming up on the outside. I accelerated as we turned into Balmoral Avenue, heading towards home in Andersonstown. The other car gave chase along Balmoral Avenue and through the lights at the Lisburn Road junction. The pursuit continued along Stockman's Lane but, when we reached the roundabout at the M1, I had gained ground. As we swung left off the roundabout and went up towards the Andersonstown Road, a single shot rang out as the other car turned back, but it missed my car. I was thankful that my pursuers decided not to follow us into West Belfast.

Shortly afterwards, as I left my home one lunch-time with my son, Peter, who was then seven years of age, and the chairman of the Falls branch of the NILP, I heard council workmen shouting at me: 'Look out, look out, they have a gun!' Just then a single shot was fired from a car passing along the road in front of my house. I have always been grateful to those council workmen who clearly distracted the gunmen in the car.

One night we were having a meal in the Dunowen restaurant in Dungannon after a party meeting when the Provos exploded a bomb outside the rear door of the building. Incidents like these worried us about our own safety but much more about our wives and children. From time to time we moved our families out of our houses to stay with friends and relatives. Some of us stayed away from home at times and we had friends all over the place, including several sympathetic hoteliers, who always made us welcome, even at short notice, at all hours of the day and night. We never developed a routine; it was safe to do things once, but not more. If we had to travel at night we always arranged to do so together or brought someone along with us. We became very circumspect about discussing our movements on the phone and only told our most trusted acquaintances of future plans. Travelling around Belfast involved us in long detours, so that as much of the journey as possible was in 'friendly' rather than 'hostile' territory. In some areas people would come over and start shouting abuse at us, even if we were momentarily stopped at a traffic light. Every post brought its handful of threatening letters, some obviously written by simple-minded, hate-filled fanatics, but many the work of articulate, clear-headed people, warped and twisted by bigotry and hatred. None of us was deterred by this avalanche of events and difficulties, however, and we stuck to the path we had mapped out.

In the opening weeks of 1972 the evil of internment was thrust to the front of the political agenda after members of the First Parachute Regiment brutally turned back a protest march at the latest internment centre at Magilligan Strand in Co. Derry. Hand-to-hand fighting took place between the Paras and the demonstrators, who were beaten with batons. John Hume and Ivan Cooper were present and were witness to the viciousness of the clashes. Both predicted that the Paras would come back harder and with more effective tactics at another march planned for Derry City the following Sunday, 30 January. Faulkner's government, the military and the police held a number of meetings prior to the event. It was clear that momentous decisions were being taken, that something very grave was afoot. We had our meetings too and, fearing the worst, four of us decided to attend the march. Gerry and John were unable to do so.

I was still on crutches after my operation and had great difficulty in getting there. We were stopped seven times before getting past the military cordon at the Waterside. When I got out of the car at the Guildhall, I had to get back in again quickly for a gang of loyalists attacked me. Although several thousand gathered for the march that day, the crowd would have been greater had it not been for the obstruction by the military. By the time I reached the Strand Road, hopelessly late for the march and rally, people were saying that trouble had broken out. Before long, others, clearly shaken and trembling at what they had experienced, began to emerge from the Bogside area to give us the first accounts of how the Paras had opened fire on the marchers, leaving bodies lying all over the place. Realising the gravity of what had happened, but still unsure of the exact extent of it, I went at once to John Hume's house where I found him in deep shock. Reporters had taken over the house and commandeered the phone to file their stories. I said: 'John, we have work to do. I'm going to clear these people out and get our own organisation going.'

'Go ahead,' he said. 'Get our own people in here to the parlour and let's agree a strategy on this.'

We deflected pressure to hold a press conference until we had authoritative information about everything that had happened. Messengers were dispatched to bring information back, but not by phone. The reports coming in indicated that at least eleven people had died (the final total was thirteen) and that controversy was raging like a forest fire in a drought. Locally the word was that the Paratroopers had indiscriminately opened fire on unarmed marchers. The army were claiming that they had been fired on. Telephone facilities were arranged for the press in local houses; they were already describing the day as 'Bloody Sunday' and comparing it with the Sharpeville massacre in South Africa. I rang Dr Conor Cruise O'Brien in Dublin for his advice. In the ensuing turmoil it was agreed to call an all-Ireland national day of mourning, initiated by the trade union movement. I got Mickey

Mullen, of the Irish Transport and General Workers' Union, on the phone and he agreed to set the wheels in motion. We also decided to set up a national fund for the victims, with arrangements for immediate payments to offset the cost of the funerals.

It was only when I left to return to Belfast in the middle of the night that the enormity of what had happened really sank in. There was a massive outcry about the shootings, especially as the British side brazened out their unsubstantiated claims that those shot had been handling firearms. Many workers throughout Ireland stopped work for two days until the dead were buried. The Irish ambassador in London was recalled to Dublin while the Lord Chief Justice, Lord Widgery, was called in by Ted Heath to carry out a judicial inquiry. Within a month, the British embassy in Dublin was burned to the ground, seven people had been killed in an explosion at the Parachute Regiment's headquarters at Aldershot, violence was rampant again throughout Northern Ireland and hardline unionists forced the Faulkner administration to ban another protest march planned for Newry the following Sunday.

In spite of the ban, at least 20,000 people turned out for the demonstration in Newry. Tension was running at an extraordinary level and we were extremely worried that the march would go off the rails and cause us international embarrassment, for the world's press, and that is no exaggeration, had converged on the town. Sean Hollywood, a local teacher, handled the organisation and kept personal control of the operations through a carefully selected band of stewards, and to everybody's intense relief the march passed off with dignity and without incident. A few days later, however, summonses were served on a number of us who had been in the front rank of the parade. We were fined £15 at Newry Magistrates' Court for breaking the public order legislation.

The traumatic effect of Bloody Sunday paralysed the political process for a time, but the Heath–Lynch axis continued to work, and on 24 March 1972 the sensational announcement was made from 10 Downing Street that the Stormont parliament had been prorogued. The Faulkner government had resigned after refusing to transfer security powers to Westminster.

9

'I'LL HAVE SOME OF
YOUR SCONES'

Once Heath decided to wind up Stormont, William Whitelaw was appointed as Northern Ireland Secretary of State and sent to Belfast the next morning to establish a new Northern Ireland Office and clear up the shambles created by fifty years of unionist misrule. The hardline William Craig, who had by this time become leader of the militant Vanguard movement, called for a two-day general strike in retaliation for the imposition of direct rule from Westminster. The strike call was highly effective because electricity cuts were imposed by the power-station workers, forcing even those opposed to the stoppage to cease work. Craig and his cohorts learned an important lesson from this episode which they were later to deploy with devastating effect. A large crowd converged on the Stormont grounds to hear Faulkner and other newly redundant unionist politicians denounce Heath and Whitelaw. The crumbling relationship between the unionists and the Conservatives was finally shattered. Unionism was shell-shocked at the loss of Stormont and all the power and patronage vested in it. For the first time the party was out of power and out in the cold. From our point of view the conditions were just what we needed for a new political start.

The blocks in our way remained immense, however. The existence of internment was still the major obstacle. Ever more dreadful violence continued, numbing our capacity to be shocked any more, forcing us to run a constant gauntlet of fear and despair. In the aftermath of the loyalist-inspired strike, sectarian trouble spread like an epidemic through the workforces in many Belfast firms. The Harland and Wolff shipyard, a traditional hotbed of sectarian feeling, employed only about 200 Catholics among its 10,000 workforce. The terrible excesses of bouts of trouble over the previous hundred years had been avoided since 1969, thanks to inspired leadership by trade unionists such as Sandy Scott, but now, for the fourth time since July 1970 the loyalists chased the few Catholics out of the yard again. This time they had been so thoroughly frightened they refused to go back. Young female Catholic stitchers were also forced away from their sewing machines at the textile factories in the Donegall Road area.

Elsewhere tribal polarisation in workplaces and housing areas set in, as hard as concrete. In Derry, the Provos had barricaded the Bogside and Creggan areas off from the rest of the city, creating a no-go area which was patrolled by armed men in Balaclava masks. In the Catholic areas of Belfast, vigilantes roamed as the soldiers and police patrolled tentatively. Tension was at an all-time high as loyalist sectarian assassins prowled the streets at night looking for victims. The city was deserted at 6 p.m. every night as people rushed home and stayed there. The pubs and cinemas closed, the buses stopped and every dawn was greeted with relief, except by the relatives of the night's victims. Every day, both at home and at the SDLP office at College Square North, brought its own tragic procession of people suffering hardship and tragedy from all the upheaval. Into my already busy life, as the death toll steadily mounted, had to be fitted the emotional burden of attending countless funerals.

We had put our opening political position on the record in a lengthy statement on Saturday 25 March 1972. 'We ask those engaged in the campaign of violence to cease immediately in order to enable us to bring internment to a speedy end and in order to make a positive response to the British government's proposals. We also ask for an immediate cessation of political arrests by the British Army and RUC.'

Recognising that there was a heaven-sent political opportunity to be seized and that this was no time for nationalist triumphalism, we made a direct appeal to those we described as 'our Protestant fellow citizens who differ from us politically. We do not regard our political achievements as a victory over you. Rather do we regard them as steps forward and an opportunity for us all . . . we recognise that many of you may feel isolated in the present circumstances. You are not. You are our fellow-countrymen and we are yours. Together a great opportunity awaits us. We ask you to join with us in meeting the challenge.'

We were encouraged by the fact that one of Whitelaw's first responses on arrival in Belfast was an undertaking to review the case against every individual internee. On 7 April he released 73 men in a clear sign of good faith, although another 728 were still in custody. By the beginning of May, when over 150 people had been freed and more releases were promised, we felt that the time was ripe to put real pressure on the Provos to stop their violence. If that could be achieved it was highly probable the loyalists would stop too. They had become increasingly restive since direct rule and on successive weekends had been holding rallies at which William Craig 'inspected' hundreds of men, wearing military clothing, formed up in ranks. An end to violence and all sorts of belligerence would clear the way for a major political initiative.

From our various contacts, Hume and I gleaned all we could about precisely where the Provos stood and what they might settle for to call a permanent ceasefire. Their terms were publicly spelled out by Seán Mac Stiofáin, the chief of staff, at a press conference behind the barricades in Free Derry on 13 June. Basically the Provos wanted the British to withdraw from Northern Ireland and let the Irish people decide how they would then be governed. He offered a seven-day ceasefire if the British

Army ended arrests, halted searches and stopped 'harassing' the civilian population. Mac Stiofáin, who was English-born, invited Whitelaw to Derry to discuss the proposals face to face.

Whitelaw promptly replied that he would not respond to what he called an ultimatum from terrorists, but from what we knew the Provos were serious and we felt we should try to pick up the ball and run with it. It was necessary before doing anything to reach an understanding with Whitelaw, so a private meeting with him was hastily arranged through officials. The meeting took place in London two days later, in the afternoon of Thursday 15 June, with John Hume and myself on one side and Whitelaw, with his senior officials, Sir William Nield and Philip Woodfield, on the other. It was our first formal meeting with Whitelaw, whom I found to be a big genial man who used his disarming laughter as part of his political equipment. The meeting concentrated upon the obstacles holding back real talks between ourselves, as a party, and the Northern Ireland secretary. At first the meeting was intense and formal but when I removed my jacket, Whitelaw followed suit and we settled down to a highly productive encounter.

Whitelaw indicated that the total ending of internment could only follow after two weeks clear of violence. With the release of about 150 internees in the week before the meeting, there were by now only some 400 men still in custody. A future amnesty for those convicted of offences arising from the Troubles, people who would not have been in jail in any other society, was also discussed at length and, significantly, not ruled out. The question of granting these prisoners political status in the meantime, to distinguish them from ordinary criminals, was raised, especially in the light of the hunger strike to back this demand which had started at the Crumlin Road prison in mid-May. Whitelaw also indicated that he was prepared to meet the Provos to discuss their policies, but not while their campaign of violence was still being waged. None of this was contained in a fairly bald joint statement at the end of the two-hour meeting. By way of amplification, Whitelaw said that if violence ceased the possibility that existed for long-term peace would be greatly extended. He said that he and the security forces would respond to any genuine end of violence.

Confident that we had the makings of a ceasefire deal in our hands, Hume and I flew immediately to Dublin. Our first step that Friday was to meet with the other four founder members of the party to secure their agreement to our initiative. We discussed the situation over a working lunch in the restaurant of the Royal Dublin Hotel and, now further armed with the approval of our colleagues, Hume and I set out to contact the Provo leaders. We had no knowledge of where exactly to find them but after being handed from one emissary to another we were eventually told to drive to a pub in Donegal town. After hanging around there for a time, we were told to go to Hume's house in Derry and wait for a further message. The Provo leadership exists on the run so getting the runaround like this was not unusual. It was also a necessary delay from their point of view to give them time to think out their approach. I was catnapping on the sofa in the early hours of the Saturday morning when a messenger came to take us to a house in the Creggan where we met Daíthí Ó Conaill and Mac Stiofáin. Mac Stiofáin was a volatile individual but Ó Conaill, who had been badly wounded in a gun battle with the RUC during the 1956–62 campaign, was altogether the shrewder and more able of the two. We first explained our mission, Whitelaw's words and assurances, and then we faced questions about them. Later that Saturday morning we went back to Belfast to report to Whitelaw on our talks.

This unpublicised Saturday meeting with him was highly successful. He agreed to create a 'special category' section for convicted prisoners at Long Kesh, which was from then on to be known as the Maze prison. He agreed to the request from the Provos that he release a young internee from Belfast, called Gerry Adams, into my custody and provide letters of safe conduct to enable the Provos to make arrangements for a ceasefire that now seemed inevitable. Most dramatically of all, Whitelaw said that he was prepared to meet the Provos face to face to discuss their policies on the future of the North. It was even suggested that he would have a preliminary meeting with the republican leaders at a private house, near Derry, belonging to a close relative of his, before flying them out to London for a meeting with the representatives of the British government. After discussion of the political risks involved it was decided that Steele and Woodfield, the two officials who were senior enough to take decisions, would participate in this preliminary encounter.

Over the weekend, in an estate car lent to me by the Provos, I rounded up a number of men who were either 'wanted', as the British Army would have said, or 'on the run', as the Provos would have put it, and brought them to Belfast under the protection of the letters of safe conduct provided for me by the Northern Ireland Office and the army. They stated that I was an MP who was not to be obstructed or interfered with in any way. There was another meeting with Whitelaw that Monday afternoon at which more details of the ceasefire package were discussed, including the immediate introduction of special category. During the day Adams was among fourteen internees released, the others freed to conceal the significance of his release. By that evening in our house at Shaw's Road we had staying with us Adams and Frank McGuigan, the first man ever to have escaped from Long Kesh (he dressed as a priest). Theresa gave them keys to the house, so that they could come and go to meetings. She was always annoyed that the keys were never given back.

Late that night the whole deal very nearly unravelled when I was told that Billy McKee, the leader of the IRA convicted prisoners on hunger strike for political status, had been taken to hospital. I discovered that the governor and staff at the prison were standing by with hot soup and milk for the striking prisoners, waiting to be told officially of the agreement reached with Whitelaw. But Whitelaw's deputy, Lord Windlesham, in my view showing an appalling degree of callousness, had not communicated the information to the governor or the prisoners. I started a telephonic bombardment of the Northern Ireland Office, finally getting Whitelaw himself out of bed in the early hours, after I failed to get Windlesham to take immediate action to end the strike. Whitelaw gave the required order and medical staff moved in to feed and examine the strikers.

With what amounted to political status safely achieved – the prisoners could wear their own clothes and receive more privileges than conventional criminals – the ceasefire efforts were fully back on course. On the Tuesday morning there was a big meeting of the IRA leadership in Belfast, which my 'guests' all attended, and afterwards we set off for Derry, again using the safe conducts. The army had been ordered to clear the route, we were told, and we had an uneventful journey except for the fact that one of the IRA group complained I was driving too fast. 'Do you think you're escaping from an operation?' he asked.

Later that day the IRA leaders met Whitelaw's two officials at the house belonging to his relative and the two sides exchanged position statements. Some forty-eight hours later, in a statement issued in Dublin, the IRA announced a ceasefire with effect from midnight, Monday 26 June. Whitelaw promised to reciprocate once offensive operations by the IRA ceased. Brian Faulkner, who had lined up with the more extreme unionists after direct rule, remarked that the ceasefire had come 379 lives, 1,682 explosions and 7,258 injuries too late. Determined to show that the ceasefire was not a sign of weakness, the IRA kept the violence going until the deadline. Five soldiers and a policeman were murdered, there were nearly fifty explosions and a wave of armed robberies which netted the considerable sum of £55,000 in Belfast on the Friday alone. In a particularly grim episode, one of the soldiers was shot dead in east Belfast, only a few minutes before the ceasefire came into effect.

Although the violence stopped and IRA leaders in the city pledged the ceasefire would be observed, all was not well within the ranks in Belfast. The old-guard leaders like Seamus Twomey and his friends in Andersonstown were critical right from scratch, and felt affronted that Dublin had gone over their heads by bringing in Gerry Adams. They felt that they were older, wiser and had more experience than Adams who, they believed, had lost his rank by being interned and should not have been included. This rampant jealousy amongst the Belfast leaders was running like a sore when Whitelaw laid on an RAF aircraft and flew the IRA leadership to London for his promised face-to-face meeting on Friday 7 July. With increasing breaches of the ceasefire being reported in Belfast I believe the Belfast faction was waiting to destroy the ceasefire at the earliest suitable opportunity. While the leaders were in London, events that would bring the ceasefire to an end were already under way back at home.

For the previous week there had been growing tension at Horn Drive, which marked the boundary between the Protestant Suffolk area and the Catholic Lenadoon estate. A dispute had arisen over the re-allocation of a number of empty houses earlier abandoned by Protestants, who had either been intimidated out or had fled after being pinned down in the regular crossfire between Provo snipers and their military targets. Plans to move Catholic families in were halted by the army after the loyalist UDA threatened to burn out the new occupants. The Provos said that if the army did not back down they would move the families in themselves on Sunday 9 July. The issue was put on hold while Twomey went off to London but on the Saturday, upon his return, he and his functionaries resumed the brinkmanship. The army refused to budge so the next afternoon the Provos provoked a confrontation. As soon as soldiers halted a quarry lorry, piled up with the furniture of one of the Catholic families, stones began to fly and within minutes gunshots rang out bringing the ceasefire to an end. I have no doubt the

Provisionals exploited the incident to engineer that outcome. Had they been genuinely interested in rehousing the families, they could have waited until the Housing Executive prepared the ground and moved them into the vacant houses by proper allocation. Since it had been set up in 1971, the executive had earned an excellent reputation for fair housing allocations and its officers were working very hard to resolve the problem that had developed.

The violence resumed that Sunday evening with a vengeance. Explosions and shooting incidents erupted all over the North. Ten people lost their lives and another 1,500 refugees flocked across the border. There were efforts by a number of people to try and save the ceasefire but the true level of the cynicism, viciousness and empty-headedness of the Belfast Provos was exposed on 21 July. During that afternoon they planted twenty-two vehicle bombs at various locations throughout Belfast. All exploded within a forty-five minute period, killing nine people and injuring hundreds of others. It was not for nothing that the day has become known as 'Bloody Friday'.

I was in Dublin when I heard about the atrocity. In my anger I could not comprehend the logic of the Provo mind, which aspired to be the democratic government of the North while bombing into oblivion the innocent citizens of Belfast. After this savagery Whitelaw abandoned conciliation and ordered the army strength in the North up to 20,000. Over the next ten days hundreds of armoured vehicles were shipped into Belfast and thousands of troops arrived by air. During the night long convoys travelled to action stations along the border and virtually every town and village. In the early hours of 31 July the army tore down the barricades around the no-go area in Derry and swamped the streets of the city with patrols in a move called 'Operation Motorman'. In Belfast, too, no-go areas were being taken over and the city centre was sealed off with a cordon to thwart any further bombings, and massive forts and observation towers were built as the army moved as never before to dominate the North, in both republican and loyalist strongholds.

On Tuesday 1 August we gathered at the Inter-County Hotel in Lifford to talk through the shape of the political response the SDLP must now make. First, though, we discussed the impact of the huge military operation. As we compared notes it was evident just how much we all strongly resented the increased militarisation, but we knew that any public criticisms we made would only play into the hands of the Provos. So we issued a statement praising the community's calm response to what was in reality a military invasion of the Catholic areas and said: 'In the present situation restraint and silence are the best expressions of resentment.'

The breakdown of talks with the Provos was a salutary lesson for us in the SDLP, for it showed that the IRA was incapable of engaging in the political process. Their agenda was shrouded in historical myths no longer relevant; their demands were unrealistic and their attitudes were sectarian and unbending. The calibre of the leading personalities was also seriously deficient. They spoke a language and subscribed to values that hadn't changed in fifty years. Given the violent horrors they had unleashed on the community, they were clearly not fit for public office. Although we were still hog-tied by the continued existence of internment, we were in a newly advantageous position in that we could move for political progress without having to take the Provos into account. Indeed the more we distanced ourselves from their futile and murderous activities the better.

Our deliberations in Lifford were interrupted by a dramatic telephone call from George Colley, Jack Lynch's deputy, to Ivan Cooper, calling us to Dublin for urgent, unspecified consultations. We were told no more than that an Irish defence forces helicopter was being dispatched to collect us. Some time later the aircraft arrived, touched down in the hotel car park and whisked John Hume, Ivan Cooper and myself off to Dublin. We were met at Baldonnel airfield and driven to the Department of Foreign Affairs in St Stephen's Green, where Colley and Dr

Paddy Hillery, the Minister for Foreign Affairs, were waiting. Austin Currie then joined us.

The discussion that followed lasted until very late that night and most certainly did not justify the mystery generated by the helicopter flight. It covered the implications of the military operation in the North, the ongoing consultations between the Lynch and Heath administrations and our common interest in the efforts to create political movement. The Lynch government was in some domestic political trouble at the time and was facing a testing by-election in Mid Cork. I was sure we were being used as pawns by the Fianna Fáil party. Ever since the 1969 arms scandal, when members of his cabinet were fired after being implicated in an alleged plot to smuggle arms into the North for the Provos, Lynch had been sensitive to criticism and so it was to his advantage to be seen to be backing the beleaguered nationalists in the North. The ploy worked and he later won the election, but I was steaming about the way we were dragged to the Dublin meeting and did not mince my words about the phony pretext. To placate me, cars were provided to ferry us back to Lifford through the night to resume our own discussions.

Despite pursuing military objectives, Heath and Whitelaw had not flinched in their determination to restore some form of conventional local politics. The day after our Dublin trip Whitelaw publicly asked us to come and see him a few days later, on Monday 7 August. We accepted. The encounter took place at Laneside, a secluded villa on the south shore of Belfast Lough, near Holywood, which the British government had set up as a clandestine listening post even before the Stormont parliament had been stood down. This meeting marked the start of the most important and fruitful phase of my entire career in public and political life. At long last we were able to get down to working out political arrangements more appropriate to the latter half of the twentieth century than the disastrous compromise of the 1920s.

The resumption of the Provos' bombing campaign upset the

understanding we had had with Whitelaw over releasing the internees. More people had actually been lifted since Motorman. We first explained to him that we could not enter any new political arrangement while innocent men were interned without trial. Before doing anything, we in the SDLP had to be mollified on the internment issue and in such a way as not to give any offence to the Protestant community, who saw our demand as nothing more than fellow-travelling with the Provos. Whitelaw, obviously well aware of our position, outlined a proposal to bring in tribunals which would be presided over by three judges and have no juries. Internees would appear before the tribunal to demonstrate their innocence. We instantly opposed this system, for it reversed the basic concept that all accused persons were innocent until proven guilty. At a time when it was one of our fundamental objectives to reverse years of injustice, we could not condone or defend such a blatant device, which would corrode universally accepted standards of justice even more. But strong as our objection to internment was, it really served as an excuse for us to remain on what we saw as the political high ground. We felt that we held the whip-hand in the situation and that by holding out we could minimise the concessions we would have to make and maximise the gains.

A few days after this meeting Whitelaw wrote to all the seven parties represented in the former Stormont parliament, inviting them to a round table conference on 25–7 September to talk about future political structures. The venue was later announced to be in Darlington. Through follow-up meetings, usually with officials, we communicated our uncompromising line to Whitelaw. In a bid to draw us to the conference we were offered a meeting with Heath. This took place at Chequers on 12 September. We flew to London and were brought to Chequers in limousines that Mafia chiefs would have been proud to occupy. We were brought into a large room and sat down along one side of a magnificent long table. Heath came in and sat in isolation opposite us. He was very relaxed. We had carefully rehearsed the order and contribution each of us would make to the discussion, ending up with Gerry Fitt, so we started off as planned, droning on about the evils of internment. Heath watched and listened intently. After the third hour the female service personnel who staff the British prime minister's country residence brought in tea and several plates of hot scones.

At the end of our first round of speeches Heath remained silent, and we were each forced to speak again. He knew our strategy – who was to speak and what was to be said – because our party headquarters had been bugged by the military. He continued to peer at each speaker. I was feeling quite hungry by now and, as I had been speaking when the scones were brought in, I had got none of them. I noticed that another plate of scones near Heath was untouched, so I stood up, leaned over, glowered at him, and said: 'Well, if we're not getting anything on internment, I'll have some of your scones.' Heath burst out laughing and pulled his chair back from the table as he roared aloud. The meeting took a turn for the better and although Heath sent clear signals that radical political concessions were on offer, he emphasised there could be no immediate ending of internment.

That meeting sealed our intention to boycott Whitelaw's conference. After Chequers we went off to a hotel at Gweedore, on the wild Atlantic coastline of Co. Donegal, for another deep examination of the options facing us. Much of my thinking was done walking along the shore in the early morning in the bracing sea air. The peace and tranquillity were light years away from the perpetual turmoil at home and I yearned to find a way out of the blood-soaked tragedy in which we were all involved. By now several guiding principles had emerged from our thoughts. We would continue to work to eliminate the religious divide. We would use the democratic route as a means to achieve our political ends. Any new political structure must be underpinned by agreement on security powers and shared responsibility. A coalition arrangement within a form of devolution seemed to be the way forward. Consensus politics and a sensitive regard for minorities were essential requirements for the successful application of our new proposals.

We had received a handwritten paper from Paddy Lane, a Belfast surgeon, on the merits of a condominium arrangement, with Britain and the Irish republic assuming joint authority over Northern Ireland. It was a practical concept he had witnessed at work in the former British Empire. Desmond Fennell, a freelance writer from Galway, was also an advocate of this idea and he came to Donegal to meet Ivan Cooper and myself to explain the idea more fully. After a weekend of talks, which involved all six of us, it was decided to issue a lengthy political blueprint, which I first drafted with Ivan Cooper. After line by line debate, and helpful amendment by our colleagues, we headed the document 'Towards a New Ireland'. Its basic thesis was that Northern Ireland should be controlled by the British and Irish governments as an interim arrangement until there was consent to full Irish unity. Hume had drafted the final version.

The document called for a declaration by Britain that it would be in the best interests of all the people in the British Isles if Ireland were to become united on terms acceptable to the entire population, north and south, and that this objective would be positively encouraged. We proposed an inter-governmental treaty accepting joint interim responsibility for the administration of Northern Ireland, reserving to both governments all powers of security, defence, policing, foreign affairs and finance. The SDLP further proposed a fifty-member all-Ireland senate with equal representation from the North and the South to plan the integration of the whole island and the harmonisation of structures, laws and services. Interim local administration in Northern Ireland was to be carried out through two commissioners, with an eighty-four-member assembly elected by proportional representation. The assembly members would elect a fifteen-strong executive, who in turn would choose the chief executive, with responsibility for allocating departmental posts. Legislation passed by this assembly would be underpinned by both the Irish and British legislatures, while all constitutional matters which were in deadlock could be referred to a court of three judges – two appointed by the commissioners, and the Lord Chief Justice of Northern Ireland. Under these arrangements the union flag and the tricolour would have equal status and be flown side by side on all public occasions. There would also be a Northern Ireland flag. We proposed that the seats for Northern Ireland MPs at Westminster should be abolished and none created in Dáil Éireann. Finance for Northern Ireland would be provided by London and Dublin, in proportion to each country's gross national product, with provision for annual review. The plan also stressed the need to provide an acceptable system of security and policing, which would ensure an effective end to political violence.

There were many merits in our proposals. They would enable us to finally shed the shackles which the Provos had steadily placed on our arms and legs by their violence. Such a radical set of ideas addressed directly, for the first time, the fears of the Protestant population. They brought us back to democratic exchanges through the ballot box and a political forum – providing a way round the military impasse. There really was something for everyone in there and it could be enlarged upon because the ideas were mainly of an interim nature. We realised only too well that the longer the stalemate lasted, the more the mainstream political parties became irrelevant. During the recent Provo ceasefire we had been alarmed to find that the public were fickle enough to support the Provos merely from relief at the ending of the violence.

Our document was published on 20 September 1972, with simultaneous press conferences in Belfast and Dublin. In the following days Heath wrote to Gerry Fitt pushing us to attend the conference. The government had commandeered a new hotel, the Blackwell Grange, for the purpose. Our strategy was now fixed and, again citing internment as the reason, we declined the renewed invitation. In reality we were on something of a high, for we were sure our document would monopolise the conference discussions and, in our absence, the other parties would be locked into our agenda. When the conference opened, only three of the seven eligible parties turned up: the unionists, the NILP and the newly formed moderate Alliance Party. We felt our decision not to attend was fully vindicated at the end of the first day, when Bob Cooper, the deputy leader of Alliance, said that what they had learned was that the unionists had learned nothing.

Putting a brave face on the continued deadlock, Whitelaw stated at the conclusion of the three-day conference that all policy statements, including ours, would be included in a government Green Paper to be published shortly. Whitelaw's peacemaking efforts suffered another major setback a few weeks later when he was forced to postpone to the spring of 1973 elections for a string of re-organised district councils. That autumn the loyalists engaged in another workers' strike, which they enforced by power cuts, and clashed with the security forces. After that they threatened to boycott the council poll, causing Whitelaw to back down rather than risk an electoral fiasco with much more serious repercussions.

One person who did not like our proposals for a new Ireland was my old acquaintance Dr Conor Cruise O'Brien, the Irish Labour Party spokesman for northern affairs. Soon after they were published he stated that they were a formula for civil war and that to seek any support for them would lead to an uncontrollable escalation of violence. Largely because of his attitude, the parliamentary Irish Labour Party did not endorse the SDLP statement. I was incensed by this behaviour and felt badly let down by it, so I wrote an open letter to the Irish Labour leader, Brendan Corish, pointing out that criticism had been made of our statement in public while the Irish Labour Party were planning a meeting to discuss its contents.

A meeting with Irish Labour Party members was promptly arranged, but it was characterised by vitriolic exchanges from the start. David Thornley backed me strongly, but Conor Cruise O'Brien and Frank Cluskey were deeply critical. By the end of the encounter we were on our feet shouting and gesticulating at one another. It was the start of a bad patch in my relationship with Conor Cruise O'Brien, which I regretted very much for I greatly admired his integrity, scholarship and courage. We repaired the damage some years later when he asked me to call on him at Queen's University where he was lecturing, and we have remained on the best of terms ever since. A final meeting on 18 October 1972 restored nominal harmony between the SDLP and the Irish Labour Party, although for years afterwards when I went south to help them at election times, none of the others from the SDLP ever did.

Whitelaw's Green Paper, designed to stimulate further political discussion, was published at the end of October. It incorporated the position papers of all the parties, including our own. The most notable development was Whitelaw's decision to hold a plebiscite among the Northern Ireland people on the future of the border early in 1973. All involved had their say about it in the round of radio and television analysis programmes and in the newspapers, but we all knew that the outcome of the border poll was a foregone conclusion and that the political horse-trading would have to take place anyway.

Heath underlined his personal commitment to Whitelaw's indefatigable efforts with a two-day visit to the North in mid-November and another meeting with Jack Lynch in London shortly after his return. Our strategy was endorsed at a full party conference in Dungiven at the end of the month. Around this time I was involved in a behind-the-scenes crackdown on the people responsible for a dreadful series of tit-for-tat sectarian murders. To date there had been 106 such killings, claiming 70 Catholic and 36 Protestant victims. On 6 December, Whitelaw announced that a specially formed 'murder squad', consisting of police and soldiers, would work in the areas where the killings were at their worst. The year 1972 ended with the political deadlock apparently as solid as ever. The death toll for the year reached 467, bringing to 678 the number of victims since 1969. As I took stock of the situation over the Christmas and New Year period the enormity of the loss of life in the year just past sickened me to the bones.

In the early part of 1973 we realised we would shortly face three crucial polls, our first as a party. Apart from our policy discussions we now had to concentrate on raising money and building up a party organisation to meet the electoral challenge. There was little point in producing fine political blueprints and policies if we could not attract support and get ourselves elected. One priority was to appoint local election agents to keep the electoral register up to date. That meant registering all new voters when they came of age and keeping tabs on voters who died or moved into and out of any area.

We decided at this stage that any of our candidates elected to a new Stormont assembly must be prepared to be full-time representatives. It followed, therefore, that we had to take steps to see they were politically astute, schooled in the ways of fighting elections and participating in parliament, in addition to being well informed about the range of issues they would have to handle. We set up a week-long seminar in Donegal for our prospective candidates and arranged for an economist and a constitutional lawyer, among others, to lecture them on a range of appropriate subjects.

Party membership had increased steadily throughout 1972 but for some reason a disproportionate number of them were educationalists, mainly teachers. They vastly outnumbered the next largest group who were businessmen. Few of those who joined up had political experience. They appeared out of the blue as though a hidden hand had moved them to join, to secure nomination and to be eventually elected. I could not help thinking that many of those who appeared were inspired by Catholic groupings, such as the Knights of Columbanus. In the rural areas many of them had links with the old Nationalist Party election machine, which overlapped with the local Catholic parish structure.

We had a lot to do to instil Labour values into our new recruits. It was to be a hard job. Some of the teachers were particularly strident, and most of the members were far too instinctively nationalist for my taste. To speed up the process of their political education we decided to prepare briefing papers on the subjects that they would have to deal with: health, social services, education, economy, transport, agriculture, law and order, development, environment and law reform.

We gathered up research material and John Hume and I took off to Dublin. Our plan was to go to the Burlington Hotel where we would work for forty-eight hours to have the papers ready for the training week. We booked into one of the large suites, pulled the curtains across the windows and commenced work, stopping only for food and sleep. On the first morning we sensed that the hotel was unusually quiet. I looked out the window and found the front of the hotel cleared and the entire staff, chefs, waitresses, porters and so on, standing across the road. There were soldiers gathered around an old banger in the car park. The crowd saw us at the window and shouted to get out quick. We dashed downstairs and ran out.

'What's wrong?' I asked.

'That old banger from the North has a bomb in it,' I was told. 'They are going to blow it up.'

I suddenly realised it was my car they were talking about. 'Hey, that's my car. There's no bomb in there. Leave it or I'll never get home.'

The all-clear was quickly given and the crowd and staff slowly returned to the hotel. P.V. Doyle, the hotel owner, came over after looking at my car in disgust. 'They say there's a lot of political graft in northern politics but it's easy to see that you're not

190

part of it,' he said.

The first of the three polls we faced was the referendum on the border which Whitelaw had fixed for 8 March. Special arrangements were made for every eligible citizen who wished to avoid intimidation at polling stations and vote by post. Fearing that postal votes could easily be abused or stolen, we told our supporters to apply for their votes but not use them. We took the view that the border referendum, which Whitelaw had designed to reassure the unionists about their position within the United Kingdom, was an irrelevance to the real problems facing us. There was no doubt about the result, which would only serve to undermine the efforts we considered vital to encourage the unionists to examine the Irish dimension. Britain now conceded that this was an important element in the political process.

Some of us in the SDLP, but not the more nationalist-minded, still gave a high priority to having a party philosophy that would accommodate progressive Protestants. It was an unlikely prospect but nevertheless an important principle. In pursuit of it we placed a full-page advertisement in the *News Letter* on 5 March 1973, in advance of the border poll. It was a mould-breaking gesture. Political advertising was normally confined to papers which championed either the unionist or nationalist cause. By putting our case directly to unionist readers we had therefore demonstrated our willingness to reach across the divide. Indeed, at this time we were engaged in regular informal dialogue with people of all shades of unionist/loyalist opinion. For instance, from my trade union days I had many lines open to individuals who had become involved in organisations like the Ulster Defence Association. The party leadership in fact encouraged such contacts, which we believed could only contribute beneficially to greater understanding and confidence.

When the predictable referendum result was declared, 591,820 people had voted for Northern Ireland to remain within the United Kingdom. That was a decisive 57.4 per cent of the 1,030,084 entitled to vote. A mere 6,463 votes were cast for a united Ireland. Only 59 per cent of the electorate turned out, indicating massive support for our boycott. As Gerry Fitt said, the exercise merely told us that there were more Protestants than Catholics and more unionists than nationalists, facts we knew already.

At this time of frenetic political activity, the British government trawled the civil service for its best and brightest to do the demanding staff work for Whitelaw. None was to have a greater impact than Frank Cooper, who became the permanent under-secretary at Stormont Castle, the most senior civil servant and effectively Whitelaw's right-hand man. A short, stocky man with a slight speech impediment, Cooper had the classic background for a senior British mandarin: Manchester Grammar, Oxford, RAF pilot in the Second World War, then a rapid ascent of the ranks in the Air Ministry and the Ministry of Defence. He was a very experienced and astute negotiator. We learned from one of his colleagues, probably very deliberately to influence us, that when Britain was trying to settle the Cyprus problem he held over one hundred meetings with Archbishop Makarios to hammer out a formula for independence. We found out quickly just what a tough operator he was, with a capacity to chill any opposition by logic. I remember his cold reply in response to our fears about the safety of RUC personnel in a certain situation: 'Never mind. That is what they are paid for.'

As the political discussions intensified I witnessed at first hand the ploys and machinations of these clever civil servants at work. When they hit a problem or an obstacle they adopted a quiet but ruthless subtlety. One of their most effective tactics was to require each party to define their actual position in writing. They would then question the party and rewrite their paper for what they called 'better understanding'. But, in doing so, hey presto, there was actually no difference at all. What a wonderfully uncomplicated world they made it all seem!

To those of us most closely involved, their fingerprints and tactics could be clearly seen when the British government finally issued its White Paper on 20 March. Under the British political system future legislation is researched by officials and a Green Paper, or discussion paper, is produced. After consultations with interested parties comes the White Paper, which is a statement of intent, but not a binding one, of what the actual legislation presented to parliament for final amendment and approval will say. The Northern Ireland White Paper provided for an elected assembly of seventy-eight members elected by proportional representation. The chairmen of departmental committees would form the executive and a Council of Ireland would be set up. The Secretary of State would replace the governor and the Northern Ireland Privy Council was to be abolished. Westminster reserved for itself the control of all finance and security matters.

A couple of days later, having chewed over the implications, the party gave the formula a cautious welcome. I found the proposals highly promising, in that many of the ideas in our 'Towards a New Ireland' document had been directly taken on board. I thought that, given a real chance to try them out in office, our traditional sectarian tension and social division could at last be replaced by something worthwhile. The party also signalled at this stage that it would be fighting the Assembly election, taking its seats and working to end internment and achieve a political settlement by peaceful means. The Provos reacted stridently, calling for a boycott and British withdrawal from the North, which reflected the continued sterility of their thinking.

The White Paper proposals had a decisive effect on the power-play within unionism, forcing the hardline loyalists, led by Bill Craig, to break away from the mainline unionists, who reluctantly remained behind Brian Faulkner for the time being.

Almost immediately, however, attention switched to the postponed local government elections, now due on 30 May. With 526 seats available on 26 newly structured district councils, we faced our first major electoral test and came through it with flying colours, getting 83 of our 166 candidates elected; this made us the largest single party after the unionists. Among our new councillors was Dr Raymond McClean, who was unanimously elected mayor at the first meeting of Derry District Council soon afterwards, only the second Catholic to hold the office in that city's long history. This was just the springboard we needed for the crucial Assembly elections fixed for 28 June.

The SDLP fielded 28 candidates in this contest, out of a total of 210 people chasing 78 seats in twelve constituencies. We produced a manifesto entitled 'A New North – A New Ireland', fleshing out in more detail our ideas on topics such as the economy, ending discrimination and restoring effective policing. On the evening of Monday 25 June, with polling due on the Thursday, we held a final organisation meeting at the College Square North office. It was about mundane matters: taxis and cars to ferry people to the polling stations, eve of poll advertisements in the papers, manning polling stations to watch out for personation. The work finished at about 10 p.m. and, as I headed off home, the others went to McGlade's Bar in Donegall Street for a much-needed drink. These were unarguably dangerous days for all of us and we were constantly warning each other to be careful. Senator Paddy Wilson, Gerry's indispensable right-hand-man who was acting as his election agent, bumped into some friends in the bar. Paddy was notably inoffensive and easy-going. One day when we had been discussing the threat of assassination he said: 'Sure who would want to do me any harm? I'm not important. I'm everybody's friend.'

Next morning I was horrified to hear on the early radio news that he had been murdered. Paddy left McGlade's with Irene Andrews, one of the friends he had met, and both were abducted at some point while giving her a lift home. Their bodies, lacerated by multiple stab wounds, were discovered at a quarry on the Hightown Road, in the hills above Belfast, after someone representing the Ulster Freedom Fighters rang the

News Letter to claim responsibility. We were all greatly shocked by Paddy's brutal death. He had worked hard for the needy of Belfast, as a senator and councillor, and had played an invaluable role in helping to found and develop the SDLP. The Ulster Freedom Fighters was a *nom de guerre* adopted by the Ulster Defence Association. I had long been concerned at their sponsorship of sectarian assassinations and I called on Whitelaw to outlaw them, just as the IRA were outlawed. Mourning Paddy overshadowed the final stages of the election and when we buried him on election day, it was a forceful reminder of just how much was at stake in reinforcing the democratic process and thwarting the men of violence, on both sides, whose only vision was of a scorched earth dotted with tombstones.

When the Assembly election count was completed on Saturday 30 June we found we had secured a 22 per cent share of first preference votes and had won 19 seats, second only to the largest grouping, the unionist faction led by Brian Faulkner. The most notable feature of the poll was the way that the once solid unionist vote had fragmented. So-called Unpledged Unionists, who did not support Faulkner, won ten seats while the hardline Loyalist Coalition, led by Bill Craig and Ian Paisley, claimed fifteen seats between them. There were three other loyalist victors, eight from the soft unionist Alliance party and one NILP representative. The arithmetic of this outcome showed that if the Faulkner Unionists (22) combined with Alliance (8) and ourselves (19), we could share power, form an Executive and operate the Assembly with a workable majority.

Whitelaw, who had done his own sums over the weekend, wasted no time in calling the party leaders to Stormont on the Monday. The same day, in London, Ted Heath met Liam Cosgrave, the leader of the new Fine Gael–Labour coalition in the republic, who had beaten Jack Lynch's Fianna Fáil in the recent general election. Cosgrave had already signalled a willingness to work with a new administration at Stormont, so the way was now clear for what the *Irish Times* the next day described as the most important Anglo-Irish talks since the successful Treaty negotiations in 1921.

Whitelaw needed the co-operation of the SDLP more than any other party to get his show on the road. Any arrangements in which we did not participate would have no credibility. We knew this and decided to play hardball on the ending of internment when he invited us to meet him again at Stormont Castle, flanked by Cooper and his team. Whitelaw knew our position and promised that he would deliver on internment. On 7 August he advised us that he had set up a review of the cases of each of the current 426 internees under the new emergency security legislation which had just come into effect. (By now there was at least a semblance of even-handedness, in that a dozen or so loyalists had been interned.) The review, of course, held out the prospect of substantial numbers of releases but he kept stalling as the talks progressed, primarily to lock Faulkner's group into support for a power-sharing arrangement. The Alliance Party was no problem. They were prepared to back any deal that Faulkner and ourselves worked out.

The unionist extremists wanted nothing less than the restoration of the old Stormont with their hands exclusively on the levers of power. Craig was jostling with Paisley to be seen as their undisputed leader, but he was sending conflicting signals about what he really wanted. On the one hand he was flirting with those on the wildest fringe of loyalist paramilitary organisations and making belligerent speeches and statements. On the other hand he was making noises about finding common ground with the SDLP. Ivan Cooper and myself met him with John Taylor, a former Faulkner minister who had defected, to explore this possibility. The talks did not lead anywhere and related more to a concealed agenda which, it became quite clear, was only designed to stop us getting together with Faulkner on power-sharing.

Inter-party and inter-government talks continued apace throughout the summer and autumn. Formal inter-party talks between the SDLP, Alliance and Faulkner unionists, convened by Whitelaw, began at Stormont with a seven-hour session on 5 October, a grimly significant day for it was the fifth anniversary of the civil rights march in Derry that had triggered off all the subsequent trouble. The work that Hume and I had done on the detailed position papers at the Burlington paid great dividends at the negotiating table. Our people were better informed, led the discussions and consequently influenced the conclusions quite substantially. Faulkner was much impressed, particularly when he discovered what lengths we had gone to. Four days later we were able to conclude our first and perhaps most important agreement, on the economy. We planned to implement a programme of economic planning which was intended to provide full employment and enable us to put industry into the areas that suffered from the most acute deprivation. Whitelaw promised ample investment capital for local projects and adequate grants for outside industrialists investing in Northern Ireland. There was a strong socialist strand in the programme and I was secretly pleased that it had won the approval of such Conservatives as Whitelaw and Faulkner.

But despite the growing cordiality between us, there was still some sniping. Roy Bradford, one of Faulkner's team, re-opened discussion about the economic plan a week or more after it had been agreed. I found it odd that he should do so because the plan had been accepted not only as the cornerstone of a new start and a new relationship between the unionists and ourselves but as a way of neutralising the Provos and other subversive elements. Economic growth leading to full employment would remove social discontent from the deprived areas which groups like the Provos thrived on. If we could get people into steady, well-paid jobs, we reasoned, they would have little incentive to become bombers or gunmen. Bradford seemed to be trying it on, playing to the gallery in his own party. As events turned out he would rock the boat again. I was angry about this but Faulkner intervened and backed us when we complained.

'It is agreed. That it is the end of it,' he said.

These rare spats apart, the atmosphere became increasingly friendly as the talks progressed. There was a steady growth of mutual support and willingness to work together. We learned that our unionist opponents were basically a decent bunch of well-meaning men, with a great desire to build something of value for the people of the North. I am sure their respect for us also increased at that time. Faulkner consistently displayed an incisive grasp of all the issues and approached every stage of the discussions constructively. A greater degree of tolerance and understanding was in evidence as we sought to meet each other's difficulties. This was a new Faulkner and we traded concessions as a result.

By November we had reached agreement to form and participate in a power-sharing Executive, but our talks became deadlocked on the 6-4-1 formula proposed to share out the seats around the table. We were unhappy at overall control being handed to the Faulkner unionists. They had had twenty-two members elected to the new Assembly, but two had been lost since the election in June. Nat Minford had been appointed to the Speaker's chair in the Assembly and David McCarthy had been killed in a car accident. As Faulkner's grouping in the Assembly was only one stronger than the SDLP delegation, we felt strongly that he was not entitled to two more Executive positions.

On 21 November the three party groups met at Stormont Castle to try to finally resolve the matter. Whitelaw and his officials shuttled between the three rooms where we were positioned, and delegates from the three parties talked in a bid to resolve the dispute. The SDLP adopted an uncompromising stance on the issue and refused to budge. We knew that everybody was up against a deadline, for Whitelaw was due to see Heath that evening to brief him, before a debate about Northern Ireland in the House of Commons in London the next day. It was a question of who would blink first and we were determined it would not be us. Whitelaw's departure was postponed several times that day as various ideas to break the deadlock were produced and tested on us without success.

After ten hours he finally decided to issue an ultimatum. The helicopter pilot waiting outside was instructed to turn on the engine and prepare for take-off. As the rotors clattered into motion and then whirred impatiently, the SDLP expressed its satisfaction with what was now on the table. It had been decided that four additional ministerial posts, outside the Executive, would be created; these posts were shared out, with two for us and one each for Alliance and the unionists. The unionists, who were well and truly against the wall, accepted. As Whitelaw flew out in triumph, the historic decision was announced. There would be a power-sharing administration of fifteen ministers – seven unionists, six SDLP and two Alliance. Brian Faulkner was to be chief executive and Gerry Fitt his deputy. Of the eleven posts in the Executive, six would be allocated to Faulkner unionists, four to the SDLP and one to Oliver Napier, leader of the Alliance Party. This was an improved position for us and allowed Faulkner to keep overall control of the Executive.

Some of the last minute haggling had centred on the allocation of the various departments. Faulkner had strongly insisted on getting the Finance portfolio, which we made a token bid for but did not vigorously contest. The job would have been John Hume's and, if he had really wanted it, I am sure we could have forced the issue. Instead Hume set his sights on the Department of Commerce, where the prime task was to stimulate the economy by promoting investment and employment. Dr Garret FitzGerald, however, sent me a note by courier, in the final stages of the talks, saying that we were wrong. 'We are convinced that you are totally wrong in not going for and getting Finance. We know that Finance in the North will be quite different from in London or in Dublin, but we also know with all the experience of government that even in its limited Northern

Ireland role, it will be immensely important because of the restricted but nevertheless important powers of allocation of resources and the right to veto expenditure in any area, which will exist as fully in your system as in ours. We know that London shares this conviction and they cannot understand why you should make this mistake.' We reviewed our attitude in the light of this advice. I pointed out that the man who pulls the purse strings holds the power but Hume was steadfast, clearly judging that the potential political advantages in Commerce were substantially greater than in Finance.

The final line-up of the Executive and administration was agreed as follows: Brian Faulkner, unionist, chief executive; Gerry Fitt, SDLP, deputy chief executive. The other unionist office-holders were: John Baxter, Information; Roy Bradford, Environment; Herbie Kirk, Finance; Basil McIvor, Education; and Leslie Morrell, Agriculture. Robert Lloyd Hall-Thompson was chief whip, outside the Executive.

Our appointments were: Austin Currie, Housing, Local Government and Planning; John Hume, Commerce; and myself, Health and Social Services. The non-Executive posts were: Ivan Cooper, Community Relations; and Eddie McGrady, Planning and Co-ordination. The Alliance appointments were party leader Oliver Napier, to be responsible for Legal Affairs and Law Reform, with Bob Cooper, outside the Executive, in charge of Manpower Services.

Although things had moved along smoothly at Stormont Castle, there was most certainly a different mood further up the hill at Parliament Buildings. A disorderly, confrontational atmosphere had steadily developed ever since the Assembly had met for the first time on 31 July. Nat Minford was elected Speaker and an all-party committee was appointed to draw up standing orders. The subsequent debates about standing orders themselves became occasions of disorder and, in the absence of rules, the Speaker was largely powerless. Recent heart surgery aggravated his impotence and the extremists knew it. We were greatly disadvantaged because we expected Nat, who was not without courage or integrity, to stand up to them. He had, for instance, severed his connections with the Orange Order on appointment to the chair as a signal that he was going to be impartial. When the report of the Standing Orders Committee was voted on in the Assembly in early November some of Faulkner's supporters voted against our multi-party Assembly majority, a gesture we found most discouraging.

We were also appalled to discover that the standing orders omitted to give the Speaker power to name and suspend a member who was constantly out of order. This allowed any member who physically assaulted another to come and go from the chamber without hindrance. Once we came into office we introduced a new set of remedial amendments, but in the meantime the community must have been highly disillusioned as the newspapers, radio and television reported on the repeatedly riotous scenes in the Assembly. The parties concerned were: the Unpledged Unionists, led by Harry West; Vanguard, led by William Craig; and Ian Paisley's Democratic Unionists. They later formed themselves into the United Ulster Unionist Council.

It was clear that additional support was coming to them outside the chamber from organisations affiliated to the Orange Order, which was traditionally and fundamentally opposed to association with Catholics. Power-sharing with the SDLP was the type of issue it was best suited to exploit. The disturbances reached a new peak once news of the formation of the Executive-designate emerged. On 28 November the Speaker had to adjourn the sitting twice because of 'grave disorder' and then abandon it. The unionist extremists started shouting at the Faulkner unionists, chanting 'traitor' and 'out, out'. A week later police had to be called into the chamber to eject some of the hardliners, when fists and boots were flying, especially at those appointed to the new Executive. Basil McIvor, who is now a respected resident magistrate, handled himself with great dignity, calmly punching every attacker who came near him. It was by far the ugliest episode I have seen in a parliamentary chamber.

As far as we were concerned, the IRA accused us of being 'collaborators', a word with a sinister ring to it in the context of turbulent Irish history. Although they knew the Catholic community would not stand for us being directly threatened, the Provos said they would attack policemen who were guarding our homes or escorting us. Shots fired at two policemen guarding Austin Currie's house at this time underlined the threat. The loyalists also warned they would attack us. One of their news sheets, distributed through bars and drinking clubs, had taken to calling us 'Six Dirty Lousy Pigs'. They were probably responsible for throwing a grenade into a bar in Lurgan owned by Hugh News, one of the elected members of our Assembly team. Mercifully there was no massacre.

Despite the power-sharing breakthrough there were still major outstanding issues to be addressed, principally internment, law and order matters, including reform of the police, and the Council of Ireland. These subjects had been thoroughly discussed at a parallel series of inter-governmental talks throughout the autumn. Heath had taken an active personal role in these proceedings, visiting Belfast for two days in late August and then Dublin in the middle of September, the first time a British prime minister had set foot in the Irish republic since partition. Liam Cosgrave, the prime minister, and Dr Garret FitzGerald, the foreign minister, were greatly impressed by his personal commitment to finding a solution to the Irish problem. In between our sessions at Stormont, we had been up and down to Dublin for regular meetings, where we were made aware that Heath was seen as an eminently fair man with a constructive attitude to the problem, quite unlike any of his predecessors.

With the Assembly and Executive-designate now in position the next step was an inter-governmental summit to tie up these loose, but fundamentally important, ends. Given the vulnerability of his position, it was also imperative that the conference should ensure the durability of Brian Faulkner's political power-base in the Unionist Party and community. At 6.30 p.m. on Wednesday 6 December, all fifteen members of the Executive and the administration and eight advisers left RAF Aldergrove on our way to the Civil Service Staff College at Sunningdale, near London, where the tripartite negotiations were due to start the following morning. It was our first real experience of the trappings of power – chauffeur-driven cars, civil service back-up, and so on. Before leaving we had been issued with comprehensive guidance about the conference, which was planned down to the last detail, such as morning tea and a wake-up call at 7.30 a.m. The actual negotiations were to take place in the conference room in Northcote House, a fine Georgian manor house, which was the centrepiece of the complex.

The previous weekend we had been surprised and disappointed to learn that Whitelaw was being appointed Employment Secretary in a cabinet reshuffle by Heath. Clearly the conciliatory skills he had used to such good effect on us were to be deployed on Britain's coal miners, who were then limbering up for a confrontation with the government over pay and conditions. Francis Pym, the chief whip, had been posted to Belfast as replacement. By contrast with the ebullient Whitelaw, he was a cold fish and certainly not as adroit a politician. This was when Frank Cooper really assumed command. Pym's opening move was to ask the anti-power-sharers to submit their views on a Council of Ireland, but he refused to let them attend the conference. The British obviously shared our view that the loyalists only intended to obstruct progress in ratifying the Executive and forming the Council of Ireland. It may well be that Pym and Cooper thought this invitation would neutralise the loyalists, but, to me, it mattered little for they were clearly determined, in any case, to pursue obstructive tactics in and out of the Assembly. Better that they were not at Sunningdale with all the opportunity that would give them. I hoped we could invite them into the process later when they dropped these tactics.

The British conference team was led by the Prime Minister and included the Foreign Secretary, Sir Alec Douglas-Home, the Attorney-General, Sir Peter Rawlinson, as well as Pym. With advisers and administrative back-up there were a total of forty-two. The Irish government delegation consisted of Liam Cosgrave, his deputy, Brendan Corish, Dr Garret FitzGerald, Attorney-General Declan Costello, James Tully, Minister for Local Government, Patrick Cooney, Minister for Justice, Richie Ryan, Minister for Finance and Dr Conor Cruise O'Brien, Minister for Posts and Telegraphs. With advisers they also fielded a total of forty-two. All the members of the Northern Ireland Executive-designate attended. There was a total of eight advisers from the various Northern Ireland parties. We had Paddy O'Hanlon on economics and finance, Michael Canavan on policing and Paddy Duffy on legal matters.

The conference got off to an early start on the Thursday morning. Heath and the British delegation occupied one side of the long table, with the component political parties of the Executive seated to his left. The Irish government party were on his right. Heath spoke in glowing terms and without notes of what harmonious results the Northern Ireland political parties had achieved on their own when the power-sharing agreement had been made. He suggested that an extension of that harmony would enable the conference to conclude in the two days scheduled. He then outlined the outstanding questions we had to resolve. These were: the measure of recognition which the Irish government would afford to the constitutional status of Northern Ireland; extradition and an all-Ireland common law enforcement area; political control of the police in Northern Ireland; the powers and functions of the Council of Ireland; and the provision of finance for the operation of the Executive.

Heath suggested that full-scale discussions on every aspect of these questions would be too unwieldy and that it would be more expeditious to set up representative sub-committees on each issue which would report back to the full conference with recommendations for action. Five sub-committees were then formed. Our members were Eddie McGrady and Paddy O'Hanlon on the Finance committee; myself on Economics; Austin Currie and Michael Canavan on Police; Ivan Cooper and Paddy Duffy on the Common Law Enforcement Area; John Hume and Paddy O'Hanlon on constitutional status; with Gerry Fitt operating between all the committees helping to draw together the various strands into a comprehensive fabric.

The general approach of the SDLP to the talks was to get all-Ireland institutions established which, with adequate safe-guards, would produce the dynamic that would lead ultimately to an agreed united Ireland. SDLP representatives thus concentrated their entire efforts on seeking a set of tangible powers for the council which in the fullness of time would create and sustain the evolutionary process. All other issues were governed by that approach, and the need to reduce loyalist resistance to the concepts of a Council of Ireland and a power-sharing Executive.

The SDLP was sensitive to the need for loyalist views to be taken into account in the deliberations of the conference. We were in need of some loyalist support to enable us to make the Executive effective. It was only by demonstrating our impartiality and skill in running the various departments that we could counteract hardline propaganda that we were only concerned with a united Ireland. We realised that by getting a sustained run in office we could syphon off the sectarian poison from the atmosphere. That way we could transform the face of northern politics for ever. We were confident that hoary issues relating to flags and symbols would be replaced by more relevant ones, relating to the deep-seated social and economic problems we faced.

It had been decided that no statements would be issued to the media unless agreed by all parties. There was thus a major row after the opening session of the conference when it was discovered that a member of the Irish delegation had leaked details of the proceedings by telephone. It was learned later that the leak had actually been approved by one of the Irish ministers, who was also planning to give a briefing to the press who were ensconced in a local hotel. The incident produced an angry response from everyone and led to a complete shutdown of communications with the outside world.

By the end of the first day it was becoming clear that Heath's two-day target had been unduly optimistic. The sub-committee on constitutional recognition and the Council of Ireland was in rough seas; the policing sub-committee was in the eye of a storm.

The unionists had insisted from the outset that the only way they could accept the need for a Council of Ireland was in exchange for a formal declaration by Dublin recognising Northern Ireland's constitutional status. The republic's constitution, of course, laid claim to the whole island. The Irish government anticipated the need for such a statement and produced a draft, which was later incorporated in the final communiqué, side by side with one by the British government. The Irish government statement recognised that there could be no change in the status of Northern Ireland without the consent of the northern majority. Britain acknowledged that if a majority of the Northern Irish people ultimately wished to become part of a united Ireland they could do so. These agreed undertakings were later formally registered with the United Nations. Faulkner and his unionist colleagues appreciated the importance of this unprecedented Dublin declaration in selling the Sunningdale package to their supporters and critics. It was the first time any Irish government had given such a totally cast-iron recognition of the constitutional position of the North.

The going was much rougher in the group working on extradition and common law enforcement. The unionists refused to concede the significance of a case heard in the High Court in Dublin the week before the talks, in which a ruling was given that an IRA offence must be regarded as political and therefore not extraditable. They failed to see that a constitutional change was necessary to make extradition possible. Neither would they attempt to understand the difficulties confronting a coalition government, holding office by a mere two seats, in having the constitution changed for this sole reason. The legal complexities of creating a common law enforcement area proved to be more daunting than had at first been thought. Faced with this situation, the British, with more wit than grace, avoided a breakdown by suggesting that a Commission of Jurists consider both proposals in more detail and report back later for formal agreement at a reconvened conference.

I was involved in the sub-committee on Economics. There was an initial clash between myself and Garret FitzGerald because he started the business of the meeting before the SDLP and the Alliance representatives were present but, that apart, progress was rapid and by the late afternoon of the first day a report was ready and agreed for inclusion in the final communiqué. We were pleased that we had achieved this so easily. It had been done by avoiding detail and keeping to the firm ground of clearly defined headings. The precise detail of the joint activities was to be hammered out later by full-time officials with the expertise of the various ministries, both north and south. It was agreed to set in hand at once a series of joint studies on areas of common interest, on which the Council of Ireland would base its executive decisions and work programmes. The studies were to examine the exploitation, conservation and development of natural resources, all aspects of agriculture, co-operative ventures in trade and industry, electricity generation, tourism, roads and transport, advisory services in public health and sport, culture and the arts. It was envisaged that it would be for the Irish parliament and the Northern Ireland Assembly to arrange for the devolution of further functions to the Council of Ireland and that the British government would co-operate fully with this.

The sub-committee on Finance also reported successfully on its deliberations at the end of the first day, reflecting a robust desire on the part of everyone to produce early, encouraging conclusions. It was agreed that finance for the council's activities would come entirely from grants provided by both governments towards agreed projects and programmes.

On the Friday night all of us attending the conference were invited to dinner at 10 Downing Street. The meal was a seven-course affair which opened with prayer and ended with a local church choir singing 'When Irish Eyes are Smiling'. The choir, in an annexe off the main room, actually sang a number of Irish songs specially selected by Ted Heath. After the meal the SDLP members, no great respecters of dignity, began to circulate freely amongst the rest of the guests and indulge in a bit of banter and teasing. Sir Alec Douglas-Home had his back slapped vigorously while being asked by Ivan Cooper, 'How is the grouse shooting in Scotland this season, old boy?' The look of surprise on his face kept us laughing for the rest of the night.

Heath was chided by Gerry Fitt that he could not expect to solve the Northern Ireland problem when he was not able to play 'The Sash My Father Wore' on his piano. He promised to play it for us on our next visit. We were conveyed back to Sunningdale by bus and we soon had all the passengers singing at the top of their voices. Paddy O'Hanlon sang a song which he had written after a riot in the Assembly. As we travelled through the London streets and out along the motorway to Sunningdale, there was a flow of songs from Ivan Cooper, Oliver Napier, Basil McIvor, John Hume and myself. Even the normally reserved Brian Faulkner relaxed enough to sing 'Galway Bay' and to recite, for our amusement, a number of Gaelic phrases that he had learned in school in Dublin.

But on Saturday morning it was back to business, where the most solid deadlock had built up in the sub-committee on policing. The SDLP believed, and was urging strenuously, that the police forces on both sides of the border should ultimately be the responsibility of the Council of Ireland. A declaration to this effect would enable the SDLP to identify with and support a reformed police service in the North, working in the context of a common law enforcement policy for the entire island. The unionists were resolutely opposed to this approach. Indeed, their position was that reform or change of any sort was not necessary. Faulkner was already on public record as wanting control of the police and security policy to be returned to the Stormont administration. In the course of long and often heated exchanges in the sub-committee, he put forward that specific case.

Work in the policing sub-committee had begun early on the Friday morning and continued on Saturday and into Sunday morning. As the other committees completed their agendas and agreed their input to the final communiqué, the impasse over policing threatened the entire outcome of the conference. At various times during the sessions the personalities changed. John Hume and Gerry Fitt joined our team for periods and at one time, Ted Heath even sat in. Around 5 a.m. on Sunday morning he tried to mediate by holding talks with each party in their private rooms. He found no joy, and gloom descended when it was reported that Faulkner was threatening to walk out of the talks. Our side of the policing sub-committee were proving intractable, especially when Hume had joined them.

At breakfast Garret FitzGerald and Conor Cruise O'Brien pulled me over to the side of the room for a few words. They confirmed that Faulkner was indeed on the verge of going home and asked me to intervene. I found Faulkner and went for a walk round the grounds with him. I asked what he needed to get the talks going again. He said he needed the SDLP, his partners in government, to recognise and publicly support the RUC. He was right. It did not make sense that we should be sharing administrative responsibility with him yet refusing to consent to the means of maintaining law and order. After our walk, I called a meeting in our party room. There were emotional and fierce exchanges before we agreed to a more accommodating stance. When the sub-committee meeting resumed, the British and Irish delegations were asked to leave the northerners on their own for a time, and a statement was drafted that brought about a break-through. It said that the Northern Ireland Police Authority would be appointed by the Secretary of State after consultation with the Northern Ireland Executive, which would have con-sulted the ministers of the Council of Ireland.

With the conference now drawing to a close, the SDLP members had a private meeting with Heath on the promised phasing out of internment. He was asked to begin releases immediately and to include this undertaking to the SDLP in the communiqué which was in the final stage of drafting. He agreed and promised to start the releases as early as possible.

The formal signing, by all members of the delegation and party leaders, took place in the main hall of Sunningdale College. Afterwards we crossed to a separate building in the grounds to give press, radio and television interviews about the package we had agreed. It was clear that another conference would be required, perhaps some time in January, to conclude outstanding matters concerning the report of the Common Law Enforcement Commission and the definition of functions for the Council of Ireland. From the SDLP's point of view, the progress made represented a fair deal on top of what had been achieved a fortnight earlier in Stormont Castle. We were satisfied that we had secured the basis for an effective and evolving Council of Ireland. We had gone beyond our wildest dreams in moving towards a realisation of Wolfe Tone's objective of uniting Protes-tant, Catholic and Dissenter. Our one nagging worry was whether Faulkner would be able to sell the package to the unionist electorate, in view of the rising tide of hostility to him back home. It was for that reason that our comments after the conference were, uncharacteristically for us, of the low-key variety and were to remain so in the trying days immediately ahead.

On 21 December we had a meeting with Lord Belstead, one of the Northern Ireland Office ministers, about internment. We handed over a list of people we would welcome being released first, largely because we felt they would be a restraining influence within the Provos. Some of those we nominated were men brought to our attention by their families, whose detention was aggravating personal, employment or business problems. This meeting was followed, on 27 December, by a confidential letter from Pym to Gerry Fitt, as party leader, setting out the government's position. 'I know how strongly your party feels on the subject and from our various discussions both the Prime Minister and myself have a clear understanding of the difficulties it creates for you, and indeed for all those who are concerned with the future of Northern Ireland. We share your hopes of the progress which can flow from the Sunningdale Agreement towards the long term resolution of the problem and all those who took part in the Sunningdale discussions have a duty to ensure that the provisions in that agreement are pursued as a matter of urgency.

'As Her Majesty's Government has repeatedly made clear, it is our firm intention to phase internment out; but as I said in my statement of 20 December no date can or should be set for bringing it to an end since we must take account of the security situation and political developments.'

Stating that he did not feel able to authorise the release of detainees before the New Year, Pym then outlined a number of concessions that had been brought in: a parole scheme, to enable detainees to spend short periods at home; more liberal granting of compassionate parole; and steps to rehabilitate those still in detention. This meant introducing provision for education. We felt there was enough in the letter to satisfy our continued concerns on internment.

A few days before Christmas, official notification arrived through my letterbox that the members of the power-sharing Executive were to be sworn in on 31 December at noon, before taking up office the next day. We duly appeared in our 'Sunday best' before Francis Pym and the Lord Chief Justice, Sir Robert Lowry. We lined up to be sworn in and receive our letters of appointment. Ken Bloomfield, secretary-designate to the Executive, the organiser as usual, caught my eye. 'Are you going to swear in?' he asked.

'Indeed I'm not. I would be a hypocrite if I did,' I said.

He rushed off with a smile to find a suitable affirmation. When the ceremony started he was moving along at Lowry's elbow, introducing him to each individual before they were sworn. When they reached me and changed the procedure there was a slight commotion among the SDLP people. 'Hey, what's going on here? He's not taking the oath.'

'Jesus Christ,' said one of them. 'What will the cardinal say about that? We'll all be excommunicated.'

10

'CALL ME PADDY'

The power-sharing Executive came into office on 1 January 1974 conscious of how much depended on its efforts to stabilise and create prosperity in a society which had suffered so much from the violence of the previous five years.

First thing that morning, escorted by my regular RUC guards Bill Wilson and Bob Colhoun, I reported at Dundonald House in the Stormont estate, the headquarters of the Department of Health and Social Services. I was directed to the minister's room beside the private office where the staff were standing by to start work. I was asked if I desired to make any changes in the staff arrangements. 'No,' I said. 'But you better let them know that when I am under stress I am liable to let loose with a few traditional swear words.'

My first task was to appoint a private secretary and I was given a list of candidates. They were all male and Catholic. I wasn't falling into that trap so I handed the list back. 'Give me a proper list of efficient people which includes "Prods" as well as "Papes" and female as well as male,' I said. From the second list I selected Margaret Gilpin, from Portadown, who was the opposite of me in virtually every respect. We made a great team once we got the show on the road and I could not have received any higher standards of support and loyalty than she provided.

When I got settled behind the desk I was given a mountain of briefing files to read about the work of the department. They were piled up on a side table in the office. I ordered them to be taken back to their authors and condensed into no more than two paragraphs each. The table full of files was an old trick to deter a new minister.

I had prepared myself for taking office by buying a new suit, although I still refused to buy a dinner jacket. My purchase caused much amusement among my colleagues who were more used to the sight of me in an anorak or a pullover. I also decided it was inappropriate for a man of eighteen stone to be the Minister for Health so I went on a diet. My resolve in this regard was sorely tested, however, by the generosity of hosts and waiters and waitresses, who always piled plenty of spuds and meat on the minister's plate. I also stopped drinking, mindful of the cautionary tale of John Wheatley, the Glasgow socialist, who was Minister for Public Works in Ramsay MacDonald's government in the 1920s. His private secretary used to draw a line on the bottles to check if he took any when left in his room on his own. The secretary believed that no Labour man could be trusted behind locked doors with a bottle of spirits. He was always disappointed, for he did not know that the minister was teetotal. I decided to emulate him, which was just as well for I found there were two drinks cabinets at my disposal, one in the private office, the other at Parliament Buildings. I used them all right, but strictly for visitors.

More seriously, I sought to learn what was expected of me by speaking with experienced friends like the senior civil servant Dr Maurice Hayes, Professor David Dennison, the British Labour MP Stan Orme, and Brendan Halligan, of the Irish Labour Party. Civil servants traditionally try it on with new ministers to test their mettle. Given that we were the first non-unionist party ever to hold office in Northern Ireland, I knew from the first day that we would be treated with suspicion and tested right along the line. There were few Catholics in the senior ranks of the Northern Ireland Civil Service, at assistant, deputy or Permanent Secretary level. The mandarins in the key areas, Stormont Castle and the Department of Finance, had seen off O'Neill, Chichester-Clark, Faulkner and Whitelaw and some of them, whose unionist views they did not even bother to conceal, made no secret of their scorn for us and doubts about our capacity to do the job.

A notable exception to this profile was my Permanent Secretary, Norman Dugdale, who was a most compassionate and civilised man. From the moment he greeted me that morning he was a model of co-operation and a sound adviser whose attitude was to keep me within my remit and not waste time in blocking my ideas.

The department which I now headed had two main divisions. One was responsible for disbursing about £170 million a year in social security payments through a network of thirty-six local offices. Another £100 million was spent by the Health and Personal Social Services division, which supervised the four area health boards and their 40,000 employees who operated the National Health Service.

From the start I adopted my usual informal way of working and getting things done. I told officials they should stop calling me 'Minister' and simply call me 'Paddy'. Some of them, brought up in the tradition of deference, would only compromise with 'Mr Devlin'. When I had a problem dealing with a file I would sometimes wander off to the department concerned and talk it over with the official handling the matter. Other times I called them to my office to resolve things. I always went to the staff canteen and mixed with the staff, which no other minister had done before. In this way I got to know the people concerned and they learned about me.

My door was always open to the staff and anyone could come in to see me. I was also prepared to take calls from members of the public, which I did. The openness was abused, however. I found members of staff coming in to look for promotion, which was not a function I carried out anyway. Some were disgruntled

Catholics claiming that they had been refused promotion on religious grounds. I told them I was not going to be a Minister for Catholic Promotion, although I clearly favoured the creation of fair employment procedures to ultimately redress the imbalance between Catholic and Protestant civil servants. I had a guy who rang me each morning looking for an increase of benefits because it was the Catholic turn to raid the cash register. I finally refused his morning calls.

It had long been my strongest conviction that the root cause of all our problems was the deep and endemic poverty that afflicted both traditions in our community. I believed it was the basic social evil that fostered all others. My greatest political ambition was to defeat poverty and I thought it ironic that we spent millions combating violence, which was the symptom of our troubles, yet we expended hardly anything on eradicating the hardship which caused it. As a preliminary move in the right direction, I set out to commission research into the matter and to involve independent academic and other specialists. Eight or nine suitable projects were identified and put in hand.

From my days as a councillor and MP, dealing with daily constituency cases and a weekly surgery, I knew that a huge proportion of our people were almost totally dependent on public welfare benefits for their survival. I could name families where the parents had never worked and where their children were brought up and went through school only to find themselves living off the state as well. I dealt with hundreds of complaints from people who could not cope with the complexities of the benefit system and suffered indignity and poor treatment in social security offices although I never encountered a case in which a person was deliberately deprived of what they were entitled to by a civil servant. The problems that did arise were occasioned by people suffering from mental thickness, misplaced loyalty to an erring colleague, or defective appointments in areas where discretion had to be exercised.

I recall one senior official in the Supplementary Benefits

Commission who regularly made my blood boil because he would not exercise any of the wide discretionary powers at his disposal. I was determined to put a stop to this and change staff attitudes. An incident which sticks in my mind was the model for the sort of caring attitude I wanted to foster. I was representing a needy soul at a national assistance tribunal. There were a number of cases being heard that morning and an elderly clerk came out with a refusal sheet to an emaciated and depressed-looking man. When he received the sheet the man attacked the clerk, a big friendly fellow who easily warded off the blows. I went to his aid and we took the angry man outside to calm him down. The clerk was clearly upset at the tribunal decision and asked the man to visit his house that evening. I learned later that he had arranged private help for him from a charity. As well as this considerate sort of treatment, I wanted to make sure that claimants were automatically given all the benefits they were entitled to instead of having to work it out for themselves.

The first step was to order the production of a booklet setting out the entire range of benefits and how they could be claimed. My officials were told it had to be in plain language, not the bureaucratic gobbledegook that was found in most social security literature. (This innovation, I am pleased to say, outlasted my term of office and still continues.) I asked for someone to be made available in each local office to advise applicants and lead them through the maze. Guidelines were drawn up to encourage the staff to deal more courteously with claimants and to foster a mutual respect. All too often someone whose name was Sean or Seamus would be addressed as John or James. I was also concerned that far too many claimants were made to feel they were being done a favour by the department instead of getting what they were lawfully entitled to. I thought these practical steps would produce a completely new, better relationship between staff and claimants and reduce the volume of long-running grievances that existed.

In this regard, it gave me great pleasure to announce the

closure of the grim old dole office at Corporation Street, in the centre of Belfast, and its replacement by a number of new, more user-friendly district offices throughout the city. Corporation Street, which was as depressing for staff as for claimants, represented all that was worst about the social security system: the long counter, the queues, the endless waiting. Its modernisation as a new district office would, I hoped, prove to be a turning point.

I got the chance for another radical gesture when I had to fill a position on the Supplementary Benefits Commission. I promptly nominated Betty Sinclair, the secretary of the Belfast Trades Council. My decision was questioned by some of the officials involved and, unknown to me, was referred to Faulkner. He raised the matter with me informally after a meeting. I defended the appointment, pointing out that Betty had tremendous experience, for years having fought cases at the commission on behalf of disadvantaged people.

'You do know she's a communist?' said Faulkner.

'Of course,' said I. 'But I thought we'd stopped discriminating against communists as well as Catholics.'

He laughed and walked away and the appointment stood.

Not all the initiatives I wished to get going were the sole responsibility of a single department. The plight of handicapped and disabled people was cause for concern. Together with Bob Cooper, the Minister of Manpower, I got work going on a scheme designed to provide employment opportunities for both the physically and mentally handicapped. The idea was to encourage employers to adapt machinery and work practices to provide access for the disabled. In turn we would compensate them for any slowdown in productivity and provide grant aid. At the time it was a revolutionary idea.

One of the most arduous adminstrative tasks was scrutinising the replies to written and verbal questions from Assemblymen. This was critically important work, for ministerial credibility and authority were at stake. Hundreds of questions were asked of departmental ministers, an average of sixty per session per member, but one industrious fellow actually asked two hundred questions. In terms of questions it was the busiest session since the Belfast parliament had been set up. I came to dread answering some of the verbal questions, those dealing with medical matters. The replies were rarely given to me until shortly before going to the dispatch box to speak and I therefore had little time to master the convoluted language and the multi-syllable medical terms, which were often in Latin. In truth, I could never make head nor tail of them so my replies were a welter of mispronunciations, fumbles, stumbles and false starts. I would finally decide to hurdle the difficult words as best I could and read on. The Hansard writers and the parliamentary reporters then obtained written copies of the replies from Margaret Gilpin to ensure they got it right for the record.

One day in the Assembly the Alliance peer Lord Dunleath mischievously raised with me the matter of massage parlours, which were then flourishing in Belfast. Most of them were simply fronts for prostitution and there was a considerable overlay of terrorist extortion and protection rackets. He wanted to know if control or supervision of these establishments was among my myriad responsibilities and suggested that it would be beneficial to my health, and stimulating, if I was to inspect some of them in an official capacity. I replied that my wife might not be too happy about that aspect of my ministerial duties, before reading the reply prepared by my officials.

Such establishments, I said, were not under the control of the department. Massage was given free of charge, on the health service, by qualified physiotherapists on the referral of registered medical practitioners. Massage, employed normally in conjunction with heat and exercise, was of therapeutic value because, locally, it produced relaxation of muscles and promoted the dispersal of excess fluid from the tissues. Within this therapeutic role, the general term 'massage' covered several well-recognised manual techniques, all of which are aimed at producing the local effects I have described. Any other services which were required by a patient would have to be sought outside the National Health Service.

There was much laughter in the House as I sat down. A few days later, in my mail, the madam of one of the establishments concerned wrote inviting me to visit and assured me of a 'warm welcome'. On a more serious note, we set up an investigation into such premises, especially the way they advertised openly in the newspapers which could have misled some innocent souls, and after some police action the majority of them eventually closed down.

The lack of accessible family planning assistance was another anomaly I had identified. Given Catholic, and even some Protestant, attitudes on the subject, doing anything to remedy the situation was going to stir up the proverbial hornet's nest. But when I learned that a Family Planning bill was being brought in at Westminster, I took unpublicised steps to have its provisions apply to Northern Ireland. I called in Brian Henderson, my information officer, to stress that the measure must go through without publicity.

'Don't draw attention to it,' I instructed.

'Right,' he replied.

When the bill was finally passed at Westminster we used the 'parity measure' formula to explain that a free family planning service would be available on request to anyone, irrespective of age or marital status, from health service clinics and hospitals. Faulkner, as ever on top of every development and issue, came over to me after a meeting and asked why the full Executive had not been consulted. I said that I didn't have to consult them and that I would not have got it through by going into a 'song and dance' about it. He smiled and walked off. Nothing happened for a few days, even though the Catholic *Irish News* covered the story on an inside page. Then there were a couple of protest letters printed. I didn't reply, since the letters were not directed at me, and the new arrangements got under way without a fuss.

Some of the old hands frowned at my methods and some were terrified when they saw me walking along the corridors in my shirtsleeves and braces. Others went white when they saw my Browning pistol stuck in my leather shoulder holster, hanging on the coatstand in the office. Those were tense and trying days and the fear of assassination was never far from any of our minds. I took the view that if I had a gun, I should carry it and be prepared to use it if the need arose. Consequently I was always ready with 'one up the spout' although I never fired a shot in anger through all those dangerous days. There were surprisingly few threatening calls either at home or to the office and I got only one abusive letter during the early days of the Executive. I became concerned that I might be getting popular! My one sorrow at this time was the death of my mother, at the age of seventy-two.

Every week we had a full meeting of the Executive in the old cabinet room at Stormont Castle. Brian Faulkner was in his element in his new role and energised the administration as never before. We had a day-long seminar in Stormont at which some of the Permanent Secretaries, Dr George Quigley, Ewart Bell, Bob Kidd, Norman Dugdale and John Oliver, delivered papers about the future work of each department. The Heath government indicated that we would have financial underpinning for this work. We were also assailed with new ideas and far-reaching proposals from businessmen, trade unionists and academics. Crucial opinion- formers in business and commercial life began to give us real, if sometimes grudging, support. Delegations from all types of organisations arrived at Stormont to meet ministers on a wide variety of matters long since abandoned or neglected by earlier unionist ministers. Even loyalist Assembly members, committed to boycotting us in public, used our private offices intensively to help them with their own constituency problems.

Ministers responded fully to the desire of Assembly members for a deeper and more democratic participation in the running of the departments. Certain issues regarded as sacred cows were trotted around the field for an airing, especially in the industrial development sector, which had always been regarded by the unionist ministers in the earlier parliaments as a closed shop. If ideas stood up to scrutiny they were kept or amended. We were committed to providing good government, not point-scoring. The central objective was to concentrate our activity on social and economic issues so that realignment of interests on a capital and labour basis would take place, paving the way for conventional right–left politics. Thus the traditional issues and symbols, which were being exploited to supply nourishment for paramilitary activities, would be superseded.

We produced a comprehensive social and economic pro-gramme, the most far-reaching ever drawn up in Northern Ireland. Three particular aspects of it were especially notable. A central planning unit was created to analyse the economic problems and marry them to the resources available locally and from the British government. Through pilot studies designed to estimate grant impact on the acute levels of poverty and depriva-tion, we adopted a highly innovative approach to disbursing grants and other benefits. Housing was given top priority in our spending plans to improve existing stock and build new homes. The situation we faced was truly appalling: 27 per cent of houses had no bath; 21 per cent no running water; 27 per cent no inside flushing toilet; 10 per cent were not connected to the public water supply and 15 per cent were not connected to a sewer.

Another far-reaching innovation was the introduction of inte-grated education, teaching Catholic and Protestant children side by side in the same classrooms for the first time. Not all of the SDLP, with their eye on Catholic church insistence on its own schools, were in favour of the move, but Basil McIvor pushed it through and although it has not become a mass movement yet, twenty-one integrated schools are today firmly established and steadily making a positive contribution to removing community division.

The growing perception that we were good for Northern Ireland was enhanced by favourable employment figures, the most accurate barometer of our local economic climate. In February the unemployment rate was the lowest for twenty-nine years and the downward trend continued during the months we were in office. Providing jobs was one of our major priorities and John Hume's responsibility. At least 4,000 new jobs were promoted in the first quarter of 1974. Once, in Hume's absence abroad on a job-promoting mission, I met Tony O'Reilly, the former Irish rugby international, in Dublin. At the time his international interests, which included the Heinz group, had around £11 million invested in Ireland. He wanted to know what he could do to help with our economic difficulties in the North. After some discussion he agreed to host a dinner at his headquarters in Pittsburgh for a number of American entrepreneurs with a view to encouraging them to establish subsidiaries in Northern Ireland.

Other multinational companies had publicly stated their intention to do so. There were setbacks, though. The German electronics firm, Grundig, based at Dunmurry, near Belfast, had intended to open a second plant at Newry, one of our worst unemployment blackspots, but after their chief executive, Thomas Niedermayer, was kidnapped by the IRA in late 1973 (his body was found in 1980) the plan was understandably scrapped. Needless to say we were all horrified by the abduction and angry that the futility of the IRA's activities had cost yet another life and destroyed the economic prospects of so many people in Newry.

On 1 February 1974 we sat down to tackle the unfinished business from Sunningdale. Cosgrave and seven members of his government arrived in three Irish Air Corps helicopters at Hillsborough Castle, and Brian Faulkner and seven of us from the Executive took part in the five-hour get-together. It was an unprecedented meeting between Irish political leaders, north and south, and significant, not least of all, because there was no

British participation. Although it was a friendly, purposeful and businesslike meeting, we faced some pretty fundamental problems.

Faulkner sought reassurance on the matter of the republic's recognition of Northern Ireland. This had been clouded in confusion since Kevin Boland, a former Fianna Fáil cabinet minister, had legally challenged the Irish government statement in the Sunningdale communiqué. Cosgrave had not backed down, and assured Faulkner the case was being vigorously contested in line with legal advice and that it would be won, which it was. After that there would be a full clarification of the position in public, confirming what had been agreed at Sunningdale.

Working parties of permanent officials were set up to plan the detail of the functions that would be given to a Council of Ireland, and it was agreed that an interim report from the Anglo-Irish Commission on Law Enforcement be produced. Their agenda included extradition. There was also a general discussion on cross-border security which revealed unionist misgivings on what they believed was the failure of the Irish government to apply effective measures to deal with IRA activity along the border. At the end of the meeting it was mutually agreed that satisfactory progress had been made and further sessions, at official and ministerial level, were to be arranged as soon as possible to expedite the final stages of the Sunningdale Agreement.

But despite the continued momentum underlined by the Hillsborough meeting, the SDLP was still exercised about the lack of direct steps to phase out internment. This was absolutely crucial to us remaining in office, whatever other benefits were accruing. Only sixty-five internees had been released at Christmas, and none of them were people whose freedom we had recommended in the list submitted to Pym. Indeed I knew some of them would not be forces for moderation in Provo circles, a view confirmed by the subsequent continuation and intensification of violence. Despite reservations, the party had issued a statement on 29 December asking for our supporters to

224

come off the rent and rates strike which we had backed since August 1971. This was a gesture to Pym and Faulkner, who both felt it was improper for us to be behind such a campaign of civil disobedience while we were in power.

The SDLP had been told by Pym that the Emergency Provisions Act would not be retained beyond July 1974, when it was due for renewal. This indicated to us that internment would be ended by then. But with only a trickle of releases since Christmas, the patience of the SDLP members on the Executive had been sorely tested. I actually accused Pym of trying to sabotage Whitelaw's promise to end internment. It was abundantly clear to us that the military were opposed to this step and that those who got out were being watched. We knew this at first hand because, during our weekly visits to Pym, reports were often produced about recently released men who, he claimed, had become re-involved. We argued passionately that this approach was basically wrong. Better to go for mass releases to take advantage of the Executive's good work, demonstrating that there was an effective political alternative to violence. This course, if followed, would have transferred pressure onto the Provos to end their campaign, pressure from the men released and from the families of those convicted of offences and serving long-term sentences, who would have called for an amnesty.

Whatever the depth of our discontent over internment, it was as nothing compared with Faulkner's highly precarious political position. Despite his courage and leadership things went from bad to worse for him within the Unionist Party. Soon after the Executive had taken office he was forced out of the party and had to set up his own organisation of pro-Assembly Unionists. But what turned out to be the first of a series of shattering blows for all of us, from which we never recovered, came in February when Ted Heath, who was locked into a life or death confrontation with the British coal miners, ran out of options and decided to call a general election. Whatever the national reasons for going to the country, the election was going to be disastrous for us. The Executive had hardly got into its stride. Heath twice called John Hume and myself to Stormont Castle to speak with him on a confidential line. The first time we pointed out to him the dreadful consequences of an election for Northern Ireland, in that all the time and energy invested in creating a political settlement could well come to nothing before there had been any real chance to deliver. It was during the second conversation he explained that all his options had run out and he was calling an election on 28 February.

The SDLP at first decided to field only eight candidates in the twelve constituencies. Although it meant splitting the nationalist vote, we felt there was no alternative to fighting Bernadette McAliskey in Mid-Ulster and Frank McManus in Fermanagh–South Tyrone. This concern intensified when we heard that the United Ulster Unionist Council, comprising the Official (anti-Faulkner), Democratic (Paisley) and Vanguard (Craig) unionists had got together and nominated a single anti-Sunningdale runner in each constituency. We then revised our strategy and nominated in all twelve contests. My own view was that none of the Executive or Assembly members should run in the Westminster election, except for Gerry Fitt, as sitting MP. It was a mistake to let the pro-Assembly Unionist Roy Bradford run, for that meant we seemed to be looking for a repeat of the mandate we had already got the previous year.

The subsequent campaign was the most divisive and bitter I had ever experienced. The Provos ranged themselves against us in the Catholic areas while the pro-Sunningdale and anti-Sunningdale factions fought it out in the Protestant community. Scurrilous abuse was heaped up against all of us. Loyalists who were engaged in widespread sectarian murder threatened to shoot SDLP Assemblymen if they did not use their influence to get the IRA bombing campaign halted. About the same time well-sourced reports from Dublin indicated that the Provos were targeting the SDLP members of the Executive for assassination, which the Provos later denied. Shots were again fired at the home of Austin Currie and a massive landmine was planted nearby, although it was found and defused. The house of our North Belfast candidate, Tom Donnelly, was badly damaged in a bomb attack. The Alliance Party headquarters was also devastated when a 100-pound bomb went off outside its premises. In the early hours of election day a very sophisticated dirty trick was sprung against Gerry Fitt: he and Bradford were the only Executive members standing for election. A story was spread among journalists drinking in the Europa Hotel that Gerry was not eligible to defend his West Belfast seat because of the provisions of the 1957 House of Commons Disqualification Act. By breakfast time the groundless allegation was being broadcast on the local airwaves and promoted by loudspeaker throughout the West Belfast constituency. Although we got a correction out first thing, when we confirmed that the devolution legislation governing the Executive superseded the 1957 act, we feared that mortal damage had been done to his vote. This was no ordinary smear. The Provo yahoos who spread it had clearly been activated by others in the background and had been given a credible peg for their campaign by someone with the requisite legal knowledge. It was further confirmation to me that there were wrong-headed people among the better informed and educated classes prepared to support the hatred promoted by the Provos at the expense of democracy.

In the event Gerry comfortably retained his seat with a 2,180 majority, although down from the 3,198 majority he polled in June 1970. It was the only glimmer of encouragement in a dreadful result. All the other eleven seats had been won by the anti-Sunningdale unionist candidates, who had run under a single umbrella to maximise their vote. Inevitably they totalled their votes and presented it as a referendum result against Sunningdale. From our standpoint the arithmetic was highly damaging. Pro-Sunningdale candidates had attracted 295,155 votes, 41.2 per cent of the poll, but 421,782 or 58.8 per cent of the poll was counted as anti-Sunningdale. Our worst fears, as expressed to

Heath, had in fact been surpassed. We knew that the election result would give a renewed, and more dangerous, impetus to the already festering campaign to topple the Executive and undermine the moves to ratify the Sunningdale accord.

The national election result was far from clear-cut and Heath only relinquished office after a vain struggle to form a new government with the support of the Liberal Party. We regretted his downfall because he had delivered. Harold Wilson moved back into Downing Street at the head of a minority government and appointed Merlyn Rees to replace Francis Pym. Although the Conservative and Labour leaders at Westminster detested everything the right-wing, anti-Faulkner zealots stood for, eleven MPs of that ilk in a hung Westminster parliament could not be ignored by the new government. Wilson was a very shrewd politician and, although Merlyn Rees assured everyone in sight that the Sunningdale Agreement would have his support and we would be given time to show the fruits of our work, we feared the obvious temptations to Labour of a policy of 'a nod and a wink' to the unionists in the corridors of power. But as long as there was no direct challenge being mounted to the power-sharing Executive or the Council of Ireland then we had no objection to any game of 'footsie' being played. The SDLP quickly put its position on the record, defiantly ruling out any rewriting of the Sunningdale Agreement and adding that we had no intention of allowing 'any ill wind or foul breath' to disrupt the basic agreements that had been reached.

The eleven new MPs retained their coalition and were well aware of their potential parliamentary power. As Craig, Paisley, and Harry West, who had emerged as leader of the Official Unionists, began a co-ordinated drive to get the Sunningdale process halted and what Craig called the 'power-sharing pirates' evicted, their belligerence triggered off virtual panic among the Faulknerites. Again threatening the integrity of the Executive, Roy Bradford suggested restructuring it to include a faction from the Unionist Coalition.

As the Executive struggled to keep its momentum, we could see that our cohesion was beginning to unravel. Bradford was the first and greatest waverer. Every time he spoke, Leslie Morrell, the Agriculture minister, who sat beside him at our formal meetings, began to put a single finger in the air behind Bradford's back and move it about. I was puzzled by the gesture and asked him to explain. Roy is like the finger, he told me, checking for lethal gas like the canary on the miner's finger down the mine.

The direct course of events that led to the fall of the Executive began on 11 March when twenty-one Assembly members, headed by John Laird, put their names to a motion calling for a renegotiation of 'the imposed constitutional settlement'. Two days later, with the Boland case out of the way and in a bid to strengthen Faulkner's hand, Cosgrave gave unequivocal recognition to the status of Northern Ireland in the United Kingdom and affirmed that Irish unity could only come about by peaceful means and consent. The following week the Assembly began debating Laird's motion. The SDLP was pretty angry when Peter McLachlan, one of Faulkner's men, called for the Council of Ireland plans to be dropped, a course, he said, for which there was considerable support in the Assembly.

The debate, which dragged on at intervals through March, April and into May, was viciously bruising at times. The loyalist opposition speeches were largely personal attacks on members of the Executive. Some members of the SDLP were accused of gun-running or of forming subversive organisations. I was accused of having the lofty rank of intelligence officer in B Company of the Belfast Provisional IRA while carrying out my duties as Minister of Health and Social Services. That was certainly faint praise, for I had had a higher rank than that when I was interned in 1942. The only speaker heard in silence was Paddy O'Hanlon, the SDLP chief whip, who ripped in to Paisley, having studied a brief that we had prepared on his controversial record and more recent activities.

The issue of making the Sunningdale package more acceptable to the loyalists, which had been publicly trailed by Bradford and McLachlan, had already been privately foreshadowed by Faulkner within the Executive in early April. He believed that gradual staging of the Sunningdale provisions would be necessary to keep his group faithful to their voting obligations in the Assembly. We had paid little heed to his fears at first, for we judged he had enough support to carry the day inside and outside the Assembly. Consequently we were more than surprised when, on 22 April, the *Financial Times* had carried a story that Faulkner was seeking to renegotiate the Sunningdale Pact, particularly the provisions establishing a Council of Ireland with executive functions, its own central secretariat and staff and the setting up of its own headquarters. Clearly he was preparing to water down the whole idea of the Council of Ireland in favour of a scheme providing only for regular meetings between members of the Northern Ireland Executive and Irish government ministers, leaving each side to take independent action to implement agreed decisions affecting north and south.

Faulkner's fears were justified, we learned later, for individual members of his group were being isolated and subjected to intense pressure in their own homes by aggressive activists and fanatics linked to the Unionist Coalition and the Ulster Workers' Council. As a result there were increasingly hysterical demands at the weekly meetings of Faulkner's Assembly group to have the main provisions, if not the entire Sunningdale Agreement, dropped. It had been reported to us that there could be as many as eight defections from the Faulkner group on the final Assembly vote, which would bring us down. We knew that the influential chairman and secretary of Faulkner's backbench supporters were among the possible defectors.

Bradford was particularly active the whole time chatting up these sore-heads with opportunistic reservations on Sunningdale. In my view he hoped to replace Faulkner as leader of the group and then bring West and the Official Unionists back into the fold. As overall leader he would then certainly have been able to redefine the Unionist Coalition with Paisley and Craig on his terms. Thus, the Executive could be brought down and replaced by a pseudo-Executive dominated by a unionist alliance, headed by Bradford himself.

While these machinations were going on throughout March and April, to ensure a full vote against Laird's renegotiation motion, the Executive decided to set up a sub-committee consisting of Morrell, Bradford, Cooper, Napier, Hume and myself to attempt to work out a staged implementation of the Sunningdale Pact. We were under great pressure from the start and by the time the UWC strike was beginning to bite it had come to bursting point.

The unionists were angered, and could not defend to their supporters the military and police impotence against the continued high levels of IRA activity and the ongoing campaign of shooting and bombing. There had been a particularly provocative IRA bomb attack in the heart of Belfast on 28 March when a huge bomb in a lorry parked outside the army base in the former Grand Central Hotel exploded and devastated buildings over a wide area. It was the second attack in the same place in three weeks and when Rees and Faulkner visited the scene the next day they were jeered and jostled. The death toll since 1969 had passed the 1,000 mark at the time and showed no sign of stopping. Although the loyalists and security forces were responsible for some of the casualties, the overwhelming proportion had been perpetrated by the Provos.

There was a significant cross-border aspect to the Provo campaign: many attacks in the border areas were mounted from the South and the attackers returned there; prison escapees fled south and were paraded at press conferences without any action being taken by the southern authorities; explosives and arms were smuggled from the South; terrorist training undoubtedly took place there; and the courts invariably refused to extradite suspects wanted for trial in the North and released them to walk the streets. This was all highly disturbing for the entire community but the Faulkner unionists failed to sympathise with the difficulties faced by the Irish government. Without a referendum to approve fundamental and emotionally charged constitutional amendments it was quite impossible for the Irish government to back extradition warrants. Neither could a judge overrule the constitutional constraints he faced when confronted with a suspect claiming a political motive for what were truly revolting crimes. It was fairly clear that the mood of the people in the South would not have favoured constitutional change in the context of anti-IRA measures alone. Any change would have had to be firmly bound to agreement on a comprehensive set of all-Ireland institutions which we envisaged. By their nature, of course, these institutions would have entirely removed at a stroke the prime justification for organised violence and would have isolated the republican mavericks who could then be dealt with on an effective all-Ireland basis.

The failure of the Anglo-Irish Law Enforcement Commissioners to come up with clear-cut conclusions in their report, which was completed at this decisive point, aggravated our efforts to re-phase the Sunningdale Agreement and move to ratification. Instead of endorsing and blueprinting the common law enforcement area they had been asked to study, the commission came up with the milk-and-water proposal of extra-territorial legislation, enabling terrorists to be tried in the part of Ireland where they were arrested regardless of where they had committed the offence. This fell far short of what we expected and we received no help from Sam Silkin, the British Attorney-General, who arrived in the middle of this grim situation to discuss the report with the Executive. His assessment of what was involved reflected a heavy anti-Irish bias and his remarks about the Dublin government were unjustifiably derisory. I gave him a hard time as a result. It must be assumed his feelings were transmitted back to the already wobbling unionist backbenchers, further destabilising them.

Events came to a head on 14 May when the matter was finally to be voted on in the Assembly. That morning the *News Letter* had carried a threatening advertisement, inserted by the UWC, which was a clear breach of privilege. It warned members of the Executive, specifically Hume and Faulkner, that a full stoppage of industry would follow if the motion to implement the Sunningdale Agreement was carried in the Assembly that evening. We had been aware for months that this body was in the background. In conjunction with Craig and Paisley, they had organised several work stoppages since the imposition of direct rule. Their real clout lay with the handful of skilled Protestant technicians who ran the Northern Ireland electricity power stations but the paramilitary groups, like the UVF and the UDA, provided them with a certain amount of direct muscle.

Before the crucial vote was taken, Faulkner moved an amendment to Laird's motion, proposing that the Assembly welcome the declaration by the Executive that the successful implementation of its policy depended upon the British and Irish governments delivering on their commitments under the Sunningdale Agreement. Faulkner was constantly shouted down, heckled and interrupted while he moved the amendment and other members on the Executive side were subjected to a similar torrent of personal abuse. The amendment was pressed to a vote at 6 p.m. and was carried easily enough by a vote of 44 to 28. The majority was trimmed slightly by three defectors from the Faulkner group: William Morgan, a former Minister of Health and Social Services; James Stronge (later killed with his father by the Provisionals in January 1981) and Herbert Whitten, both from Armagh. The vote was cast in a strangely subdued atmosphere, with a few catcalls from loyalists in the public gallery indicating that we had triggered off a general strike. Leading figures from the UWC were waiting for the result in Parliament Buildings.

The stoppage had already been well planned. There had been several rehearsals in previous months with strikes called over a range of issues. They were only scantily supported but they enabled the UWC to perfect its control of the electricity generating system, the master-stroke that we failed to recognise would be our undoing. The UWC organisers had met Unionist Coalition leaders the night before the vote at a hotel in Larne to tell them of their detailed plans. Their already militant mood could hardly have been more stupidly aggravated than it was by Wilson in the House of Commons in London earlier in the day. Drawing on so-called IRA 'doomsday plans' captured by the RUC at a luxury flat in the Malone Road area of Belfast a couple of days earlier, Wilson frightened the wits out of everybody by revealing a 'specific and calculated' plan to take over public buildings and entire suburbs of Belfast. As he was speaking, Rees was holding a press conference at Stormont where the maps and documents were put on display.

The first any of us on the Executive heard about the plot was from the news bulletins and reporters seeking our reaction. It was cloud-cuckoo-land material outlining an impossible strategy that could have no reality. How could anyone seriously believe that the IRA could hold off the British Army, the police and indeed the loyalists? They were always hit-and-run merchants, rarely engaging in face-to-face combat. I knew they always invested as much time in planning their escape as in planning the actual attack. All too often they would shoot their victims in the back or detonate their bombs from a distance so as not to endanger themselves. Never in their history had they become involved in the sort of full-frontal assault envisaged. If we had been consulted about the documents we would have said this and more. But even if the plans had been plausible, what was the Prime Minister doing giving the Provos such a propaganda boost? We were incredulous, to say the least. The Wilson bombshell played into the hands of the hardline loyalists. It added to the fears and anger of the Protestant population. Moreover, it gave yet another reason for the loyalist paramilitary organisations to take steps outside the law and let the strike go ahead.

The unionist politicians, who were uncomfortable at having to work with the hard men, doubted if the strike call would be effective. They tried to advise against it, stating their preference for a campaign of civil disobedience. When the stoppage began, Paisley, it was said, took off in haste for Canada to bury a dead aunt, creating the widespread impression that he was lying low, waiting to see how things turned out. Harry West, equally perplexed, showed by his early interventions that he had little sympathy with the stoppage. Only William Craig concealed his doubts but he kept, nevertheless, such a low profile that he managed to avoid public notice until the winning 'nag' of the UWC was being unsaddled in the paddock after the race, where he jostled with Paisley and West to appear as the winning owner.

After the Assembly vote, there was no sign, either that evening or the following morning, that the call for a general stoppage of industry was having any immediate effect. Estimates of absenteeism during the first morning were put at less than 5 per cent of the total labour force. Even then it was confined to the Lagan Valley engineering firms. (It should be noted that by my reckoning only 40,000 workers were absent from their jobs at the peak period of the stoppage, while more than 170,000 workers defied the strike call and continued working, albeit with difficulty because of the rotated electricity power cuts.)

Around lunchtime on Wednesday 15 May, however, armed and masked paramilitary groups appeared and started to close down mills and factories by intimidating workers and management. Main thoroughfares were immediately blocked and all traffic came to a standstill. The main power stations were occupied and generators were gradually run down to shut off supplies to industrial users. Within a couple of days they were running at only one-third capacity, preventing those who wanted to work from doing so. The lack of power also affected the intensive farming industry, and pictures of suffocated chickens being incinerated, fresh eggs being destroyed and milk being poured away helped to create an atmosphere of crisis that proved contagious throughout the community. Fuel distribution points were also taken over, tightening the UWC's stranglehold on the community. No one was immune from their regime of hardship. Some hospital patients were sent home, medical operations were postponed and emergency generators had to be brought into action to protect those undergoing treatment. The UWC established a headquarters at Hawthornden Road, provocatively close to Stormont, and began issuing passes and permits for essential services and products. The absence of UWC authorisation meant that vehicles, no matter how vital their occupants and loads for the well-being of the community, were turned back. This amounted to the staging of an unadulterated coup d'état for entirely political reasons.

The truly astonishing fact is that all this was carried out without the intervention of a combined security force of over 30,000 soldiers and policemen, who did not lift a finger to stop it. Incredibly, not one single case of arrest was reported, yet, for fourteen whole days there was a state of complete lawlessness in the North. The fact that not one single case relating to the stoppage was brought before the courts created the impression in the minds of the loyalists that the police, the military and Rees acquiesced in their illegal actions. The British military, who carried out a cursory evaluation of their ability to intervene and run the power stations, decided to opt out and were obviously withdrawn to barracks in large numbers to avoid contact with the strike leaders and activists. It was this apparent immunity from security and legal retribution, more than any other single failure by the authorities, that caused thousands of law-abiding people who had earlier given support to the Executive to switch sides. In all the years since I have never been given a believable explanation of why the strikers were allowed to gain such an initial grip. As events in 1977 were later to prove, tough police and army action at the beginning would have been effective and halted the progressive escalation that finally crippled us.

As a dedicated trade unionist I regretted the failure of the movement to influence the situation. A few days into the crisis there was still a chance left that the drift of supporters away from the Executive could have been arrested. The Irish Congress of Trade Unions invited Len Murray, general secretary of the Trades Union Congress in Britain, to lead a march back to work from the centre of Belfast where a substantial number of workers were still keen to go back to their jobs. The march was a complete flop, for the military and the police failed to prevent the loyalist paramilitary oganisations blocking off every housing estate during the night and closing the roads the workers would be using the next morning to get to the starting point of the march. Moreover, the military failed to protect adequately the couple of hundred brave workers and union leaders who marched. They were immediately intimidated by a howling mob of thugs, male and female, and were identified by fanatics who were later able to single them out for more savage treatment.

The no-warning car bombs exploded by loyalists in Dublin and Monaghan on Friday 17 May, when thirty-three people died and over a hundred were injured, undoubtedly heightened the impetus of the loyalist action and raised tension even more.

Every morning I had to run a gauntlet of hostile loyalists at road blocks to get from my home in Andersonstown to the office at Stormont. I preferred to drive myself in my own car with a police escort following in another vehicle. I have to say that some of the police were less than helpful and others downright hostile, directing me into the path of blocks despite taking circuitous routes. The priority for my department was to make sure that social security benefits continued to be paid. Apart from making routine unemployment, pension and family allowance payments, we had to deal with people laid off from their jobs. The postal service was disrupted and many post offices closed, so we had to open up emergency pay-out points in our district offices. This entailed running armed convoys with cash to meet the payments. I cannot pay sufficient tribute to the staff, who braved the toughest circumstances to get to their posts and keep this vital public service going. The fact that strikers benefited as well stuck in my throat, but the needs of the overwhelming majority of ordinary people who depended on the money had to come first and it was their position I was determined to protect.

By the middle of May, with the strike biting ever more damagingly into the fabric of life in Northern Ireland, the Executive sub-committee had been in almost constant session to find a form of phasing in the pact that could be recommended to the British and Irish governments. We had been deadlocked throughout. The sessions were tense and often quite abusive with frequent clashes between Roy Bradford and myself. Everybody recognised that if the Executive was to survive we would have to find an accommodation. In the end, against the votes of the SDLP, a modified implementation of the pact was forced through. The Alliance members supported the unionists against us. I was opposed, as were certain other members of the SDLP, to the new recommendations being made public at that time. We were of the opinion that a public announcement would only strengthen the UWC position at a crucial period in the stoppage. At a meeting of the SDLP Assembly party held on Wednesday 22 May, at Stormont, the modifications to the Council of Ireland proposals in the Sunningdale Agreement were rejected by a vote of 11 to 8. Faulkner was informed of this and he immediately left for Stormont Castle to inform Rees and draft a statement of resignation from the Executive which, of course, meant that it would collapse.

Meanwhile Stan Orme, deputy to Rees in the Northern Ireland Office, asked Fitt to convene another meeting of the Assembly party as he wished to speak to them about the implications of the vote just taken. By now the Assembly was in session and Faulkner had been persuaded to hold off making his resignation announcement in the Chamber. I was asked to go ahead with Ministry of Health and Social Services estimates which were scheduled as the business for that day. News of the crisis spread like lightning through the building and by the time I got to my feet rumours were already flying that the Executive had fallen. Ivan Cooper had whispered to me as I was going into the Assembly to spin out my speech over as long a period as possible, but few people were bothered about my planned expenditure of £300 million. All attention was focused on the drama that was being enacted behind the door of Room 16 in the the Parliament Buildings. Alone on the front bench, I kept going for nearly ninety minutes until I was informed that a new SDLP statement was agreed and ready for publication.

The clinching factor in getting the SDLP to change its mind was a new undertaking from Orme that, finally, internment would be ended. Given our links with the Labour Party, we had confidently expected, ever since they came to power in February, that they would not only swiftly release the internees, but compensate them for their period of detention without trial or conviction. We were quickly disillusioned, for honey words were all we received from the new Secretary of State. Rees felt no obligation to live up to the Conservative promises to end internment, having been thoroughly nobbled from day one, in my view, by the uncompromising views of Frank Cooper and Frank King, the current army commander. The trouble with Rees, I said at the time, was that he constantly wrestled with his conscience and sat on the fence and ducked taking decisions. I did not mind that. It was the rare time he came off the fence that caused all the trouble.

After my stint at the dispatch box I was told that Orme had given strong indications at the meeting that the agreement on ending detention would be honoured and that the government would at last fully back the Executive in trying to bring an end to the stoppage. But to keep the Executive show on the road, we had to accept and support the amended version of the Sunningdale Pact. A further vote was then taken by the SDLP, reversing the earlier decision. Faulkner was informed and a new statement was quickly drafted by him; this was read into the Assembly record when the assistant Speaker quite improperly stopped the moving of my departmental estimates to allow for the intervention.

On behalf of the Executive the Chief Executive said: 'The Executive stands united by the principles embodied in the Sunningdale Agreement as a basis for the development of mutual trust and confidence and looks to their implementation in accordance with the need for consent.' The agreement was now to be implemented in two phases. The first phase would involve the setting up of a fourteen-strong Council of Ministers, seven from each side of the border, whose function it would be to consult, co-operate and co-ordinate work in the social and economic areas which had been identified earlier in the negotiations. The joint meetings would be held alternately in the North and South, and would be serviced by the secondment of staff to a new joint secretariat. Every other initiative was off until the second phase, which would not be activated until after a test of opinion of the Northern Ireland electorate, probably at the next Assembly election, not due until 1977 or 1978.

Following this uneasy compromise, the attitude of all Executive members hardened in favour of immediate action to break the ongoing stoppage and restore the authority of the Executive. The Alliance member and several unionist members indicated that they would resign unless Rees acted decisively to clear the road blocks, to take over fuel distribution and to increase electrical power capacity, the lack of which meant that the workplaces of those who wanted to work had had to be closed. Next morning, on 23 May, a joint ministerial committee was set up, chaired by Orme, with Executive members involved. Hume, the minister responsible for fuel and power, placed before them a plan designed to take over complete control of oil and petrol supplies. Distribution to the public would be through a limited number of petrol stations which would be fortified and protected by the army and serviced by Ministry of Commerce officials. If necessary, military drivers would deliver petrol to these stations. It was expected that the remaining power workers would leave the main generating stations. When that happened three hundred experienced technical personnel from the army and navy, whom we were given to understand by Rees were standing by, would take over and restore full power. No difficulty was anticipated after the initial period of this exercise, for the generators were of a conventional type said to be familiar to these technicians.

Rees had repeatedly failed to act on this plan over the preceding weeks and now all on the Executive, with one or two exceptions, were determined not to tolerate further stalling. A meeting with Harold Wilson was demanded and granted. On Friday 24 May, Faulkner, Fitt and Napier were flown to Chequers to meet Wilson and a group of British ministers. Present were: Roy Mason, Minister of Defence; Sam Silkin, Attorney-General; Rees, and Wilson himself. The meeting commenced before lunch and continued until 4.40 p.m. – a five-hour period of discussion. The members of the Executive were under no illusions about the gravity of the perilous situation back home. They said that if decisive action was not taken immediately by the British government, then a number of members of the Executive would resign and Northern Ireland would be plunged into a whirlpool of community and constitutional turmoil with unforeseeable consequences.

The Chequers discussion centred on what precise courses of action could be taken and what the implications were likely to be. At its conclusion those from the Executive who attended came away with a clear understanding that all road blocks were to be removed, power plants taken over and fuel points instituted in line with the Hume plan. We reckoned that the loyalists were largely the products of a law and order community and, apart from a handful of extremists, would not operate outside the law once it was established that they were in breach of it. We predicted that the Hume plan, if vigorously activated,

241

would create the type of confrontation that the loyalists could not face. This was never really understood by Rees or Wilson at any time during the stoppage.

Overnight, after the Chequers talks, we learned from some journalist friends in London that Wilson had ordered the Hume plan to be fully implemented to coincide with a televised speech he was scheduled to make during peak viewing time on Saturday night. It was his intention, we were told, to describe what action the military had taken and warn the loyalists of the consequences of any action which opposed the army. For the first time in weeks we felt events were turning in our favour and we all waited for Wilson's speech with great anticipation. On the Saturday morning, however, we feared that something had gone wrong when the journalists reported to us that embargoed copies of Wilson's speech, which were to be available at 10.30 a.m. in good time for the Sunday newspaper deadlines, had been delayed. Regular phone calls throughout the day indicated that a discussion of unusual depth was taking place at 10 Downing Street involving Roy Mason and members of the Defence Council. We suspected that the Cooper–King combination was totally opposed to deepening army commitment and were of the opinion that the Executive should be allowed to fall. Only a token military operation should be mounted to ensure that British hands could be seen to be clean.

It appears that they won the day. The Wilson text, which was finally delivered to the journalists around 5 p.m., exploded upon the scene with the impact of a cotton-wool snowball hitting a battleship. His television address was a massive anti-climax offering a pathetic intervention that delivered nothing of what was promised. After the IRA 'doomsday' nonsense it was his second major miscalculation over Northern Ireland within a month. He ended up again in total absurdity by doing nothing more than calling the loyalists 'spongers'. Whatever else may be said about them, the loyalists are mainly people who have worked hard all their lives for their families and community. They have rightly earned everything they received from private or public employment, and their entitlement to state benefits. Their political and constitutional fears I understood and sympathised with. I could not, of course, approve the methods they were using to express them.

Faulkner was scheduled to broadcast immediately after the Wilson speech and, given the complete change of plan that had occurred, he was left in a very exposed position. In the early hours of Sunday morning, as we expected, certain superficial operations were embarked on by the army. Some road blocks were removed outside the houses of SDLP Assembly members. The craziest exercise was a convoy of heavy military vehicles which were repeatedly sent out the Antrim Road gates of Girdwood Park, in the sight of Gerry Fitt's bedroom window, after circling in through the back gate of the barracks in Cliftonpark Avenue. He was told that convoys were being sent out to take down road blocks and deliver petrol.

By breakfast time on the Sunday morning it was clear that any hope of effecting a rescue operation for the Executive was gone. Even the government car pool at Stormont had run out of petrol and could not get its tanks refilled. Fitt saw Rees that morning at Stormont and afterwards all the SDLP members of the Executive gathered at his house to review the situation. We decided it was hopeless to carry on any longer and agreed to resign unless the plan proposed to Wilson by the Executive was implemented without further delay. Rees had meanwhile left for Cornwall to see Wilson, while Cooper and myself left for Dublin to inform the Irish government of the worsening position. Over recent weeks we had used a variety of couriers to carry messages between us and the Irish government. It was the type of information that we could not risk passing on by telephone. This arrangement also meant that we were able to get fresh bread and milk brought over the border for our families. On this occasion, when Cooper and I reached Dublin that evening we first met Cosgrave and members of his cabinet in Garret FitzGerald's house. They were left in no doubt as to the grimness of the situation. We went from there to the home of former Prime Minister Jack Lynch to deliver the same ominous message.

Driving back to Belfast the following morning, we stopped at Dundalk to telephone ahead and arrange a rendezvous with our police escort on the northern side of the border. They were in position when we crossed at Killeen a short time later and they travelled ahead of us as we headed through Newry towards Belfast. After passing Banbridge we ran into a road block near Dromore which had been mounted by flag-waving farmers, many with cudgels and other weapons, who had drawn their tractors and machinery across the dual carriageway. The police vehicle was waved through a gap but before we could follow it was closed off again and some of the farmers ran menacingly towards us. Our driver, from the Stormont car pool, acted with great presence of mind, swung the car across the central reservation of the dual carriageway and headed back the way we had come. We noticed a number of cars were giving chase, so he took to the side roads near Banbridge, retraced our journey to Newry and Dundalk and then headed to Cavan hoping to reach Belfast safely this time via Armagh. Eileen Fitt, one of Gerry's five daughters, who was travelling with us, was as terrified as we were. Ivan and I had both drawn our guns when the confrontation developed and we sat with them on our laps for the rest of the very frightening journey back to the border. On our way through Cavan we were flagged down by a policeman who asked if we were Cooper and Devlin. 'There's a phone call for you from Stormont,' he said. I went in to his station and took the call, which was from Faulkner telling me that all his people were resigning and pulling out of the Executive.

While we were travelling, the Executive had met that Monday in a mood of total depression. After all the political and military prevarication, the army had entered the Belfast Harbour Estate that morning to begin petrol distribution, but it was too little, too late. Executive discussions by this time were neither full nor frank. Bradford's earlier call for direct talks with the UWC had greatly irritated us. We were also of the opinion that much of our earlier business had been leaked by someone to the UWC and we had no desire to give them further assistance by the same route. We learned, for instance, that information on the internal difficulties in the Sunningdale sub-committee had been leaked to the UWC leaders. There was one particular occasion when West came rushing into the Assembly chamber shouting to the Speaker that the Executive had fallen. On another occasion after a discussion in the Executive room on an emergency fuel plan, we found that the UWC had taken pre-emptive action based on our plan. Their action was too coincidental in detail to be anything other than a direct feed from within the Executive. We had since limited discussion quite considerably to maintain our dwindling hopes of survival in the face of this monumental disloyalty.

These restrictions were to have unfortunate repercussions. Over the last few days of the committee's existence we tended to take decisions on our own – reporting to Faulkner in private. As a result the scope of our discussions reduced in scale, we tended to feed exclusively off party colleagues and inter-party cohesion suffered. This also left the way clear for the undermining of our functions. A small sub-committee of departmental assistant Permanent Secretaries was set up by Orme to keep the Secretary of State informed of events, and met on a daily basis at Stormont Castle. But away from our political scrutiny in those last dramatic few days, it was diverting valuable information from Executive members. Confusion was created between ourselves and the Northern Ireland Office on the odd occasion that joint decisions had to be taken. We were by no means happy with the functioning of this committee and the way in which it succeeded in by-passing the Executive even though we were still meeting daily. We were unable to get to Stormont by road during this time and were flown in by helicopter for these daily consultations.

Faulkner was coming under tremendous pressure from even his most supportive backbenchers to get Rees to negotiate with the strikers. This course of action had been turned down frequently by the Executive and Rees for weeks, although it should be pointed out that Orme had fruitlessly met the strike leaders on 15 May while the stoppage was still escalating. Now even some Faulknerite members of the Executive were lending support to the backbenchers' demand for negotiations.

That Monday night, Faulkner, who showed rare courage throughout the preceding week in resisting the demands to negotiate with the UWC, received a telephone call at his home in Seaforde, Co. Down, from a senior civil servant who informed him that the gradual run-down of the electricity system was fast reaching the point of no return. When the power stopped and the water pumps failed, raw sewage was likely to flow back into the pipes and flood large parts of central Belfast.

It was perfectly clear that the psychology employed by the UWC was to pick off key pro-Sunningdale personalities one by one and subject them to inexorable pressure. They had done this successfully earlier, before the Sunningdale vote was taken, when three members of Faulkner's group had defected. They had turned at least two of his supporters within the Executive. Now Faulkner himself was the target. The nightmare scenario that had been painted for him was too much. He decided he could not risk it happening. The growing conviction that, doughty fighter though he was, he could not win through was confirmed by a virtual mutiny among the most senior civil servants at Stormont when he arrived the next morning. A number of the Permanent Secretaries met Faulkner on his own, something quite unprecedented, and indicated to him that they could conceive of a situation where they could no longer support the Executive. It was an incredible statement that shook Faulkner to his very toes.

Outside Stormont the building was gridlocked by lines of tractors towing farm machinery, with farmers calling for our resignations. At the ninety-minute Executive meeting later that morning, in Parliament Buildings, Faulkner revealed that his mind was made up in favour of opening up lines of communication to the UWC by using an agent like Lord Grey, the former governor, or Sir Fred Catherwood, the industrialist, as go-between. His proposal did not receive the full support of the Executive, nor was it expected to, and he left to attend a meeting of his own group which had convened in the adjacent Unionist Party room. About 1.20 p.m. he was back in the Executive room to announce that his party had decided he should go to Rees to tell him to negotiate with the UWC or all the Faulkner unionists would resign from the Executive forthwith. Everyone in the room knew that Rees could not accept that from the Faulkner group or anyone else. All knew it was the end, and everyone shook hands. Many had tears in their eyes. Cooper and I, of course, missed this defining moment as we were still on the road back.

As Faulkner went outside to read his resignation statement for the television cameras the Assembly met at 2.30 p.m. on 28 May 1974. It was a bizarre atmosphere and after Austin Currie vainly tried to interest the chamber in a scheme to assist intimidated householders, after less than half an hour it was agreed to move for adjournment. Rees had announced there was no longer any constitutional basis for the Executive's existence but we decided to wait to be sacked rather than resign. Some of my colleagues adjourned to their offices to clear their desks while waiting for the sack. It came in a letter from Rees the next morning saying that he had signed warrants terminating our appointments. Direct rule resumed and the UWC called off the strike.

From my point of view, there remains one further element to be fitted into the story of the last days of the Executive. Early in April, as part of a drive to clear up the rent and rates strike we had backed since 1971 as a protest against internment, Austin Currie, as housing minister, announced there would be no amnesty for those owing money. At the time 11,000 tenants of publicly provided housing owed arrears. This issue was inextricably bound up, in my mind, with the failure by Rees to end internment. But the final straw for me, was that, after a brief pause, until 20 May, to allow arrears to be cleared up, tenants would face a 25p per week collection charge. Many of them were already subject to compulsory deductions at source from their social security. I had supported the strike myself by not paying the rent on my Housing Executive house but I had paid my arrears off before Sunningdale. Now Currie was actually being forced to introduce this additional levy. There were clear divisions in SDLP circles on the issue. When the matter was raised in the Executive, Hume and I voted against it and I was appalled when Currie announced in the Assembly that he was going ahead with it, especially since I was the minister who was to make the collection by deducting it from benefit payments. I was totally out of sympathy with this policy. I felt it fairer and more effective to solve the problem by appealing to the tenants to clear up their arrears. I had expressed vociferous reservations as soon as the levy was mooted and so strongly did I feel that I wrote a letter of resignation from the Executive which I handed over while attending a meeting with Rees on 17 May. The letter said:

> I stated to you last week and to Stan Orme a fortnight ago that I would not remain on the Northern Ireland Executive in charge of a department which would be used as an instrument to impose penalties on rent and rates strikers unless there was hard evidence that internment or detention was being seriously phased out.
>
> My attitude to this matter has been made known to a limited range of people since the issue arose in the first place. I have remained passive in the hope that the written commitment we received on a number of occasions by your predecessors in government would be honoured by you. Instead, I find that you have promised to bring into being a small committee of five people to assist with resettling the problems of released detainees and you have done nothing else towards that commitment.

Against that, I receive weekly reports of mass assaults by military on detainee compounds; the female population detained in Armagh prison has doubled; the number of people detained in the Long Kesh is increasing daily; assassinations of isolated members of the minority soar to the deafening sounds of your inertia; and six weeks ago you announced at Westminster without consultation with the SDLP that you intended to reactivate the Emergency Provisions Act 1973 though we in the SDLP had been given to understand by the Secretary of State, Francis Pym, last December that the opposite course of action would be followed.

I had been told on two separate occasions that large scale releases were to take place on the week the Westminster elections were announced. Based on that, one could conclude that the arrangements had already been set up for the releases. These releases were never brought into effect. The responsibility for that decision is yours entirely. You have had ample time to produce proof of your determination to end detention. I am now of the opinion that this issue, which was one of our prior reservations before we entered a power-sharing Executive, is not to be met.

Thus, I am faced with a personal decision regarding my position on the Executive, in view of my belief that you are not seriously intending to honour this commitment.

In these circumstances, I could not participate in the imposition of penalties on householders suffering from the same misgivings about the ending of detention that I myself share. My only honourable course is to withdraw from the Executive. I request you to recognise this letter as my resignation.

In ordinary circumstances this issue might well have brought the Executive down. Hume, McGrady and Cooper all told me that if I resigned on that issue they would go too. The Executive could not have outlived such a haemorrhage. But that Friday afternoon, while I was arguing with Rees, the news of the dreadful death toll from the loyalist car bombings in Dublin and Monaghan began to come in. With the UWC strike already beginning to bite hard, I asked Rees to postpone discussion on the matter and freeze my resignation letter. By the end of the month it had, of course, become academic.

Several days after the Executive had fallen, Margaret Gilpin invited me to come to the private office for a farewell drink later that week. I agreed, of course. I had made so many friends and developed a lot of respect for those I worked with in such a short spell that I wanted to thank them and say a proper goodbye. When I got there I was surprised to see just how many people had packed into my former ministerial office. Several of the senior officials made friendly and supportive speeches which deeply moved me and I thanked them for all their help. I thought to myself that the Department of Health and Social Services was so competent it could work every bit as well without political leadership – though I did not advocate that policy.

There was little recrimination on the workings of the short-lived and ill-fated power-sharing experiment. What it had demonstrated beyond all doubt was its effectiveness and the necessity that it would have to be incorporated as a mandatory principle in any future formula to create peace and political stability.

The SDLP team in the executive had performed well. We were anxious to make the power-sharing arrangements work, to show that a joint operation of this kind could function effectively and that everyone would receive fair play from an efficient set of ministers. This turned out to be the highpoint of my life and political career, and I still have feelings of great satisfaction from having served in the Executive and from having achieved what we did regardless of religion or tradition. While we did not have the power or time to divide the wealth of the nation more fairly and squarely, we did reduce the hardship and distress.

The collective effort of the ministers, so ably led by Brian Faulkner, is still an unexcelled model and legacy for future attempts to govern our perplexed community. There was ample evidence throughout those days that political traditions or party allegiances were no obstacles to administering the North with even-handed professionalism. But for me the lasting surprise of this period will always be the emergence of the other Brian Faulkner, not the dour, scheming sabbatarian, but the courageous visionary who relaxed with us, shared our jokes and even accompanied us to the Members' Bar and bought his round.

There is no doubt that he was by far the most effective politician ever to walk the corridors of Stormont. He was leagues beyond the yardsticks of mediocrity that measured the ineffectiveness of generations of unionist politicians. Where they were tongue-tied, he was articulate. He had political and business know-how; they had little. He had purpose and direction; they relied on tribal instincts, an automatic uncritical party vote and a biased civil service. In the 1960s he created jobs on a scale unprecedented then or since, bringing to the North such firms as Courtaulds, Rolls-Royce, Goodyear, Michelin, Ford, Grundig and Hoechst, providing the diversity necessary to transform the local economy from its traditional dependence on ships, linen and ropes. His greatest achievement, as far as unionism was concerned, was his decisive handling of the IRA campaign of 1956–62. As Minister of Home Affairs he set up a small coterie of civil servants, led by the infamous William Stout, and interned suspects from republican areas. These tactics paid off.

Faulkner never quite made it because he was not part of the 'big house' gentry. The feudal lords alone were considered fit to be prime ministers, not the self-made entrepreneurs or their sons. Faulkner was drafted in only when the roof had lifted and the walls were crumbling. It was too late to shore them up but he tried manfully, as he had done in everything else he attempted for his party and Northern Ireland. He died all too prematurely in a horse-riding accident on 3 March 1977.

11

AN UNWORTHY SQUABBLE

The fall of the Executive was followed by a massive political inquest. The SDLP held several sessions to reconsider its position, which not surprisingly was to reaffirm the party's whole-hearted commitment to the Sunningdale process. Faulkner, who said he was a born optimist, made favourable noises about trying to get another power-sharing Executive together, an initiative which we, of course, would have eagerly backed.

I was always uneasy that Faulkner, whose political support was already haemorrhaging dangerously, had been asked to swallow too much in one gulp at Sunningdale. In retrospect it seems to me that if we had adopted a two-stage approach, by allowing power-sharing at Stormont to establish itself and be seen to be both non-threatening and effective, he might have been able to sell it. Then we could have moved forward to establish the Irish dimension from a secure base camp.

On the other hand, had it not been for Heath's election undermining us and giving the political high ground to our opponents, we might have been able to demonstrate the credibility of the Executive. We were going to be bogged down for some time solving all the detail of the Sunningdale process before getting the Council of Ireland going, so, without the disastrous election result, the goodwill we were rapidly generating might have been decisive.

I regard the successful negotiation which brought about the Executive and the work we were able to do in our all too brief time in office as the defining episodes of my private and political life. The term 'power-sharing' has since become politically suspect in Northern Ireland but my experience has convinced me that whatever it is called, responsibility sharing, in one form or another, will be an integral part of any future political deal between unionists and nationalists. It is the only practical way to reconcile the conflicting objectives of both communities and to create an acceptable and fair political framework for government.

Whatever the political might-have-beens in early 1974, our willingness to try again was greeted without any enthusiasm by Rees. After what was only a ritual consultation with the parties, he set out to pursue an ambiguous and cynical policy, passing the political buck to the local politicians and starting what inevitably turned out to be a fruitless flirtation with the Provos. In his own post-strike reflections Rees had referred to the emergence of what he called 'Ulster nationalism'. This phenomenon, which has never been heard of since, was one of the topics he suggested could be discussed by an elected constitutional convention. The idea was that we would argue with each other about the political future of Northern Ireland while Rees could sit on the sidelines and continue wrestling with his conscience.

He first set about writing a White Paper to provide an agenda for the Constitutional Convention, which was published in July. The hardliners on the unionist side (who very surprisingly called off their strike without demanding any political concessions from the British government) were understandably cock-a-hoop and triumphant and in no mind to make the sort of concessions we would want. Although we had to go in there and try, I was fairly sure there would be deadlock.

As we were all limbering up for the planned election of the seventy-eight members of the Convention, Rees and Cooper moved to open up dialogue with the Provos. I am fairly sure their intention was to encourage the Provos to call a permanent ceasefire and lure them into mainstream politics with a view to arranging a comprehensive political settlement that would allow Britain finally to get out of Ireland. This was the Provos' basic demand, and an objective openly stated on a number of occasions by Wilson himself. Rees had earlier lifted the proscription of the UVF, more evidence of his strategy to stage-manage an end to violence, bring all factions together in the Convention to force a solution to the Irish question.

I am utterly convinced this was the real mindset of the Rees–Cooper regime at Stormont Castle. Cooper was, after all, the man who had negotiated with Makarios in Cyprus to secure the British exit from an equally debilitating commitment. The loyalist strike had cost Northern Ireland 10,000 jobs and over £200 million, bills which Britain would have to pay. International embarrassment, especially in the United States and with the partners in the European Community, was becoming a major factor. Above all, with advances in aircraft technology and the advent of satellite communications, Britain no longer had any economic or strategic interest in remaining in Northern Ireland. The days when Derry was a vital staging point for trans-atlantic shipping or when Ireland was an outpost for radio relay beacons between Europe and North America had long gone. Increasingly to British eyes, Northern Ireland amounted to nothing more than a painful, and costly, boil on John Bull's backside.

Disenchantment with our problems was increasingly evident on what has come to be called the British mainland. Irish products, like Kerrygold butter, would be boycotted after soldiers had been killed in Northern Ireland but the real aggravating factor was the extension of the IRA campaign across the Irish Sea. Since the first attack in March 1973, when hundreds were injured in co-ordinated car bombings at the Old Bailey and Whitehall in London, others had taken place in the capital and in provincial cities like Birmingham and Manchester.

Cooper tried to involve me in his operation. Over a meal at Stormont Castle he sounded me out about the political situation as I saw it, with specific reference to my assessment of the Provos and what they might be prepared to settle for. I saw no justification for their futile violence and was keen to see it halted, so, with the help of a legal friend, I drew up a number of practical suggestions for responses that could be made to encourage a ceasefire. These mainly related to military tactics on the ground. I refused to be used further as a direct conduit. The ideas I had articulated were, however, picked up by Cooper, christened 'the PD formula' by his officials and formed the basis of the talks he eventually held. Cooper's biggest difficulty in opening dialogue with the Provos was in finding an honest broker. Ever since the ignoble end of the 1972 truce, politicians, including Rees, had publicly pledged they would not meet or negotiate with the Provos. This undertaking meant that anything Cooper did had to be at arm's length and deniable in parliament by Rees.

There were significant levels of distrust on both sides and the first efforts to create dialogue were unsuccessful. However, after the horrific Provisional IRA bombings at two pubs in Birmingham in November 1974, when twenty-one people were killed, contact was established and a ceasefire came into effect in December. The mutually chosen intermediaries were a group of Protestant clergymen from Northern Ireland who met the IRA leadership in a quiet hotel at Feakle, Co. Clare, on 9–11 December. The first talks broke up in some disarray when the Irish police stormed the hotel. It is said that a few locals saw three or four of the clergymen and asked: 'Is Paisley one of them?' Word then reached the Garda Síochána who arrived to find the clergymen taking tea and their guests gone. Despite the interruption the clergymen shuttled between the Provos and government for a period, effecting a ceasefire and clearing the way for face-to-face contacts between the Provos and British officials.

Rees in the background, and Cooper with officials, then played an ambiguous game with the Provos for several months, allowing them to believe that Britain was seriously preparing the ground for a withdrawal from Northern Ireland. The Provos were kept sweet partly by the steady release of internees. (The gates of the internment centres finally closed at the end of 1975.) I was instrumental in shedding the first public light on the discussions some months afterwards when I was slipped a copy of a twelve-point plan purportedly under discussion by the two sides. The Irish government was deeply concerned at the dialogue between the British and the Provos and obtained the plan when Dáithí Ó Conaill, the most influential member of the IRA leadership at the time, was arrested in Dublin.

The points on the table were as follows: the eventual withdrawal of all military to barracks and then to Britain; an end to arrests, screening of suspects and persistent searching of Catholic homes; immunity from arrest for certain named people; the issue of personal firearms permits to certain people; the establishment of incident centres to monitor the ceasefire; the release of one hundred detainees within a specified period of time; the ending of detention without trial by a certain date; discussion at local level between the security forces and Provos; the lifting of permanent road checks around Catholic areas; the RUC not to be re-introduced into Catholic areas; direct talks between the government and the Provos to be started; and the preparation of a formal ceasefire agreement.

The process was well under way by the time I got hold of the copy, and developments that I was aware of convinced me that the twelve-point plan was genuine. Internees had been released. Incident centres had been set up in Provisional Sinn Féin offices with public money provided for staff, typewriters, duplicators, telephones and even telex machines. Although they were ostensibly set up to monitor the ceasefire, in line with the aim of Rees and Cooper to get the Provos into politics, they were quickly given a wider role. Instructions were sent out to all government departments to co-operate with the centres. Large-scale funds were made available for job projects. Much of the money from one such scheme, renovating houses at Bally-murphy, was actually diverted into paramilitary hands. While all this was going on Rees and Cooper created a whole series of 'withdrawal symptoms' as evidence that Britain was intending to withdraw, like the failure to include the shipbuilders, Harland and Wolff, and the aerospace company, Shorts, both publicly owned, in government nationalisation plans. The closures of a Foreign Office communications post, an air traffic control centre, two Royal Air Force establishments and a Royal Navy depot were also presented as signs of withdrawal. Even the ending of the long-running ferry service between Belfast and Heysham was cited.

It speaks volumes for the political naïveté of the Provos that they were deceived by such sleight of hand. As I had easily predicted from my experience in 1972, the ceasefire gradually unravelled and by mid-1975 the Provos had resumed their destruction of property and life. The exercise was totally mis-handled and gave the gunmen and bombers a boost and a role in politics that almost legitimised their violence. The British government had learned nothing from the 1972 debacle and the lasting effect was to give the younger Provos a taste for politics which enabled them to run in future elections, although they were to do so 'with an Armalite in one hand and a ballot paper in the other', which is, of course, a perversion of the democratic system. What was also disgraceful was the way the Provos had been nourished with public money to the disadvantage of other parties.

Rees and Cooper had hoped to draw the Provos into the Con-vention and for a time there were signs that they would rise to the bait. However, when the election took place on 1 May 1975, twelve months after the collapse of the Executive, they were conspicuously absent. I stood in West Belfast and was elected on the first count with 6,267 votes against a quota of 5,103, taking

Dr Joe Hendron in with me on my transfers. Altogether we took two out of the six seats in the division and although our support was marginally down on the Assembly poll two years earlier, I was well satisfied.

The Convention gathered for the first time at Stormont on 8 May under the chairmanship of Sir Robert Lowry. I asked my friend Turlough O'Donnell about his fellow judge. 'Hard and fair. He'll stand no messing,' I was told. The assessment turned out to be totally accurate. Two distinguished local civil servants were appointed as advisers: Dr John Oliver and Maurice Hayes. They too made a valuable contribution to our work. The terms of reference from Rees were for us to come up with a form of government that would command the most widespread acceptance. The Unionist Coalition held forty-six of the seventy-eight seats, giving them a majority of fourteen over all other groups, a position they interpreted as a mandate to oppose change. Predictably they called uncompromisingly for a return to British parliamentary standards – code for a return to an old-style Stormont with majority rule and control of law and order. The power-sharing group – ourselves, Alliance and the tiny rump of Faulkner unionists – renewed our demands for another try at partnership in government.

When we got down to debate the unionist views were rigid. I caught them off guard when I said that we would agree with the Independent Orange Order manifesto drafted by Lindsay Crawford in 1905. They were overjoyed at this and said they were off to the parliamentary library to look it up. 'No need to,' I said. 'I will tell you all about it.' I then explained it was a plea for unity and tolerance and understanding on this island. ' "Bone of our bone, flesh of our flesh" was how it described us, your fellow countrymen,' I told them. 'If you start from that premise we'll be able to do business,' I said. The only effect my offer had was to add the forgotten name of Lindsay Crawford to the long list of Popish demons despised by inflexible unionists.

Despite this unpromising start we felt obliged at least to go through the motions of seeking an accommodation with the unionists who opposed us. The key to any deal was Paisley and the key to Paisley was Desmond Boal, an eminent barrister who had once been a member of the Unionist Party before defecting to Paisley's Democratic Unionists. As a unionist MP at Stormont, he had been one of the main critics of Terence O'Neill, but after direct rule he seemed to lose interest in politics and concentrated on criminal work in the courts, where he achieved a formidable reputation as an advocate and cross-examiner. He was an uncompromising stickler where the law was concerned and many suspects were prepared to wait weeks or even months on remand until Boal was free to represent them. About the time the Convention came into being Boal was voicing some pretty radical ideas, given his hardline background, about a new federal relationship between north and south which we felt were worth further exploration.

Boal lived on the Irish Sea coast at St John's Point, near Ardglass in Co. Down, and back in 1971 a discreet meeting had been set up there to discuss his ideas. John Hume and Austin Currie accompanied me to the meeting at which Paisley was also present. It was a cordial and positive occasion, where the private, charming and constructive Paisley was on display. Looking back on his turbulent career, I am always struck by the contrast between the public, demagogue orator, thundering away from religious pulpit or political platform, and the friendly, personable and often warm private figure I have had many encounters with over the years.

Our talk that night ranged widely over the potential mechanisms for a new federal north–south relationship. Boal and Paisley were clearly motivated to seek ways of protecting unionist rights and governance, as they had serious doubts about the British commitment to keep Northern Ireland within the United Kingdom. Their idea was for a return of the old Stormont with broadly similar powers. By the uncompromising standards that they had previously set themselves, this was the sort of far-reaching stuff we thought was the bones of any lasting settlement. At the end of our talks we agreed to meet again after reflecting on what had already been said. News of our encounter quickly reached Faulkner however. After he publicly attacked Paisley about seeking an Irish dimension at Stormont, Paisley made it clear our talks were at an end. Not for the first time he headed for the safety of the hills even before the going got tough.

When the Convention broke for the summer in 1975, with the prospect of making any advance halted, I turned to consideration of other options. Glenn Barr, one of the leaders of the loyalist strike, had become a member of the Convention. Although our political standpoints differed on constitutional questions, we found that we shared a lot of common ground on the bread and butter, social and economic, issues. I was keen to use this rapport to develop political co-operation on the things we agreed about. Trust built in this way would then enable us to approach the more divisive points from a shared rather than an opposing position.

Given the uninterested stance of Rees and Cooper and the solid conviction among both nationalists and unionists that the British were indeed preparing the ground for a pull-out, it was not surprising that attention began to turn to the idea of a negotiated independence for Northern Ireland. The closure of the government-owned Rolls-Royce plant at Dundonald, near Belfast, was only one of a series of economic blows that hit primarily the loyalist working-class community at this period. The damage was as much psychological as economic, for the traditional emotional links with Britain were now being questioned as never before. Glenn Barr, who was associated with the UDA, was one of the first proponents of independence. Although mainstream political opinion, especially among unionists, was horrified at the proposal, a surprising cross-party alliance of individuals supported at least a serious consideration of the options.

Barr did some amazingly good work, producing an interesting

document advocating the adoption of the American system of government, with checks and balances applied between a president and a parliament. There would also have been a comprehensive bill of rights to underpin and guarantee the position of each individual citizen. I was in favour of this approach and seriously flirted with the concept of independence for quite a time. I eventually lost active interest when a loyalist group, who claimed to have invested great energy investigating the merits of independence, only produced the design for a new flag. This was an idiotic position. In my view independence has still not been studied and debated seriously enough and until it is it must remain on the list of future political options.

A potentially more fruitful political opportunity did open up in August 1975 when the Convention gathered again after the summer break. My years of working as a trade unionist had developed in me the instinct to negotiate, conciliate, compromise and seek a solution to any deadlock I encountered. This stance had carried me successfully through my political life, most notably the Whitelaw negotiations in 1972–3. So when I spotted David Trimble, a university lecturer who was one of Bill Craig's leading lieutenants in the Vanguard Party element of the loyalist coalition, in the corridor at Stormont I stopped him.

'You fellows promised to talk to us. What about it?' I said.

'OK,' replied Trimble. 'What about tomorrow?'

Thus began what became known as the Voluntary Coalition talks. Bill Craig came up with a proposition for the Unionist Coalition to join with the SDLP in a temporary or emergency coalition to run Northern Ireland for a four- or five-year parliamentary term until the security situation improved and the political deadlock was resolved. Craig argued that this approach was justified at a time of national crisis and he said it was compatible with the national government formed in Britain during the Second World War. At first the SDLP was sceptical, but faced with barren inter-party dialogue and the looming collapse of the Convention we reconsidered our position and

261

through Sir Robert Lowry we indicated we would at least explore what the terms for such a coalition might be.

During our subsequent discussions we were able to reach a broad measure of potential agreement with the unionists, including support for a tough campaign against terrorists on both sides. The Provo campaign was back in full swing after the cynical ceasefire ended and loyalist paramilitaries too were rampant. I encouraged the view that the programme for a voluntary coalition could be widened out to include not only security, but an agreed social and economic policy. The favourable response to this from the unionist negotiators was highly promising.

By 3 September, after a week of exploratory but consolidating discussions, the broad shape and outline terms of a voluntary arrangement were clearly emerging. But there were signs that the Unionist Coalition was far from unanimous about what their negotiators were leading them into. These rumblings, and pressure from within his church and party, were causing Paisley to develop cold feet. Despite the fact that his party had already decided to end the inter-party discussions, he had been consulted and had approved all the steps and terms agreed until that point. Indeed, I understood his only condition was that any deal should be put to the community for approval by referendum. Late that day the unionist leaders approached Lowry and asked him to prepare a paper on what had transpired, specifically so that any doubts about our position, what we had said and what we had agreed to, could be put down in black and white to ensure there were no misunderstandings within all sections of the Unionist Coalition. Lowry asked us to approve this request and we agreed immediately.

Overnight, while his paper was being put together, the cracks within the unionists widened out. By morning Paisley was walking the corridors at Stormont saying the price of regaining a parliament was too high. His immediate hangers-on were already denouncing the proposals as a 'sell-out'. The next day, Friday, the Official Unionists and Craig's Vanguard Party were in disarray and divided. Over the weekend pressure grew against a deal. On the Sunday, as I understand it, Paisley's religious flock rebelled against any involvement of the SDLP in power. The elders and ministers told him that they would sit in the freezing cold in spite rather than share a warm fire with us. This was the sort of unadulterated bigotry I had hoped was well behind us. By Monday, when the Unionist Coalition gathered together to discuss the issue, it was smothered outright. Craig alone voted in favour of his idea. Afterwards I said that 'there wasn't a million miles of difference between us. It would not have been beyond the ingenuity of man to work out a form of words.'

It became clear later that apart from Paisley's political reticence and Craig's lonely optimism, another more malign influence had helped to wreck the initiative. Enoch Powell, the maverick British Conservative who had been ostracised because of his extreme views on race relations, had jumped on the unionist bandwagon in 1974 to pick up the safe South Down seat in parliament after losing his own in the British midlands town of Wolverhampton. The unionists were mesmerised by this Edwardian figure with his hissing voice and convoluted language. They thought he had a hot line to the British establishment and would be able to protect them from the wiles of Rees and Wilson. Behind the scenes Powell had plotted to frustrate any political development other than continued direct rule, which he reckoned was the supreme form of unionism, binding Northern Ireland tightly into Britannia's bosom. This attitude, of course, arrogantly trampled on the rights and aspirations of the minority community.

The unionists went on to write and bulldoze through a report demanding nothing less than the return of the old Stormont and majority rule. Power-sharing and an institutionalised Irish dimension were both ruled out. After Christmas 1975, Rees sent the report back and asked them to think again. The Convention was briefly recalled in February to allow them to do so, but inter-party talks with us did not even last an hour and Rees wound up the Convention in March, putting the unionists' unacceptable report in the vaults at Stormont Castle where I assume it is still gathering dust.

Not long after that I went off to do a three-week course in social policy at Salzburg in Austria. When I returned there was a message for me to get in touch with the Reverend Martin Smyth of the Official Unionist Party. He wanted to set up some informal talks with the SDLP about the political situation, so it was arranged that John Hume and I would meet him at Captain Austin Ardill's house near Carrickfergus. We held a series of discussions there throughout the spring and early summer. The agenda was a wide-ranging one and we found in Ardill and Smyth a surprising willingness to be flexible. However, we doubted the full sincerity of this approach, for we suspected there might be a willingness to make cosmetic compromises with a view to forcing the British government into reconsidering the Convention report. In the event it is my view that the two unionist negotiators were indeed prepared to look seriously at our demands, as were their own party leaders.

Early in June Ardill and Smyth were so pleased at the solutions being outlined that they decided to seek a mandate from the other elements of the Unionist Coalition for the talks to go on. Yet again Paisley delivered the knock-out upper-cut, leaking details of the talks and pile-driving the rest of the coalition into bringing them to an inconclusive end. That proved to be the last formal political initiative I was involved in. To my regret and frustration, like the others, it only demonstrated what it was possible to achieve by compromise, without actually achieving anything.

In September 1976 Rees was recalled to London to become Home Secretary and was replaced by Roy Mason, a tough, pugnacious wee Yorkshire man who had started out in the coal mines. He was always surrounded by clouds of smoke for he puffed away incessantly at his pipe. Soon after his arrival Mason decided that there was little scope for political progress and concentrated on trying to bolster the local economy while launching a vigorous effort by the police to convict paramilitaries through the courts. Twelve months afterwards he finally signalled an end to the Rees–Cooper policies when he announced that the myth of British withdrawal was dead for ever. Since then none of his successors at Stormont Castle have fared well in securing political advance. Direct rule remains, although nationalists have been given a limited say in events through the 1985 Anglo-Irish Agreement; this provides for Dublin to advise and be consulted about a range of matters in the North. The formula for a stable and widely acceptable solution is still as elusive as ever.

Once the Executive had fallen and the Assembly was dissolved, my income disappeared. There was no severance pay or redundancy payments or notice. One day we were on salaries and allowances, the next we were left in what we stood up in. As a politician, unemployment did not suddenly lead to idleness. On the contrary, the demands continued. Constituents' houses still needed repair, social security benefit payments were still being disputed, people were still being screened and arrested by the security forces. Apart from meeting the needs of my own family, the telephone bill and the cost of running my constituency advice centre was prohibitive. I had to have a job.

I knew the trade union scene better than any other and, during my days at Andrews', had been close enough to getting a full-time job with my union. Michael Mullen, general secretary of the Irish Transport and General Workers' Union whose headquarters were in Dublin, knew of my predicament and asked me if I would help to carry out a survey with a view to organising a northern region for the union. I was romantic about the Irish Transport Union in the way that young football supporters are about Manchester United. My father had, of course, been a shop steward in the 1920s, when Billy McMullen, a Shankill Road man, was secretary. When I was subsequently asked in 1975 to become the union's northern organiser I was therefore more than pleased. There was little other opportunity for me to get a job. My political career had been too controversial and jobs were never available, especially in the private sector, to stirrers like me. Few employers wanted to risk having someone in their firm who might attract violence from paramilitaries, cause offence to one section or other of their customers or be identified with one faction or another.

When I settled in to my union office on the Antrim Road in Belfast, there was an economic squeeze on and redundancies faced us throughout the North. For instance, the Derry shirt factories, which provided substantial female employment and made the wife the breadwinner in many homes, were facing tremendous problems because of competition from cheaper products coming in from the low-wage countries of South-East Asia. At the time the ITGWU had few members in the North. Indeed membership was confined to the deep-sea docks and a few adjacent factories in the Belfast Harbour Estate. It was without members in rural areas and very few were Protestants. In terms of expanding the activities of the union there was really limited scope. The well-paid jobs were organised by other unions, all of which could be described as British-based. The only workers not organised were the low-paid who had little tradition of joining unions. Some members of the more established unions attempted to freeze my union out, especially in parts of Belfast. The fact that it was Dublin-based was used as a smear and my members were disparagingly referred to as 'Fenians'.

I started off amongst the unorganised manufacturing workers in rural areas. After meeting workers on social and sporting occasions to get to know them, I introduced union matters, and this usually led to membership. Next I tried large stores and shops and hotels, which were relatively unorganised. I made inroads there too. In September 1978, the ninety-nine members I had recruited in the Belfast Europa Hotel stopped work and walked out one morning after months of fruitless talks with management about recognising the union and negotiating pay and conditions through it. Within one hour of our pickets being positioned the management caved in and genuine talks were started. Disputes like this built up my reputation as an able trade union leader and workers with grievances soon sought me out. I was pleased as punch when skiff fishermen from the staunchly loyalist areas of Kilkeel and Annalong in Co. Down invited me down to address them. The meeting was held in an evangelical hall and despite the Dublin dimension to the union they were happy to join up because they were sure I could improve their lot.

My biggest success was in recruiting five hundred Belfast City Council workers, of whom two-thirds were Protestant. The deep-sea dockers at Belfast Harbour, so called because they unloaded the long-distance ships, were a tower of strength to me. They had a long tradition of loyalty to the Irish transport union; indeed many of the members were sons of founding members who had joined up when James Connolly and James Larkin first formed the union in 1908. The dockers had fought many battles from those days and always responded to me when I required their help outside of the docks. I remember on one occasion a big supermarket owner in Andersonstown Road, Belfast, locked a young woman out for recruiting members to the union. I rang for the dockers and, after they arrived in their cars and blocked off the entrances, the owner quickly backed down, restarted the girl and even found her a more senior position.

Their finest hour, in my view, came when five Belfast dockers left for Liverpool docks to train in the use of new mobile cranes. Before they left on a Sunday night we took the precaution of informing the police, for one of them had been interned and we feared that the Liverpool police would stop and detain him at the airport. This is precisely what did happen. We immediately informed the police in Belfast and Liverpool and explained to the Home Secretary, at that time Merlyn Rees, that the nature of the men's mission to Liverpool was entirely innocent. All day Monday we were constantly on the telephone to the police in Belfast and Liverpool and to the Home Office, but no one listened.

With our man locked up for a second night, we warned that if he was not released promptly the next morning we would disrupt Belfast city and the harbour. On Tuesday morning, when there was still no sign of our missing member and no information about what was happening to him, we went out on to the main motorways and trunk roads and stopped the traffic in and out of Belfast. The police were brought in from everywhere to break it up but we played cat and mouse with them all morning before calling off our pickets and releasing the traffic jams at lunchtime.

Later in the day, when there was still no sign of our friend, the Belfast police were more frantic than we were. I had telephone calls from several contacts, including the Home Office, promising their co-operation but the Liverpool police dug their heels in and refused to free our man. That they could do so was yet another indication of the iniquity of the Prevention of Terrorism Act and the reckless way it was being used to harass travellers between Ireland and Britain. We knew that next morning the RUC would not let us sit down on the motorways again. They had called up larger numbers of police and arranged for transport to carry us away after arrest. Our tactics this time were different. We marched round the main streets of Belfast city centre and spread out across the road, effecting the same amount of disruption. On Thursday morning we organised lots of cars for points away from our usual starting place and dispatched them to the four main gates of the Stormont estate in east Belfast. There we blocked the gates with cars and prostrate bodies, preventing the entire civil service from getting into work until 10.15 a.m. and also forcing the United States ambassador to Great Britain to cancel a visit to see Roy Mason in Stormont Castle. A few hours after that exercise we got our brother back!

Since taking over the union job in Belfast I had been bitterly critical of the Harbour Board for not investing in new equipment and for failing to improve working conditions for the dockers. New health and safety legislation had been introduced and the board seemed to be opting out of its responsibilities. I was recognised as their enemy because of my protest letters to the press and to the Westminster government.

The Harbour Board was unique: it had been set up two hundred years earlier by a private members' bill and it had unusual powers. It had its own police force and could virtually do anything it wanted and was run by business people for their own interests – the direct opposite to any other harbour commissioners in the UK.

In the late 1970s, shortly after I started my campaign against the commissioners, a by-election to the board was held. I nominated a trade union candidate who was refused the right to stand because he had no resources (he needed to own shipping and have a certain sum of money in the bank). I persuaded Guy Burns, a sympathetic stevedore, to run instead. Only property owners in the city of Belfast could vote, so I made sure that a good vote of my friends was mobilised. I intended to record everything and bring it to the attention of the Labour government at Westminster and finally have this ancient farce abolished.

On the day of the election the chairman of the board opened a room beside the voting station, offering hospitality to some of his voters and the cold shoulder to Burns's supporters. The abuses of that election played right into my hands. I took my information to Don Concannon, who was then Northern Ireland Minister for Commerce and Manpower Services; he notified the Labour government and the board was disbanded. Some time later a new board was put in place, and Belfast City Council was invited to nominate a member on to it. Because of my personal campaign for reforms, they appointed me.

Many of the old members had been reappointed and they were furious when I appeared as the representative from the

269

city council, one member demanding at the first meeting that I be made to apologise for my criticisms of the board. I laughed at him when he said he would make me apologise. Afterwards we became friends when he realised the foolishness of his threat. I enjoyed my stint on the board and took the initiative in opening up the harbour commissioners' facilities to women.

Earlier I had recruited members in a factory in West Belfast which produced hand-cut crystal glass products. It had been mainly established to train young people in the skills of glass blowing and cutting and to create a viable company to meet a growing demand at home and abroad for such quality products. Father Eustace, who formed Tyrone Crystal, a similar project in Dungannon, took them under his wing and some activities were interlinked between both factories. However, rivalry between them led to disputes about quality, pay and other matters, including the division of the cost of overheads. This was crucial, for some of the expenses of the Tyrone factory were loaded on to the Belfast budget. With government investment in the factory in Belfast tied to a plan to achieve viability and quality standards, targets which it was not going to meet in time, I went to see Don Concannon, the minister concerned, to seek a reprieve and further financial aid. He turned me down. I feared it was curtains for the factory and the workers. However, I soon learned that the Tyrone people had withdrawn from the Belfast operation because of Concannon's unwillingness to provide further backing. The enterprise therefore had no proper or legal owners. A few days later, after a meeting with the workers, we occupied the factory and declared it a co-op. I reckoned that if the quality of the product was good enough, we could sell it and create a cash flow to keep the factory going and the jobs intact.

We opened up a shop on the premises and placed adverts in newspapers that brought consumers from all over Ireland to buy our glass. We brought in the lead mixture for the glass from Cavan. There were controlled explosive substances in it and so we had to keep it under lock and key while it was not in use, arrangements supervised by a local police superintendent. In six weeks we sold £42,000 worth of products, out of which we paid wages and bought raw materials. The enormous publicity about the success of the enterprise attracted predators. Not least because of where the factory was located, in Andersonstown, we found ourselves under pressure from the Provos to hand it over. At the time they were building up a whole financial network to support their campaign. Some of their enterprises were founded on extortion and other criminal practices, others were carefully run legitimate businesses designed for laundering hot money and to give an aura of respectability to their other activities. In our case they offered £75,000, which was turned down by the steering committee. When some workers wanted to strike because a toilet door would not close, I recognised that pressure was starting on us. Meanwhile, when I heard that pieces of cut glass were being sold around the doors in Andersonstown I knew that organised pilfering had been instigated.

Recognising that we could not stand up to a prolonged campaign to force us to sell, I advised the co-op to put an end to the whole enterprise. The risk of a paramilitary takeover was too great, and I did not want to be regarded as having set up something which would undoubtedly have become a major money-spinner for the benefit of the Provos. By forcing us into that position the Provos delivered a serious economic blow to ordinary people whose interests they claimed to protect. In reality what they did was deny employment, and all the benefits that flow from it, to a number of very decent, deserving people who had worked conscientiously to make the glass factory a success and provide jobs for themselves and others in one of the worst unemployment blackspots in the North. While they were ultimately betrayed by the Provos, the Labour government was also significantly to blame. With more help and the muscle that would have given us, we would probably have been able to stand up to the Provos.

I continued working for the ITGWU until I retired in 1985 at the age of sixty. During my ten years' service I was pleased to have increased membership in the North fourfold, to the point where Protestant members outnumbered Catholics. This is not designed to be making a sectarian or bigoted point. Instead, I believe it shows that a professional trade union service provided to workers can succeed and offer good benefits regardless of where the union headquarters is located or the religion of the officers and members. The trade union movement always had great healing potential in our divided society but despite the sterling efforts of people like John Freeman, Sid McDowell, Bobby Dickie, John Coulthard and Brendan Harkin, it failed to deliver at the times of greatest test, notably in the 1974 stoppage. By contrast, when Paisley tried a similar *putsch* in 1977, the unions gave a decisive lead, persuaded people to stay at their work and significantly undermined him. The present generation of union leaders, like Inez McCormack, Terry Carlin, Al Keery, Tom Gillen and Jim McCusker, are showing great courage confronting discrimination and intimidation and fostering anti-sectarian attitudes besides fighting for the more conventional rights of all their members. They are already a force for reconciliation in the entire community and as the divisions of the past continue to thaw, albeit far too slowly, I am sure the unions will play an ever more constructive role in creating a better future.

After my removal from Belfast City Council in 1958 and an unsuccessful effort to win re-election in 1966, I had managed to win a seat in May 1973 representing the Lower Falls area in what was called Divis Ward. Despite the parallel political frustrations and setbacks I suffered at the Stormont level, my time in the City Hall was more notably marked by achievement. After the Executive was toppled I was of course able to give more serious attention to the workings of the council. The Orange block no longer dominated the voting arithmetic and I found it relatively easy to get decisions through that would satisfy the entire community, providing care was taken that the terms of the motions were outside formal party lines and the party whips were not applied. By working with the liberal unionists like John Carson, Sir Myles Humphries, Victor Brennan and others in the Alliance Party and Workers' Party, I could muster a majority against the Sunday-closure lobby. Independent-minded people like Hugh Smyth, Frankie Millar, Seamus Lynch and myself were effective debaters on the motions we backed which often brought waverers over to our side.

This was one of the most rewarding periods of my life, for the co-operation we effected in the council demonstrated that there was a lot of common ground to be ploughed and harvested despite the bigger issues that still divided the community. There appears to have been considerable support for this strategy, for at the council elections in May 1977 I polled 7,000 first preference votes in Andersonstown, three and a half times the quota and the largest single personal vote ever recorded in a local government election. I took three other councillors in on the distribution of my surplus.

My commitment to council co-operation was so strong that I even agreed to play in goal for an all-party team against a Birmingham Council eleven in May 1978, at the start of our civic week. It was the first time I had played football for twenty years and at the age of fifty-three and weighing fifteen stone it took quite a bit out of me. The result was a satisfactory 3–3 draw, however, a good outcome for what was my last game.

But from time to time stupid rancour did erupt. John Carson, a unionist businessman, who was a particularly courageous and pragmatic councillor, fell foul of the Unionist Party and had the whip withdrawn from him for supporting the exchange of a bit of council land for a plot at St Gerard's Catholic Church in north Belfast. In 1980 I asked if he was prepared to let his name go forward as lord mayor and he agreed, winning the post by a single vote after a couple of weeks of corridor campaigning. I vigorously supported him and was delighted by his victory. As I knew he would, he made an excellent, broadminded lord mayor who was acceptable throughout the city. His term of office coincided with all the community tension and upheaval associated with the IRA hunger strikes at the Maze prison but despite this John ventured into both Catholic and Protestant areas, proving himself to be the first citizen of all the people of Belfast.

The initiative of which I am most proud, however, is the award of the Freedom of Belfast to John Hewitt on 1 March 1983, four years before he died at the age of eighty. Apart from the thought-provoking poetry he had written, John Hewitt was a major force in the artistic and cultural development of Northern Ireland in the 1940s and 1950s. As the deputy director of the Belfast Museum and Art Gallery he made many shrewd purchases for the city collection. He was also a prime mover in the Council for the Encouragement of Music and the Arts in the 1940s and 1950s. CEMA was the forerunner of the Arts Council and Hewitt played an important part in making Belfast less of a cultural wasteland. As a man of radical socialist ideals he was, of course, unpopular with the unionist worthies who dominated the Belfast Corporation at the time. After being unjustly denied promotion to director of the Belfast Museum and Art Gallery, he left Belfast in 1957 and became director of the Herbert Art Gallery and Museum in Coventry. He remained there until his retirement in 1972 when he returned to his native city.

I realised that Belfast had not appointed any Freemen for many years and that of those who had been honoured only one, the painter Sir John Lavery, had any connection with the arts. After taking soundings among all the parties in the council about the possibility of honouring both Hewitt and the Belfast-born flautist James Galway, I calculated that there was enough approval for Hewitt to get it through the full council, although probably not for Galway. It was a well-deserved honour and symbolic recompense for a talented man who had been betrayed by the city fathers in the past.

During my time on the council, I always worked to support the arts and cultural projects. When the Linen Hall Library in Belfast was in debt and danger and threatened with closure, I became heavily involved in the campaign to get it financial support from the council and elsewhere, to revitalise the membership and to have it preserved as a priceless and irreplaceable resource for the city. I also fought for council support for the Arts Theatre and when a bout of BBC fund-cutting led to a decision to wipe out the only locally based orchestra, I raised the matter in the council and was appointed to lead a deputation to plead for the decision to be reversed. Jimmy Hawthorne, the Northern Ireland Controller, who had to defend the decision against a musicians' strike and a public campaign to save the orchestra, came up with the suggestion of starting our own Ulster Orchestra with local sponsorship and the help of the BBC. We took him at his word and set out to find ways to turn the idea into reality. The council was persuaded to offer the Ulster Hall as a home base and to provide a substantial annual grant towards running costs. Together with financial grants from private enterprise, we were able to bring a fine quality orchestra to life. It gives me pleasure now to hear of the Ulster Orchestra's high reputation and prestige throughout the music world. It is a cultural asset which Belfast needs and deserves and I hope it will long prosper.

I have always deeply valued our rich and diverse cultural heritage and, although I was primarily a trade union and political figure, I enjoyed the company of lawyers, writers, artists and poets, many of whom were labour men like myself. In the heady days of the 1950s and early 1960s, when it seemed as if we might be on a new political path, I was part of a group that used to gather in the Duke of York bar, tucked away in a narrow alleyway off Donegall Street, in the centre of Belfast. The pub, run by Jimmy Keaveney and his family until they were forced to abandon it after an IRA bombing in the 1970s, was the focal point of radical Belfast. The best spielers in the city also turned up constantly to display their wares. The regulars included Martin McBirney QC, later a resident magistrate who was murdered by the Provos, Charles Brett, the solicitor, and

275

the irrepressible Bud Bossence, whose daily column 'As I See It' in the *News Letter* chronicled the exploits of himself and his great journalist friend, Jimmy Kennedy, in their perpetual search for a drink and a bit of crack.

Bud was a brilliant comic, whether writing prose or speaking *ex cathedra* from his long-legged stool at the end of the bar. His eyes glittering behind his thick glasses, he would attack his purported enemies like Cecil Orr, the last of the British imperialists, or Kennedy, who deliberately staged debates with Bud to get him angry. He was at his best on these occasions and visits to Bud in the Duke were to me like a pilgrimage to Lourdes for Catholics.

Another member of this circle was the playwright, Sam Thompson, who wrote a hard-hitting play *Over the Bridge*, based on his experiences working in the hothouse sectarian atmosphere of the Harland and Wolff shipyard. The story had a lethal theme as far as the unionists were concerned, for he exposed the sectarianism and discrimination against Catholics as no writer had done before. It was a sadly prophetic plea for action to eliminate the bitterness, to close down the divisions in Northern Ireland society before disaster struck. The row that started over attempts to stage the play was one of the first shock waves that ultimately heralded the earthquake which subsequently engulfed us.

I was first introduced to Sam by the trade union official, Billy Blease. I liked him instantly. He was an uncomplicated straightshooter who always appeared to be smouldering on the verge of explosion into flames at the sight or sound of injustice and deceit. Everybody within earshot knew where Sam stood on every issue. If they did not it never took Sam long to tell them. I think it was me that persuaded him to join the NILP. It was not hard to do as all his other friends were in the party or sympathetic to its aims and aspirations.

Sam had got the bug to write and under the guidance of Sam Hanna Bell he started producing scripts for BBC radio. He learned his craft well and eventually produced his most power-ful work, *Over the Bridge*. The play was scheduled to go on at the Group Theatre, beside the Ulster Hall, but when the directors saw the uncompromising script they demanded cuts. Sam Thompson and Jimmy Ellis, the actor who later made a big name for himself in the television series *Z Cars*, turned down direc-tions to censor the script, challenged the board's right to inter-fere with it and refused to put the play on at the theatre. The tentacles of the unionist regime were so all-embracing that they extended to control of the arts. Consequently Thompson and Ellis faced great difficulty in finding an alternative theatre. In the end the Dublin-owned Empire Theatre in Victoria Square decided to put the play on where it packed the house for weeks. By taking the stand they did, Thompson and Ellis helped to free the arts in Northern Ireland from the narrowmindedness and shackles of the dominating political party. The *Over the Bridge* saga is therefore one of the most important milestones in our cultural history.

The late 1970s were a lean political period. Many of the SDLP constituency representatives who had given up work as teachers and the like to sit in the Assembly were without jobs or incomes. Apart from the people immediately around Gerry Fitt and myself, the character of the party had changed. The few Protestants we had as members had drifted away and no effort was made to keep the door open for them. The party was now populated with straightforward nationalists who were Catholic by religion and conservative in economic and social policies. Unless I was there riding shotgun, the party acted in a way that was alien to my values. It also tended to gravitate towards the Fianna Fáil party in Dublin. Some of the SDLP people were far too cosy with Charlie Haughey's hardline wing in the party for my liking. At meeting after meeting I would cringe when some of them would intervene with 'Charlie said this' or 'Charlie said that'.

I noticed, moreover, that the media was now continually

referring to us as the 'mainly Catholic' SDLP. On many occasions when SDLP spokesmen took part in radio and television programmes they allowed the party to be described without protest as being a 'Catholic party'. I complained about this and challenged the designation in letters to the newspapers. Only one other member, Denis Haughey, ever wrote in support. No one else cared. It seemed to me that party strategy was solely directed towards consolidating the Catholic vote. The direction we were travelling in was in line with the old Nationalist Party, most certainly not the way I wanted to go. I had left all that behind, apart from the period when the Catholic population in Belfast was under attack. I had been drawn into that unwillingly. I was determined not to be drawn into it again.

I found myself being left out of discussions and of committees that involved policy matters. I would read in the papers that SDLP delegations had been involved in things that I did not even know about. More and more the party was being autocratically run from Derry by John Hume and his cronies. Although he met loyalist personalities, including the notorious John McKeague, to discuss negotiated independence in line with party policy, at the same time he was pursuing his own initiatives and making policy on the hoof. He had, for instance, been building up his contacts in Washington, DC, and was instrumental in getting a pledge from President Jimmy Carter that the United States would provide cash aid to help underpin any new political settlement. Again, without formal party nomination procedures taking place, Hume announced he was going to stand for election to the European Parliament in 1979. He was pro-European, a view that was absolutely different from mine.

If I was to go along with SDLP policy I would have my say on it. Changes by stealth were not acceptable. The deteriorating relationship between us caused differences at meetings. I was openly furious at the way the party was being stripped of its socialism and being taken over by unadulterated nationalists. Their attitude to IRA violence was sometimes doubtful, as

278

evidenced by silences in the aftermath of some dreadful outrage, and they were viciously opposed to the RUC in every shape and form. This was one of the particular issues that infuriated me. I was persuaded that the force had changed irrevocably since 1969. Jamie Flanagan, the first Catholic to head the force, had responded thoroughly to everything we asked of him, yet in turn the SDLP refused to give the police the wholehearted support they needed. Gerry Fitt and I regularly stood alone from the party on this issue and made our views clear. A new breed of officers like Jack Hermon, who later became a mould-breaking chief constable, had transformed attitudes and promoted professionalism within the force.

My dear friend, Bill Wilson, who died in 1989 only a few days after retiring, was typical of the new, more open force. When the Pope came to Ireland in 1979 the organisers of a youth rally at Galway could not get enough tents to house young people travelling down from the North. Bill heard about the problem, got in touch with the British Army GOC at Lisburn and borrowed tents. He then sent them to Galway by freight service and paid for it out of the RUC's Community Relations budget. As the Church of Ireland Archdeacon of Down said at his funeral, he was a 'people's policeman'.

My growing differences with the SDLP came to a head in the summer of 1977. On 26 August I resigned as chairman of the parliamentary group and issued the following statement which could well serve as my political credo:

> In view of the implications of the SDLP's recent policy statement and my own deepening disenchantment with the party as the result of an obvious drift of policies and attitudes away from that of a social democratic party, I am compelled, therefore, to examine my position relative to that party.
>
> The statement issued a fortnight ago is no more than reiterated verbiage culled from earlier party statements and emphasises once more several well established points of policy, which, incidentally, I support.

The exercise of drafting and issuing the statement, apart from some rather odd features of process, was a total waste of time. It looked at no new matters and ignored the last local government election, which produced the most significant results of any elections in Northern Ireland since 1925. It did not encompass the large-scale review of policy involving, amongst other concepts, a look at ideas of negotiated independence, which by resolution we were committed to do at last November's conference in Newcastle.

The statement was a hastily drafted piece of froth released to coincide with President Carter's expected intervention supporting SDLP policies on the North. Certain leading members of the SDLP had passed to them confidential information on President Carter's statement, and had hoped in addition to exploit its content and timing for other reasons as well as those connected to the party.

These members of the SDLP could not resist the temptation of making a public demonstration of their connections in the heady atmosphere of the political power game.

Ignored completely in the writing of the statement were the changes that were taking place in the patterns of traditional Unionist support, as evidenced by the failure of the recent stoppage in which organised workers, for the first time, passed the pickets on the way to their jobs; again in the massive abstentions of Unionist voters from the polls at the last election; a trend that can become more pronounced as Paisley's Sunday closure campaign begins to bite throughout the local councils of the North.

These changes to the Unionist support patterns were exactly what the SDLP sought since its formation in August 1970, when Gerry Fitt as leader made a strong appeal for moderate Unionist support for the party.

It was sought on several occasions since that in newspaper advertisements aimed at the Loyalist people over the heads of their politicians.

The last full page advertisement published at the beginning of the Convention election contained an assurance on the status of Northern Ireland not being changed without the consent of the majority of its people and that the SDLP would work at all times for the best interest of the people of Northern Ireland.

Yet, at a time when the work done by the SDLP to persuade voters to stop supporting Unionist politicians was beginning to pay off, the party is choosing, by its current political statement, to turn its back on its earlier policies and spurning the fruits of its own efforts.

The present policies do not suggest a better way of securing the consent of the majority for political work for the best interest of the people in the present situation. Indeed, it is to the contrary. The suggestion in the party statement is, because of intransigent Unionist politicians and the rank deviousness of the Labour Government, that the Irish Government should actively participate in the preliminary negotiations that would lead ultimately to an administration being imposed on the people of the North.

I have grave doubts that this particular suggestion can be reconciled with the policy expressed in those advertisements. Moreover, I do not believe that it can be reconciled with that sentence in the introduction to the statement which states that the SDLP recognises the path of political negotiation as 'the only peaceful way forward'.

It must be obvious to everyone, even to the person who wrote and leaked that statement to the press before the party executive considered it, that the Unionist Party will not extend a primary role in negotiations to the Irish Government. To push the Irish Government into the front line of talks at this stage is an invitation to the Unionist Party to apply a veto on any movement forward. Hence, we have collision politics on a grand scale – the ingredients of which total warfare is made.

In any case, negotiations for a future administration in the North in the initial stages are a matter for Northern Ireland parties. The second stage brings the sovereign powers into the negotiations to underpin an inter-party agreement. However one may desire it otherwise, practical results can only be achieved by following this peaceful course of action.

One thing else is certain, and that is that those Unionist voters at the last election, especially those in the trade union movement with Labour leanings, may have been forced back into a polarised political stance of a traditional type because of the failure of the SDLP to encourage them to move closer to a social democratic position.

I referred earlier to the drift, if not departure, from the aims and ideals of Social Democracy which has caused me increased concern as a party member since May, 1974, when the NI Executive fell. I am a Democratic Socialist and compromised to some extent my philosophy to assist in the creation of a strong collective voice to promote policies, which, as stated in Article 2 of our aims and objectives issued in 1970 on the formation of the party, were to be based on left of centre principles.

These policies were to secure a just and adequate distribution of wealth; to uphold and support the democratic rights and principles of organised labour; to promote the spread of financial, consumer, industrial and agricultural co-operatives; to work for the provision of a minimum living wage for all workers, and to support the principle of equal pay for equal work; to ensure public ownership of fishing rights of all inland waters; and to work for the establishment of state industry in areas of high unemployment.

With one or two notable exceptions, none of the leading members has done anything to promote these policies since 1974, and little enough before that. In spite of the fact that we are confronted with the worst figures for unemployment, poverty, housing and general incomes levels in Western Europe, we have rarely heard a cheep of protest from men who a short time ago had Ministerial responsibility for those very Departments.

Our behaviour on entry to the EEC was simply reprehensible. We issued statements at the time of the referendum in favour of entry and allowed advertisements, which we did not pay for, to be published in newspapers in which voters were promised 'steak and kidney' pie in the sky. The pie in the sky did not materialise, nor was anyone seized with remorse over the fraudulent nature of the publicity campaign. Even now, at a time when our farmers are being so severely screwed in comparison to those in other countries, the SDLP's reaction to the disastrous policies of the EEC is one of monumental indifference to the effects.

Originally, I thought we had strong hopes that as a party the SDLP could have straddled the religious divide and drawn support to the party from all interested groups because of the radical nature of our policies and the strong thrust from most of our earlier group of representatives towards Socialist solutions.

Indeed, the social and economic programme that we entered the power-sharing Executive on reflected our approach on many of the issues we had to deal with. The records of our work in office demonstrate the growing support there was for bread and butter politics of the type we advanced. Flag-waving was a non-runner in this race.

Meanwhile, I intend to carry on as an individual member of the SDLP, for my belief is still strong in what is contained in the party constitution, whatever misgivings I have otherwise.

A few days after I fired this broadside the SDLP executive voted to expel me and I ended my links with the party I helped to found. On reflection I regret the way events ended. It was a most unworthy squabble in which I was not the innocent party. I had nothing to be proud of in the exchanges. Several members of the party immediately contacted me and I advised them not to leave but Ivan Cooper, who had shared much of my thinking, left after a short time. In 1979 the party leader, Gerry Fitt, followed us into the wilderness for very much the same reasons. Hume then assumed pole position.

I tried to start a broadly based Labour party on several occasions afterwards but never succeeded. This was the reasoning behind my decision to stand in the first European Parliament elections in 1979. By providing a rallying point for socialists in a six-county-wide election I hoped we could attract enough support to float a Labour party. Most of the 572,239 votes cast were allotted on a tribal basis. The three candidates elected, unionists Ian Paisley and John Taylor, and John Hume, reflected the broad two to one Protesant–Catholic ratio in the community. I only got 6,122 first preference votes, 1.1 per cent of the total, was eliminated on the second count and lost my deposit.

In 1980 the Provo prisoners in the H-Blocks at the Maze prison went on hunger strike in an attempt to secure a restoration of the political status I had helped to win for them in 1972, which had been withdrawn by Merlyn Rees four years later. The unprecedented barbarity of the Provos' campaign and their wanton disrespect for human life had long removed from me all vestiges of sympathy for them and I was no longer in favour of them having these privileges.

Inevitably the Provos put heavy pressure on me to support them, clearly influenced by how I had handled the issue of our union member arrested in Liverpool. They knew that a deep-sea dock strike could cut off the intake of grain at Belfast Harbour, causing serious problems for bakers, animal feed manufacturers and ultimately the consumers. I resisted the call for such a political strike. The Provos then supplied a list of prisoners with the claim that they were in our union. The books were checked and, as I expected, they were not members at all. The Provos then set up a publicity campaign against me. I was attacked in newspaper reports, and articles and leaflets criticising me were put through letter boxes. I answered them all.

Statements were issued by Provo organisations claiming that loyalists were about to attack Andersonstown. Phoney organisations were formed to defend the areas, with each street having its own leadership. I denounced these activities on TV and was visited by one of the self-appointed leaders whom I chased from the door. They even tried to force me to resign my seat on the City Council but I refused. Meanwhile, just before Christmas 1980, the hunger strike was called off when the Secretary of State, Humphrey Atkins, offered terms that met the criteria laid down by the strikers. Disputes about implementing the deal led to ill-feeling among the prisoners in the H-Blocks and in March 1981 the fast was resumed, this time led by Bobby Sands.

The untimely death of Frank Maguire, the independent

Nationalist MP for Fermanagh–South Tyrone, shortly afterwards, created the need for a by-election. The disgraceful failure of the SDLP not to fight the election enabled the Provos to nominate Sands and gave him a free run. He was subsequently elected and as he continued on his fast to death the hunger strike became the top story on the international news diary. When Sands eventually died in May 1981 our Andersonstown house was the immediate target of organised attacks by mobs of young people. They arrived at the door on a whistled signal and hammered it with hurling sticks. Petrol bombs were made up outside the house to frighten us. They shouted obscenities. 'Get out to fuck you Protestant lover' was one insult I particularly remember.

The strength of feeling against me at that time was more than clear from the result of the local council election the same month. I polled only 1,343 first preference votes and just managed to hold on to my seat by being elected on the tenth count. It was a dramatic reversal of my triumph in 1977. As other hunger strikers died at intervals throughout the month fresh attacks were launched on the house. Neighbours came out to push the attackers away and were themselves threatened or had their windows broken for their trouble. One of my daughters had to go to hospital for treatment for nervous disorder and the boys were being assaulted so regularly at school they were too frightened to attend. We had to keep buckets of water and sand all over the house to douse petrol bombs if they came in. After a month of this persecution we finally decided to move, after seventeen years living in that house. Apart from the effect on my own family of living under siege, the intimidation was blighting the lives of our innocent and supportive neighbours. A team of dockers came up to shift our belongings and after a spell living with relatives we finally found a house on the Oldpark Road in north Belfast.

Peter, one of the twins who was then aged fifteen, described the experience in a school essay a short time later. 'My father had given our family three days notice in which to have our belongings ready to go in case our house was to be attacked again by people who had a different political point of view. I was really saddened the day we left because I lived in that house for fifteen years and suddenly my whole way of living was upset within a few days. I had no time to say good-bye to my friends or even give them an address so they could keep in touch. I had good times in that house and it was always full of joy and now as I walked out I could feel the emptiness because of echoes of voices from the removal men talking.'

A few days after our move my morale was boosted when I went to Cranfield College of Technology to receive a Master of Science degree. After I had left the SDLP, I had time on my hands, being used to working long hours. I always had an ambition to study for a degree and this appeared to be such an opportunity. After making enquiries I was offered the chance of a degree if I submitted a sociology thesis to Cranfield. It was first agreed that I would do something on comparisons of social security payments here and in other regions of Britain. However, when I got down to work, reading extensively through parliamentary Hansards and the minutes of Belfast Corporation and the Poor Law Commissioners, I found myself diverted and increasingly fascinated by the joint efforts of Protestants and Catholics to fight poverty in the early years of the Northern Ireland state. Cranfield agreed to make this the focus of my research and I got through it and produced a 65,000 word thesis with a generous measure of help from my tutor, Jack Winkler, with whom I shared an admiration for the Arsenal football team. Some of my friends thought the thesis should be issued as a book and Michael Burns and Anne Tannahill of the Blackstaff Press agreed and duly published it. I called it *Yes We Have No Bananas* after the tune the bands played in 1932 when leading the outdoor relief workers to the mass demonstration at the Custom House steps.

Sometime after the book came out I was approached by Jim

McDowell, editor of the Belfast *Sunday News*, to write a column each week. I could be as radical as I liked and, true to his promise, I wrote without restraint. Several years later, when a dispute occurred between workers and management, Jim and I were sacked along with Tommy Sands, of the famous Sands musical family. The *Sunday World* then took me on on the same basis and I parted company with them only when my eyesight started to fail in 1985. That year too I fought and lost my last election, this time in north Belfast around my new home but where I had no power-base.

In the early 1980s I also turned my hand to writing drama for the stage. My first effort, *Strike*, which went on at the Arts Theatre, was based on the detention of the docker in Liverpool and our campaign to free him. In 1985, with the permission of Sam Thompson's widow, May, I abridged his original two-and-a-half-hour play *Over the Bridge* into a 105-minute version which was presented at the Arts Theatre. More recently I have written a stage play called *Yes We Have No Bananas* adapted from my book.

My eyesight has now failed and I can no longer drive or read but I enjoy chatting with the many friends who keep in touch and make sure I am abreast of events by telling me things they know I haven't been able to read. Theresa is still a tower of strength to me as she has always been.

Our family has of course grown up now and carved out their own lives. Anne, our first child, lives in Birmingham with her husband, Chris Parr, who is a well-known television drama producer. We see them frequently and adore our grandson, Connel. Anne has made her own name as a writer. Her play *Ourselves Alone* has been performed all over the world and she wrote the screenplay for the film *Wuthering Heights*. Moya is the only member of the family still at home with us; Patricia now lives with her husband, Brian Strong, in Perth in Australia, where she works as an accountant. They have a daughter called Ciara. Peter is married to Christine Lyons and lives not far from us in north Belfast. He works as a chef. His twin brother Joe is building a career for himself as a theatre director having graduated from Liverpool Polytechnic.

Theresa insists that I must know little of the children growing up for I was always out and about on trade union or political business. She cites one occasion when she took ill during a Westminster general election campaign and I could not be found. 'If I die put me under the bed until the election is over,' she told her mother. 'He'll look after the funeral arrangements after that.' As politics meant everything to me, looking back I suppose my family always seemed to have come second-best but Theresa, and indeed the children, supported me all the way and I am grateful for all they did. I well remember in my early elections how Theresa canvassed streets on the Springfield Road and Unity Flats, wheeling her pram with Moya in it while Anne pushed the election address through the letter boxes. Anne worked in all the elections right up to 1969, writing election addresses, delivering them and helping in the tally rooms on election day. Moya and Patricia helped too but were not just as interested.

I suppose that Irish history will describe me as a controversial and at times stormy politician. I held strong views and vociferously expressed them. I never prevented anyone else from saying their piece but I always hoped they would be sensible enough to accept my views. I certainly did all that I could to persuade them of the logic of my case. Of course I clashed, on occasion physically, with others who were as set in their views as I was. I know I made lifetime enemies for not being able to curb my tongue or put down my pen. I was always a diabetic, for many years undiagnosed, and the symptoms of that often aggravated my own hair-trigger temper. I recognise now that I often went too far too quickly. I usually regretted those occasions as quickly as they occurred and hastily apologised. Looking back I appreciate how my close friends stuck by me throughout the various storms and ups and downs.

I don't really know how much I achieved in my career. Certainly I have a sense of satisfaction that I scaled heights that no one among my school mates has ever done, but, politically, I have a great feeling of disappointment that a labour movement did not emerge to break the cycle of sectarian conflict. In the early 1960s, the days of hope, the IRA had failed to make an impact. They had examined their failure and were promoting the ballot box, not the gun barrel, as a means of reforming the North. This was the right direction to go.

Generally the Unionist Party, under O'Neill, was accepting that the 'Orange card' type of politics was on the way out. We were heading for a political realignment with a new emphasis placed on the social and economic issues until the Provisionals emerged. The labour movement in Northern Ireland, which was growing in strength and influence before that, failed to pick up and take over the leadership of the growing campaign for civil rights reforms. If they had done so they would have been strong enough to create a bulwark to prevent the exchanges between 'Green' and 'Orange' trouble-makers. Is it not incredible that the Stormont election of February 1969 brought forth a number of MPs who represented civil rights interests, while the NILP, apart from myself, appeared to have no interest in civil rights whatever?

Liverpool and Glasgow had much in common with Belfast. All were major seaport cities and highly industrialised. Glasgow and Liverpool became labour strongholds but never Belfast, for it was caught in the grip of a perpetual 'holy war'. All its politics were determined by the sole issue of keeping the Pope's influence at bay. The NILP was influenced in the same way. Although the four NILP MPs elected to Stormont in the 1960s were able energetic men who kept the unionists on their toes, they confronted them on their own ground. They were thus under no pressure to move leftwards. Their election remit was merely to offer a better 'surgery service' at their local election rooms. Their main failing, which proved to be fatal, was that their political philosophy was not radical enough to embrace the entire community. With the NILP out of the way there was nothing left between the tribes. It remains my greatest wish that some day in the future a labour movement will effectively assert itself in Northern Ireland.

When I was a boy of eight or nine my father took me to the boxing tournaments. I always remember the peerless Jim Driscoll, a Welshman who was featherweight champion during the First World War. He was a great exponent of the straight left, and my father taught me how to use the punch. I always associate him with that, and remember him telling me that the best way to deal with an opponent was a straight left. I never forgot that advice, whether in the sporting or the political context. Indeed, I would like to be remembered as a straight left, straight in my dealings with everyone and left in my politics.

INDEX

retirement, 271–2
on Belfast City Council, 272–5
cultural activities, 274–7
breaks from SDLP, 279–83
attacked over hunger strikes,
284–6
receives M.Sc., 286
as writer, 286–7
health, 287
family, 287–8
self-assessment, 288–90
Devlin, Patricia (daughter), 64, 151,
287, 288
Devlin, Patrick (grandfather), 2
Devlin, Peter (great uncle), 9–10
Devlin, Peter (son), 64, 151, 167,
285–6, 287–8
Devlin, Rose (sister), 3
Devlin, Stevie, 58
Devlin, Theresa, 51–3, 56, 59, 64,
76, 86, 114, 177, 287
marriage, 57–8
and vigilantes, 110
home as advice centre, 148–9
attacks on, 151
role of, 288
Devlin, Thomas (father), 2–3, 8,
9–17, 25, 29, 43, 50–1, 265, 290
in Andrews' flour mill, 58–9
Devlin, Tommy (brother), 3
Diamond, Harry, 82–3, 84–5, 87
Dickie, Bobby, 272
Divis Street, 34
Dock Labour Party, 71
Donlon, Sean, 160–1
Donnelly, Mary, 2
Donnelly, Tom, 227
Doran, Lapsy, 25, 26
Douglas, Billy, 77
Douglas-Home, Sir Alec, 204, 208
Doyle, P.V., 190–1
Driscoll, Jim, 290
Dublin, 8, 24, 30, 243–4
NILP MPs appeal for help, 108–9
British embassy burned, 170
loyalist bombs, 237, 249
Duffy, John, 163
Duffy, Mamie, 57, 58
Duffy, Paddy, 204, 205
Duffy, Theresa *see* Devlin, Theresa

Dugdale, Norman, 215, 221
Duke of York bar, 275–6
Dungannon, Co. Tyrone, 89, 167
Dunleath, Lord, 219
Dunlewey Street school, 13

Easter Rising commemorations, 32
Eastwood, Barney and Frances, 85
Egan, Bowes, 99
elections, 13, 80–2, 85
local, 1958, 76–8, 82
general, 1964, 80, 91
general, 1969, 84–5
senate, 139
local, 1973, 193–4
Assembly, 1973, 194–5
general, 1974, 225–8
Ellis, Jimmy, 277
Emergency Provisions Act, 225
European Community, 254, 282–3
European Court of Human Rights,
160–1
European Parliament elections, 278,
283–4
Eustace, Fr, 270
extradition, 207, 231–2

Fabian Society, 63, 139
Falls Baths, 11, 32, 52
Falls Road, 13, 16, 18, 19, 22, 23, 33,
58, 133
NILP branch, 83–4
Catholics burned out, 106, 117
troops, 107
barricades, 109–13
curfew, 128–31, 134
Fanning, D.I., 23, 35
Faulkner, Brian, 96, 97, 153–5, 168,
172, 193, 201, 215, 218, 229, 231,
243, 245, 252
and internment, 157–63
government resigns, 170–1
Assembly elections, 195
power-sharing talks, 196–200
chief executive, 199, 200, 221
Sunningdale Conference, 202–10
Hillsborough talks, 1974, 223–4
forced out of Unionist Party, 225
undermined in Assembly, 230–1
warned by UWC, 233

295

296

299

abstention proposed, 155–7
civil disobedience campaign,
    161–2
attacks on members, 165–8
statement on violence, 1972,
    173–4
talks with Whitelaw and Lynch,
    175–7, 181–3
Darlington conference, 183–4
'Towards a New Ireland', 185–8,
    193
preparing for Stormont Assembly,
    189–90
border referendum, 191
Assembly election, 193
local government elections, 1973,
    193–4
power-sharing talks, 195–202
Sunningdale Conference, 202–10
general election, 1974, 226–8
Assembly debate on
    renegotiation, 229
rejects Sunningdale modifications,
    238
drafts new statement, 239–40
agrees to resign Executive, 243–4
split on rent and rates arrears,
    248–9
and Constitutional Convention,
    257–64
talks with Boal and Paisley,
    259–60
Voluntary Coalition talks, 261–2
talks with OUP, 264
character changing, 277–9
Devlin breaks with, 279–83
and hunger strikes, 285
socialism, 12–13, 14–15, 55–7,
    60–1, 142
and partition, 68–9
in power-sharing programme, 197
disappearing from SDLP, 278–9, 282
Spanish Civil War, 68
Special Powers Act, 92, 112
Springfield Road, 34, 124, 125, 158
Stalin, Joseph, 35
Stewart, John D., 139
Stewart, J.U., 65
Stormont see Northern Ireland
    Parliament

Stout, William, 251
Strabane, Co. Tyrone, 159
Strike (Devlin), 287
Strong, Brian, 287
Stronge, James, 233
Sullivan, Jim, 110, 117, 128, 152
Sullivan, Mary, 152
Sunday News, 287
Sunday Times, 90, 160
Sunday World, 287
Sunningdale Conference, 202–10
    issue of policing, 209–10
Supplementary Benefits
    Commission, 216–17, 218
swimming, 31–2, 52

Tailor and Garment Workers'
    Union, 69
Tannahill, Anne, 286
Taylor, John, 196, 283
Thompson, May, 287
Thompson, Sam, 276–7, 287
Thornley, David, 188
'Towards a New Ireland' (SDLP),
    185–8, 193
Tracy, Spencer, 120
trade unions see labour movement
Trainor, Danny, 38
Trimble, David, 261
Tully, James, 204
Tuzo, Harry, GOC, 149–50
Twomey, Seamus, 53, 179
Tyrone, Co., 31

Ulster Defence Association (UDA),
    191, 195, 233, 260
Ulster Defence Regiment (UDR), 114
Ulster Freedom Fighters (UFF),
    194–5
Ulster Hall, 30–1
Ulster Labour Unionist Association,
    66
Ulster Orchestra, 275
Ulster Television, 167
Ulster Volunteer Force (UVF), 31,
    102, 151, 233, 254
Ulster Workers' Council (UWC), 230
    strike, 231, 233–47
Unionist Coalition, 230, 231, 264
    and UWC strike, 234, 235

302

in Constitutional Convention, 258
Voluntary Coalition talks, 261–3
Unionist Party, 6, 49, 60, 69, 77,
  78–9, 226, 228, 230–1, 262–3,
  264, 273, 289; *see also* Northern
  Ireland Parliament
  Belfast City Council, 71–4
  vote-stealing, 81–2
  split on civil rights movement, 102
  Chichester-Clark ousted, 152–3
  Darlington conference, 187
  split, 193
  Assembly elections, 195
  Unpledged Unionists, 195, 201
  power-sharing talks, 195–202
  Sunningdale Conference, 202–10
  Faulkner forced out, 225
  and SDLP, 280–2
United Irishmen, 24
United States of America, 223, 254,
  278
  fund-raising trip, 118–21
United Ulster Unionist Council
  (UUUC), 201, 226

Vanguard movement, 172, 201, 226,
  261, 262–3
Voluntary Coalition talks, 261–2

Walker's shop, 19–20
Warnock, Jimmy, 10
West, Harry, 201, 228, 230–1, 235,
  245
West Belfast Accordion Band, 4
Westminster, 186, 234
Whale, John, 160
Wheatley, John, 214
Whelan, Danny, 43
White, Mayor Kevin, 120

White Paper, 1973, 193
Whitelaw, William, 173, 174, 215,
  225
  meets SDLP, 175–7, 182–3
  agrees political status, 176–8
  increases army strength, 180
  Darlington conference, 183–4
  Green Paper, 187, 188
  border referendum, 188, 191–2
  power-sharing talks, 195–202
  leaves NI, 203
Whitten, Herbert, 233
Widgery Tribunal, 170
Williams, Tom, 32–3
Wilson, Bill, 166–7, 213, 279
Wilson, Harold, 88, 90, 91, 107, 263
  12-point plan, 163
  visits NI, 165
  back in office, 1974, 228
  on IRA plot, 234
  and UWC strike, 241–2
  'spongers' speech, 242–3
  and British withdrawal, 254
Wilson, Senator Paddy, 144
  murdered, 194–5
Wilton, Claude, 139, 140
Windlesham, Lord, 178
Winkler, Jack, 286
Wolfe Tone commemoration, 23
Wolfe Tone Societies, 88
Woodfield, Philip, 175
Woodvale, 79–80
Workers Educational Association,
  65
Workers' Party, 273

Yes We Have No Bananas (Devlin),
  286
Young, Sir Arthur, 114, 115